The IEP Checklist
Your Guide to Creating Meaningful and Compliant IEPs

Second Edition

by

Clarissa E. Rosas, Ph.D.

and

Kathleen G. Winterman, Ed.D.

with invited contributors

Baltimore • London • Sydney

Paul H. Brookes Publishing Co.
Post Office Box 10624
Baltimore, Maryland 21285-0624
USA

www.brookespublishing.com

Typeset by Progressive Publishing Services, York, Pennsylvania.
Manufactured in the United States of America by
Integrated Books International, Inc., Dulles, Virginia.

The individuals described in this book are composites or real people whose situations are masked and are based on the authors' experiences. In all instances, names and identifying details have been changed to protect confidentiality.

Library of Congress Cataloging-in-Publication Data

Names: Rosas, Clarissa E., author. | Winterman, Kathleen G., author.
Title: The IEP checklist : your guide to creating meaningful and compliant IEPs /
    by Clarissa E. Rosas and Kathleen G. Winterman; with invited contributors.
Description: Second edition. | Baltimore : Paul H. Brookes Publishing Co., 2023. |
    Includes bibliographical references and index.
Identifiers: LCCN 2022011421 (print) | LCCN 2022011422 (ebook) | ISBN 9781681254722 (paperback) |
    ISBN 9781681254739 (epub) | ISBN 9781681254746 (pdf)
Subjects: LCSH: Individualized education programs—United States. | Children with disabilities—
    Education—United States. | School management and organization—United States.
Classification: LCC LC4031.W557 2023 (print) | LCC LC4031 (ebook) |
    DDC 371.90973—dc23/eng/20220411
LC record available at https://lccn.loc.gov/2022011421
LC ebook record available at https://lccn.loc.gov/2022011422

British Library Cataloguing in Publication data are available from the British Library.

2026   2025   2024   2023   2022

10   9   8   7   6   5   4   3   2   1

Contents

About the Online Materials

The IEP Checklist: Your Guide to Creating Meaningful and Compliant IEPs, Second Edition, offers online companion materials to supplement and expand the knowledge and strategies provided in this text. All purchasers of the book may access, download, and print the **IEP Checklist, IEP Rubric, IEP Rubric/Correction, parent surveys** (available in English and Spanish), and **blank forms** and **resource materials** from the text.

To access the materials that come with this book:

1. Go to the Brookes Download Hub: http://downloads.brookespublishing.com

2. Register to create an account (or log in with an existing account).

3. Redeem the code gIssuhDYk to access locked materials.

About the Authors

Clarissa E. Rosas, Ph.D., holds a doctorate from the University of New Mexico with a focus on bilingual/multicultural special education and educational administration as well as a bachelor's and a master's degree from the University of San Diego. Her 40 years of experience in the field of education in three different states includes teaching general education; special education, both mild to moderate and moderate to intense; English as a second language; and bilingual multicultural education. Dr. Rosas also has served as an administrator at the district, building, and university level. Her expertise and research interests include developing innovative programs and curriculum to prepare preservice and in-service teachers to meet the social and educational challenges of children with disabilities who come from vulnerable populations.

Kathleen G. Winterman, Ed.D., has more than 30 years of experience working in the field of education. Her experience includes teaching as an intervention specialist serving children ages 3–10 in inclusive settings, serving as an elementary principal, an associate professor, a special education program director, and Director of the School of Education at Xavier University. She holds seven licenses from the state of Ohio. Dr. Winterman is a published author, and her areas of research interest include teacher preparation, IEP preparation, early childhood special education, autism, educational leadership, the use of instructional technology, and services for students with mental illnesses.

About the Contributors

Leo Bradley, Ed.D., is the author of nine professional books on administrative leadership, total quality management, and school law. In his 57-year career as an educator, he held the positions of teacher, high school principal, curriculum director, assistant superintendent, and superintendent. Dr. Bradley has served as an educational consultant both nationally and internationally, from Alaska to New Zealand.

Lisa M. Campbell, Ed.D., has more than 30 years of experience working in general and special education. She began her career in Cincinnati Public Schools, where she served as an elementary teacher, an intervention specialist, a teacher leader, and a curriculum developer. She also served for 12 years as an instructor in the multicultural special education program at Mount St. Joseph University in Cincinnati. Dr. Campbell holds a bachelor's degree in elementary education (K–8), a master's degree in special education (K–12), and a doctorate in literacy education with an emphasis in educational leadership. Her dissertation—titled "Beyond Fragmentation"—was a study of the sustainability of professional development over time. Dr. Campbell is employed as an educational consultant for the Hamilton County Educational Service Center in Cincinnati, Ohio, where she works with teachers and administrators in multiple districts. Her focus for professional development offerings is primarily related to the development of effective language arts curriculum and literacy practices to meet the needs of diverse learners within multi-tiered systems of support.

Laura Shipp Clarke, Ed.D., is a special education consultant with the Northern Kentucky Cooperative for Educational Services. She has coauthored several articles for *TEACHING Exceptional Children* and serves on the board of the Kentucky Council for Exceptional Children. Dr. Clarke is the mother of three wonderful daughters and a fantastic adult son, Daniel, who has a diagnosis of autism and epilepsy. Daniel is preverbal and is learning to use augmentative and alternative communication to communicate.

John P. Concannon, Esq., has practiced education and employment law since the 1990s, focusing on representing public and private schools, teacher unions, employment, and labor matters. Prior to working as counsel in education and employment law, Mr. Concannon represented the city of Cincinnati as the assistant city attorney as well as the assistant prosecuting attorney. Throughout his work, he has had a guiding principle to advocate for those in need and share his knowledge of the law with numerous graduate students who aspire to become educational leaders.

Kathryn Doyle, Ph.D., is a special education faculty member at the University of Cincinnati. Dr. Doyle is a board-certified behavior analyst (BCBA-D) and a licensed intervention specialist. Prior to her role in higher education, she taught in the public school system for 12 years and worked in the adult developmental disability system for 3 years. She has worked in center-based services, in home-based services, and in the community with individuals with disabilities across the lifespan. Her research interests include developing academic and social communication interventions for individuals with significant disabilities as well as teacher and paraprofessional training.

Melissa Jones, Ph.D., is Professor of Special Education at Northern Kentucky University and Founder and Co-director of the Supported Higher Education Project, an inclusive postsecondary program for students with an intellectual/developmental disability. She received her Ph.D. from Miami University in Oxford, Ohio, and has dedicated her life to building inclusive communities.

Stephen Kroeger, Ed.D., is an associate professor at the University of Cincinnati. In addition to his 16 years at the university, his teaching experience includes work in the West Bank of Palestine, the West Indies, the Peruvian Highlands, a suburban middle school, and a high school in Detroit. His current research includes the investigation of microteaching as a pedagogy of enactment for preservice teachers.

Rosemary Rotuno-Johnson, Ph.D., has 25 years' experience in the special education field, in both public and parochial K–12 settings and as a visiting instructor at two Cincinnati-area universities. Her driving passion is the responsible schoolwide inclusion of students with disabilities by the empowerment of all stakeholders. She is also active in the Ohio Council for Exceptional Children.

Acknowledgments

We would like to acknowledge our parents, who instilled in us the love of education so much that we have dedicated a lifetime of service to teaching and learning.

Introduction

Throughout history, as political climates change, new technologies emerge, and public awareness builds, a shift occurs in the way people look at schooling. These ways of knowing about schools and educating children can be considered paradigms, or conceptual schemas, in which our beliefs and practices are framed. This book reflects a shift in educational paradigms in special education since the reauthorization of the Individuals with Disabilities Education Improvement Act (IDEA) of 2004 (PL 108-446). We provide insight into the underlying spirit of the law and subsequent revisions, as well as practical applications of this more results-oriented focus, prioritizing student success over documentation of deficiencies.

Along with explicit instructions, concrete examples, demonstration scenarios, and practice activities, we provide a rubric to serve as a critical lens through which one can explore an actual individualized education program (IEP) development process that builds on students' strengths and interests, resulting in positive outcomes for students. Components of this inclusive process include creating a shared vision for the learner's future through collaborative partnerships, fostering student empowerment activities through an exploration of the student's personal abilities and leadership capacities, and generating measurable action plans to support and document learner progress.

Since the 1970s, much has been learned about educating learners with disabilities, and the modern paradigm shift reflects the learning that has resulted through years of practice, reflection, and research. Understanding this evolutionary process is critical to embracing the implications and requirements of current laws and subsequent IEP processes.

Prior to 1975, most children with disabilities were not afforded the rights they now receive and were often disregarded by the educational system. Although some learners with mild disabilities did attend school, the support they received to gain access to the curriculum was minimum to nonexistent. At times, children with disabilities were banned from school due to behavior difficulties, and children with significant cognitive challenges, such as intellectual disabilities, were ignored altogether.

In one real-life example, a young man named Jack, born in 1954, was considered to be exempt from school due to his lack of language and communication, resulting in low intelligence quotients and an "untestable" status for standardized, norm-referenced assessments. Without the benefit of a law protecting his right to an education, Jack was denied access to the public school systems in which his sisters were enrolled. Each time the upwardly mobile family moved to a new state due to a work transfer, Jack's mother would dutifully enroll her three daughters in the neighborhood school. Yet, when she asked about education for her son, she was consistently told that the district did not have a program for "children like him," leaving his mother to her own devices, making phone calls, and conducting research in order to find a special school program that would accommodate him.

The last time this happened, the local school district suggested the family contact a sheltered workshop in a neighboring county. The conditions at the workshop were so deplorable that Jack's family eventually quit transporting him to the workshop, allowing him to stay at home and work in the family business instead. Jack was about 17 years old at the time, and no one came looking for him when he stopped attending the workshop. There were no systems in place to track children with disabilities, signifying a lack of value of their schooling.

The rules changed with the passage of the Education for All Handicapped Children Act of 1975 (PL 94-142). This federal law afforded learners with disabilities the opportunity to attend public schools, based on the belief that children with disabilities had the same right to an education as children without disabilities. Learners with both mild and significant disabilities were provided an education that was considered appropriate for their abilities. The programs that were created, however, were often housed in separate buildings or segregated in classrooms away from peers without disabilities.

As time passed, and laws and systems evolved, the scenario has changed. Consider a positive example in 2022: Joey, a 12-year-old student with disabilities, attended the same school as his siblings without disabilities. Each morning, he exited the school bus and was greeted by a teaching assistant who escorted him to his seventh-grade class. The classroom teacher encouraged Joey to follow the classroom procedures for hanging up his coat and putting away his belongings along with the rest of the students in the room, and eventually Joey was able to follow these simple routines independently. On a monthly basis, a group of individuals including Joey, his older sister, his father or mother, his seventh-grade teacher, his teaching assistant, and a special education teacher all met to share Joey's progress and discuss changes in his educational programming. Occasionally, a regional autism specialist would be invited to the meeting to help provide input on the various behavioral, communication, and academic strategies needed in order for Joey to continue to make educational progress.

How do positive results like this happen? It starts with a good IEP, the foundational component of an effective response to the needs of students with an identified disability. All members of the team involved in a student's education share the need to "get it right," and getting the IEP right is critical to setting up programs like Joey's in which his educational needs can be met and monitored so that small missteps are noted immediately.

The Every Student Succeeds Act of 2015 (PL 114-95), which replaced the No Child Left Behind Act of 2001 (PL 107-110) and the reauthorization of IDEA 2004, has increased the inclusion of students with disabilities in the general education classroom (U.S. Department of Education, 2002). Although inclusion has become a generally widespread reality with 95% of students ages 6–21 with disabilities being taught in general education settings (National Center for Education Statistic,

2021), most general educators do not feel prepared to teach children with disabilities (National Center for Learning Disabilities, 2019). Making it more challenging, the IEP, which should be a resource to help guide educators on how to work with a student, often seems like a document that is difficult to decipher, much less implement in a coherent and meaningful way. This book is meant to help with this challenge.

For any member of an IEP team—educators, therapists, parents, administrators, and others—this book will walk you through an unbiased rubric to assist in understanding the IEP document, contribute to its design, and effectively implement its contents. We hope to deepen your sense of ownership of IEP writing, a task that may previously have been perceived as just one more thing a teacher has to do or as a parent's chore. Together, all IEP team members can design instruction that includes educational team members from the beginning. What follows is a short summary of each chapter and the skills you will develop within each. We hope to join you on your journey to developing meaningful and legally compliant IEPs.

Numerous laws have been enacted to ensure that the rights of students with disabilities are protected; yet, the history and legal aspects of special education can quickly fade, as parents often feel they are starting from scratch when their child's educational needs are not being met. Our goal in Chapter 1 is to offer you the background knowledge of the history and legal aspects of special education with the hope that you will understand the reasons these laws were enacted and you will better understand your role within the student's educational meeting. A concluding activity is provided to help ensure your understanding of the laws and how they have affected services for children with disabilities.

Throughout the rest of the book, we explore key considerations and components of the IEP, offering foundational guidance as well as practical activities based on the rubric. In Chapter 2, we discuss the importance of developing culturally responsive IEPs to address the unique needs of a child with disabilities who also comes from a culture that is different than the school's environment. Because many of these students come from homes where English is not spoken or is not the primary language, we discuss the stages of second language acquisition and the different language proficiency levels. This chapter also provides best practices in using interpreters at IEP meetings. The chapter concludes with the importance of using the child's home language and culture as assets to address their unique needs.

Collaboration is the next major consideration and consists of a complex set of interactions that build on and influence the types of relationships being established. Although collaboration is considered an integral component to the IEP team process, many individuals lack the necessary skills needed to effectively collaborate. Chapter 3 introduces collaboration through a real-life scenario of two individuals, a parent and teacher, trying to decide on the next steps for supporting a young student with a disability. Each comes to the table with their own set of experiences and expectations, leading each to a different approach to working toward the desired outcome. The scenario is not only used to introduce the topic, but also to encourage problem-solving skills because the reader is left to guess what happened next. Because the student is the main focus of collaboration during an IEP meeting, a section of this chapter is devoted to honoring the perspective of the student by using student-centered planning to promote student empowerment and eventual leadership. The chapter concludes with activities that allow team members to consider factors and collaborative issues that may have an impact on the student's learning.

The Present Levels of Academic Achievement and Functional Performance (PLAAFP) is one of the most important components of the IEP. This section of the IEP provides the basis on which future instructional plans and educational services are determined. In Chapter 4, you will learn how to write meaningful descriptions of a child's PLAAFP and how their disability affects academic achievement and functional performance. We provide various assessment strategies because data is critical in determining a student's progress and needs. The chapter concludes with activities to help the learner gain a deeper understanding of compliant and meaningful PLAAFP sections.

Goals are at the heart of the IEP and describe the achievements that a child will strive to accomplish as a result of specific intervention(s). In essence, goals form the basis from which instruction, interventions, and services are determined. In Chapter 5, you will learn to write meaningful and compliant statements (i.e., goals) that can easily be measured and communicated to all stakeholders. The checklist provided in this chapter will assist the learner in identifying measurable goals. The activities will also assist the learner in the technical aspects of writing quality IEP goals.

Chapter 6 details the importance of writing meaningful and measurable short-term objectives that are aligned with the IEP's goals. In this age of accountability, short-term objectives serve as interim steps toward a goal and are used to monitor whether sufficient progress is being made to reach the annual goal. In this chapter, you will learn about the importance of all children meeting state standards and the charge of IEP teams to develop goals and objectives that address any gaps. This chapter concludes with activities that provide the learner opportunities to develop practical skills of writing interim objectives to meet the IEP goals.

Although the measurement of annual goals has always been a function of IEP teams, teacher accountability has increased, now requiring more diligence in the use of ongoing, relevant progress monitoring data. Chapter 7 focuses on the practice of measuring and reporting student progress in relation to goals and objectives from the IEP, using data to make instructional decisions, and collecting data for academic and behavioral goals. In this chapter, you will learn about data collection, frequency of reporting, the use of multiple measures, and time lines for collection processes. Examples of progress monitoring assessments are provided to allow you to transfer this information into classroom and school practices.

When determining an appropriate place for a student with disabilities to receive services, the IEP team should begin by first considering how the student can meaningfully participate in the general education curriculum and environment. This exploration should not be influenced by a particular disability label but, rather, by recognizing how the student might benefit from interactions and involvement in this setting and with this curricular focus. Chapter 8 discusses the importance of the least restrictive environment (LRE) and what that looks like for students with disabilities. Supplementary aids and services are described along with a summary decision-making plan for factors addressing the LRE.

Chapter 9 shows how to identify specific accommodations and supports that can be implemented in the classroom and foster divergent thinking, encouraging the development of further suggestions for accommodating the student's academic needs. The chapter concludes with activities that engage the learner in determining the best placement for a student based on their unique learning needs.

Decisions related to making accommodations and modifications form one component of IEP writing that has often been inconsistently interpreted. Chapter 9 provides guidelines for determining student accommodations and/or modifications for academic necessity, using the needs of the student as the foundation for decisions. We present a Challenge Scenario illustrating the classic conundrum involving ethical issues of fairness. The discussion reveals common misconceptions about the socially constructed nature of disability and focuses on how the nature of the task and the skills of the individual intersect to create an academic need. The accommodation and testing scenario is simply an extension of the vignettes already discussed. The activities in this chapter will assist you in developing the skills and knowledge to identify the accommodations and modifications possibly needed for students with disabilities.

Chapter 10 addresses the process of planning for transition from school to adulthood and not only provides in-depth information on the required components of a transition plan, but also leads you through a philosophical awakening related to the vast array of options available to students. What is demonstrated throughout is how all team members benefit from a thoughtful transition process that actively engages all stakeholders and is culturally respectful to the family's long-term goals for the student. Specific changes in regulations are highlighted, providing you with a thorough understanding of the current transition requirements. The checklists, rubrics, and activities help facilitate your understanding of current transition practices by allowing you to look critically at the different skills students need to be successful within the community.

Chapter 11 discusses how to design behavioral interventions plans to address challenging behaviors and provides an explanation of the importance of using positive interventions when designing IEPs to help students learn acceptable behaviors. Readers will learn about the impact disruptive behavior has on student learning and how to develop goals to address challenging behaviors.

In the final chapter, we discuss services that are provided within private and parochial schools. Chapter 12 also explains the differences between an IEP and an individualized service plan.

The IEP Checklist, an inventory for confirming the presence of required elements, is included at the end of this book. Full versions of the tools introduced throughout the book are available online for download from the Brookes Download Hub; these include the IEP Rubric for evaluating the completeness and quality of each element of an IEP, a template for making corrections based on the IEP rubric, and photocopiable versions of the activities and forms. Finally, this new edition includes a glossary of useful terms that you can reference throughout reading this book or whenever you need a reminder. Glossary terms are in bold at first mention in the text, with a full definition in the glossary.

REFERENCES

Education for All Handicapped Children Act of 1975, PL 94-142, 20 U.S.C. §§ 1400 *et seq.*

Every Student Succeeds Act of 2015, PL 114-95, 20 U.S.C §§ 1001 *et seq.*

Individuals with Disabilities Education Improvement Act (IDEA) of 2004, PL 108-446, 20 U.S.C. §§ 1400 *et seq.*

National Center for Educational Statistics. (2021). *Percentage distribution of students 6 to 21 years old served under Individuals with Disabilities Education Act (IDEA), Part B, by educational environment and type of disability: Fall 2018.* U.S. Department of Education. https://nces.ed.gov/fastfacts/display.asp?id=59

National Center for Learning Disabilities. (2019). *Forward together: Helping educators unlock the power of students who learn differently.* https://www.ncld.org/wp-content/uploads/2019/05/Forward-Together_NCLD-report.pdf

National Institute for Urban School Improvement-Leadscape. (2013). *Part B SPP/APR 2012 indicator analyses (FFY 2010).* http://ectacenter.org/~pdfs/sec619/part-b_sppapr_12.pdf

No Child Left Behind Act of 2001, PL 107-110,115 Stat. 1425, 20 U.S.C. §§ 6301 *et seq.*

U.S. Department of Education. (2002). *A new era: Revitalizing special education for children and their families.* President's Commission on Excellence in Special Education. https://ectacenter.org/~pdfs/calls/2010/earlypartc/revitalizing_special_education.pdf

This book is dedicated to educators, parents, and caregivers who work tirelessly serving children with exceptionalities. May you be blessed with successful IEP meetings that provide a plan to improve educational outcomes for each child that you serve.

I

Foundations
for Understanding
the Development
of a Meaningful IEP

1

Overview of the History and Legal Perspectives of Special Education

Kathleen G. Winterman, Leo Bradley, and John Concannon

After reading this chapter and engaging in activities related to this chapter, you will be able to meet the following outcomes:

- Explain the importance of the laws that lay the foundation for services for children with disabilities.

- Identify the court cases that shaped the laws that currently exist.

- Discuss the parameters of the current context of special education services in public and private school in the United States.

In the fall of 2019, 56 million students in the United States headed off to elementary and secondary schools, which includes 5.8 million students who attend private schools (educationdata.org). Of this population, 13.7% of the students were identified as having some type of disability, and 9.6% of the students were learning English as a second language. Today, it is considered normal for students with disabilities to be educated in their neighborhood school with their same-age peers, but this has not always been the case.

The passage of the National Defense Education Act of 1958 (PL 85-864) provided the first federal funding to train teachers to work with children with intellectual disabilities. During the subsequent decades, various pieces of legislation were enacted related to special education, all culminating in the United States' most current special education law: the Individuals with Disabilities Education Improvement Act (IDEA) of 2004 (PL 108-446).

> In this text, we define *parents* as a child's biological parents as well as those who are legal guardians.

IDEA'S KEY COMPONENTS

- **Free appropriate public education (FAPE).** Requires that the student be educated in a manner that meets their educational needs by a public educational agency that is free to the family.
  - *Zero Reject.* Mandates that the school cannot deny a child an education due to the severity of their needs.
- **Least restrictive environment (LRE).** The student is educated in a manner that is most like their typical peers.
- **Procedural safeguards** (due process). The family has the right to disagree with the placement, services, and educational plan for their child and can bring the school district to court.
- **Parental participation** (shared decision making). Parents have the right to participate as part of the education team for their child.
- **Nondiscriminatory evaluation.** Requires schools to utilize a team approach in assessing a student in all suspected areas of a disability using measures that are valid, reliable, culturally relevant, and linguistically appropriate.
- **Individualized education program (IEP).** The IEP team assesses current evaluation information and develops a written document designed to meet the unique educational needs of each student with a disability.

Did You Know?

One of the most transformational changes to the law occurred in the 1990 reauthorization, which was subtle but significant. The title of the law changed from the Education of All Handicapped Children Act to the Individuals with Disabilities Education Act, which mandated **people-first language.** This seemingly insignificant variation of terms reinforced that the individual is a person first who has a disability. They are bigger and more encompassing than their disability.

Prior to 1975, students with disabilities were systematically excluded from public education and were often thought of as uneducable and therefore not worthy of being educated with their typically developing peers. Since the enactment of the Education for All Handicapped Children Act of 1975 (PL 94-142), federal legislation has required that all public schools provide a **free appropriate public education (FAPE)** and related services to children with disabilities. In addition, this law mandated that students be taught in the **least restrictive environment (LRE)**; therefore, eliminating the practice of arbitrary exclusion based on a child's disability. The plan for providing these services, and thus a foundation for the student's appropriate education, is referred to as an **individualized education program (IEP).** IEPs act as a product and process in guiding the instruction of children with disabilities (Lee-Tarver, 2006). Rotter (2014) conducted a study and found that many general educators did not refer to students' IEP documents after they were written; they treated the IEP as an artifact rather than a vital guiding document that outlined a student's educational plan.

Stop and Think!

In 2001, President Bush reenacted the Elementary and Secondary Education Act of 1965 (PL 89-10) as the No Child Left Behind (NCLB) Act of 2001 (PL 107-110). This law is based on four pillars: 1) stronger accountability for results, 2) more freedom for states and communities, 3) proven education methods, and 4) more choices for parents/caregivers.

- How has NCLB had an impact on the education of students with individual-ized education programs (IEPs)?

- How do the four pillars relate to the development of meaningful and effec-tive IEPs?

The **Every Student Succeeds Act (ESSA)** of 2015 (PL 114-95) was passed by President Obama and continued the reauthorization of the Elementary and Sec-ondary Education Act of 1965 but furthered the initiatives of NCLB.

ESSA includes provisions that help ensure success for students and schools. The law

- Advances equity by upholding critical protections for America's disadvan-taged students

- Requires—for the first time—that all students in America be taught to high academic standards that will prepare them to succeed in college and careers

- Ensures that vital information is provided to educators, families, students, and communities through annual statewide assessments that measure stu-dents' progress toward those high standards

- Helps to support and grow local innovations—including evidence- and place-based interventions developed by local leaders and educators—consistent with Investing in Innovation and Promise Neighborhoods

- Sustains and expands access to high-quality preschool

- Maintains an expectation that there will be accountability and action to effect positive change in the lowest performing schools where groups of students are not making expected progress and graduation rates are low over extended periods of time

---

The most recent federal mandates under IDEA state that all children with disabilities must have access to the general curriculum. IEP development and implementation necessitate active involvement of all members on the child's education team. Being knowledgeable about the IEP process is not an option, but a requirement of all.

To ensure procedural safeguards are in place, students' IEPs must adhere to the IDEA mandates. Teachers, school administrators, and staff are responsible for holding IDEA-compliant IEP meetings by ensuring that the team is developing educational programs that 1) are based on relevant assessments, 2) contain meaningful ambitious goals, and 3) provide services that are based on peer-reviewed research as mandated by the **No Child Left Behind (NCLB) Act** of 2001 (PL 107-110) rather than on convenience for or the preference of the teacher.

Intervention specialists or special educators are directed to monitor students' progress toward achieving their goals and make the necessary programmatic changes if goals are not being met. The following components should be present to ensure a student's goals are educationally meaningful: 1) a condition under which the goals will be met, 2) a targeted behavior or skill to be measured, and 3) a criterion of expected performance. Data must be collected to monitor the student's progress toward achieving their goals. Students' IEPs also must include a schedule in which caregivers will be informed about the student's success in attaining their academic and performance goals.

The last reauthorization of IDEA included multiple changes to the required components of the IEP (Council for Exceptional Children, 2013). The IEP must be developed, reviewed, and revised according to Section 614 of the legislation (Wilkinson, 2010). When revising IDEA, Congress established the following changes to eliminate what it perceived to be excessive paperwork requirements of the law:

- Team members can be excused from the IEP meeting given that the parents and school agree in writing that the member is not needed.

- Revisions can be made to the IEP without holding an additional meeting if an initial IEP meeting has been held and all parties agree with the revisions. The agreed-on changes should be signed by all team members and attached to the active IEP.

- IEP meetings may be conducted via alternative methods such as videoconferencing and conference calls.

- When students with IEPs change school districts, the receiving district must provide comparable services until the child's current IEP has been adopted or until a new IEP is written (Smith, 2005; Yell et al., 2006).

A 15-state demonstration program was established under IDEA to develop a multiyear IEP (not to exceed 3 years) with written consent of the student's parents or legal guardians. States wishing to participate in this pilot program must request this option.

All main components were continued with the latest reauthorization of IDEA, but the law also extended the IEP to include objectives and benchmarks for students who take alternate assessments. The law added response to instruction for identification of students with learning disabilities, which moves beyond the discrepancy format that typically had been employed to determine eligibility for services—especially for students with specific learning disabilities. Special educators now need to be highly qualified in the areas they teach. Finally, students may be removed from school for up to 45 days under special circumstances (e.g., bringing weapons to school), even if the behavior was a manifestation of their disability.

Darrow (2016) contended that the IEP remains the cornerstone of IDEA. With the 2004 reauthorization, changes were enacted that bring IDEA into alignment with NCLB, and ESSA continues to support these amendments. Given the fundamental focus on the IEP as the linchpin of a child's academic program, teachers are mandated to have advanced training in its development and adherence to the law. As such, all teacher training programs include coverage of IEP development and other legal topics related to the education of children with disabilities. The IEP must include specific components for it to be considered an appropriate program in accordance with the legislation.

LAWS THAT SHAPED SPECIAL EDUCATION

Although education for children with disabilities was legally established by the Education for All Handicapped Children Act of 1975, which was reauthorized as the Individuals with Disabilities Education Act (IDEA) of 1990 (PL 101-476), the Individuals with Disabilities Education Act Amendments (IDEA) of 1997 (PL 105-17), and IDEA 2004, and then the **Americans with Disabilities Act (ADA)** of 1990 (PL 101-336), neither of these statutory initiatives could begin to anticipate the legal questions and controversies that implementing special education policies and procedures would create.

Thus, federal court systems had to perform three functions to clarify the intent of federal law regarding children with disabilities and how the laws should be implemented. First, the constitutionality of the laws had to be upheld; second, the court system had to interpret the law in areas of ambiguity; and third, the courts had to apply legal principles to decide controversies among schools, parents, and children.

The primary principles of IDEA are examined further in the following section. The tenets are explored based on their legal precedence, which clarified the implementation of the law.

Stop and Think!

The Americans with Disabilities Act (ADA) of 1990 (PL 101-336) established the definition of a *disability* as a physical or mental impairment that substantially limits major life activities.

- How do the Individuals with Disabilities Education Improvement Act of 2004 (PL 108-446) and ADA intersect and apply to the lives of children with disabilities?

Due Process

When education for children with disabilities was mandated, schools wrestled with applying educational pursuits within this new paradigm. Schools began to question how to educate children with disabilities. Should students be educated through different kinds of curriculum design or alternative instructional strategies? Should their educational attainment be assessed differently than children within general education? Although these questions were eventually answered through pedagogical decisions by educators, the court system defined parameters and weighed heavily into the decision-making process, sometimes supporting the educational establishment and sometimes totally reversing the educational institution's stance.

The requirement that all children with disabilities receive procedural and substantive due process is at the heart of the law regarding special education. When Congress passed the Education for All Handicapped Children Act of 1975 and later IDEA, it included due process procedures as one of the basic tenets of the law. In addition to ADA, these laws clearly spell out the fundamentals of procedural due process. Substantive due process, however, has had to be further clarified through landmark court cases.

Procedural Due Process   **Procedural due process** ensures that children with disabilities receive a proper hearing, notification, and impartiality regarding their eligibility for special education. This aspect of due process is assured through the multifactored evaluation or evaluation team report to determine if the student is eligible for special education; the IEP development, implementation, and ongoing assessment; and all the other requirements that are defined in the remainder of this chapter.

Substantive Due Process   **Substantive due process** involves acts that deny or inhibit a person's life, liberty, and property rights. Included in property rights are the right to an education and the right to earn a living. Needless to say, neither of these property rights were being granted to children with disabilities prior to the laws requiring FAPE. Therefore, both Congress and the courts have passed legislation and issued court rulings that guarantee both procedural and substantive due process rights to children with disabilities.

A review of the cases that form the precedents for special education law can be categorized through the following questions.

Can schools opt out of due process for children with disabilities due to insufficient funds?   Because many public school districts in all states are sometimes in precarious financial situations, the issue of providing an appropriate education for students with disabilities has raised the question of affordability. This issue had to be resolved so that services for children with disabilities would not be reduced or eliminated due to financial problems. Prior to the passage of the Education for All Handicapped Children Act of 1975, two significant cases clearly determined that educating children with disabilities would not be determined by financial consideration.

In the case of *Pennsylvania Association for Retarded Children (PARC) v. Commonwealth of Pennsylvania* (1971), a federal court ruled that children with cognitive disabilities in Pennsylvania were entitled to a free public education. In the case of *Mills v. Board of Education of the District of Columbia* (1972), the district court ruled that the District of Columbia school must provide a publicly supported education for exceptional children. The court stated that

> Their failure to fulfill this clear duty to include and retain these children in the public school system, or otherwise provide them with publicly supported education, and their failure to afford them due process hearing and periodic review, cannot be excused by the claim that there are insufficient funds.

What is the definition of FAPE with regard to children with disabilities?

As the Education for All Handicapped Children Act of 1975 was implemented, it was inevitable that the definition of FAPE for children with disabilities had to be clarified. Such a definition for general education students had never been universally addressed. A question was whether FAPE for a child with a disability meant that the child must reach their maximum potential as a result of an LRE and their IEP. In the landmark case of *Board of Education of the Hendrick Hudson Central School District v. Amy Rowley* (1982), the U.S. Supreme Court ruled that the law was to provide for a "basic floor of opportunity to learn," as opposed to the achievement of maximum potential. The decision clarified that the state would need to meet the definition by providing personalized instruction with sufficient support services to permit the child to benefit educationally from that instruction.

If maximizing potential had been the ruling, then many questions concerning valid assessments would have needed to be addressed. It is difficult to see how those decisions could have been reached for children with disabilities when there was no universal operational definition in place for any aspect of education. The court was wise in defining FAPE as an opportunity, as opposed to an unmeasurable outcome such as maximum potential.

In *Endrew F. v. Douglas County School District* (2017), the U.S. Supreme Court made this standard a bit more substantial when Chief Justice Roberts stated, "A student offered an educational program providing 'mere more than a de minimis progress' from year to year can hardly be said to have been offered an education at all" (p. 11). As the courts have evolved, the services and expectations of the students' educational opportunities continue to clarify what constitutes FAPE. The IEP is no longer looking at the minimum access but, rather, considers whether the student has a reasonably robust set of goals to encourage growth so that they can benefit from the educational opportunity.

Are there disabilities so severe that public schools will be exempt from the requirement to educate the child?

This question centers on the definition of education. To some, education means that some benefit will be derived from the experience. This perception is based on the traditional view of education resulting in the acquisition of knowledge, skills, or dispositions. Clearly, there are individuals who have such severe disabilities that such a definition is more challenging to determine. During its initial stages, some felt that the Education for All

Handicapped Children Act of 1975 meant that the child in question would have to demonstrate the ability to benefit from participation in a school's special education program. In the landmark case of *Timothy W. v. Rochester School District* (1989), the First Circuit of the U.S. Court of Appeals ruled that the Education for All Handicapped Children Act of 1975 mandated the education of all children with disabilities and did not require a child to demonstrate a benefit as a condition precedent to participation. Therefore, the Zero Reject principle was clearly enunciated and followed. The Zero Reject principle is one of the core principles of IDEA and states that a child cannot be denied an education due to the severity of their disability. This supports the concept of FAPE, in which all children have the right to an appropriate education. Also see the U.S. Sixth Circuit Court of Appeals opinion, *Emily Thomas v. Cincinnati Board of Education* (1990).

What related services are schools required to perform?   Many children with disabilities need medical services so that they can participate in FAPE. The courts were called on to determine what services teachers and schools could perform that would not create excessive liability potential based on how the Education for All Handicapped Children Act of 1975 defined *related services*. The act states

> The term "related services" means transportation, and such development, corrective, and other supportive services (including speech pathology and audiology, psychological services, physical and occupational therapy, recreation, and medical and counseling services, except that such medical and counseling services shall be for diagnostic and evaluative purposes only) as may be required to assist a handicapped child to benefit from special education. (PL 94-142, 20 U.S.C. §§ 1401[17])

Most of the confusion that was created by this section of the law regarded which medical services fell under its domain. In answering this question, the courts asked themselves two questions: 1) Is the service required to assist the child to benefit from special education? and 2) Is the service excluded from the definition of a medical service by serving purposes other than diagnosis or evaluation? Therefore, if the service can be performed by someone other than a physician and does not involve a medical diagnosis or evaluation, then the service would be declared a related service and included in a student's IEP. If the service includes diagnosis or evaluation, then the service would be considered a medical service and would have to be performed by a physician. Sometimes this line of separation is not clear enough for universal application and requires a judicial decision. *Irving Independent School District v. Amber Tatro* (1984) was one such landmark case that looks at this question. The courts decided that a medical service that allows the child to benefit from special education is a supportive service required of the schools. This opinion was again affirmed in the U.S. Supreme Court decision in *Cedar Rapids Community School District v. Garret F.* (1999) (see Osborne, 2022), which further clarified that the exception for medical services not being provided is when such services must be provided by a physician.

Are disciplinary procedures different for children with disabilities?   As **inclusion** increased, the need for legal guidelines surfaced regarding disciplining students with disabilities. Neither the Education for All Handicapped Children Act of 1975 nor Section 504 of the Rehabilitation Act of 1973 (PL 93-112) addressed this issue, thus leaving it to the courts to determine the legal ramifications involved and principles to be followed. Two IDEA provisions must be considered when deciding cases involving the discipline of students with disabilities—LRE and FAPE.

Serious disciplinary actions usually involve either suspension or expulsion. They must be considered separately; however, the courts have consistently ruled that students with disabilities must be given special consideration for either suspension or expulsion (Friend, 2011).

Suspension has been viewed favorably by the courts as an appropriate disciplinary action for students with disabilities when it has been determined that the student's misconduct is not related to their disability. If it is determined that the misconduct is in some way related to the student's disability, then an alternative placement such as home instruction or an alternative school whose mission is to serve students with behavior and emotional disorders should be considered in lieu of suspension or expulsion.

A "stay put" provision was derived from the Education for All Handicapped Children Act of 1975, however, which mandates that school authorities cannot remove a child with a disability from their regular classroom placement during review procedures to determine an alternate placement. The student must remain in the current placement until another placement is determined. In *M.R. v. Ridley School District* (2014), the court found that when a hearing office determines that a child's educational placement is appropriate, the child is entitled to "stay put" in that placement throughout all the following disputes about the placement until a final decision has been reached.

The "stay put" provision did, however, raise the question of what a school could or should do if a student exhibited dangerous or disruptive behavior as a result of their disability. In *Honig v. Doe* (1988), the court made clear that the Education for All Handicapped Children Act of 1975 conveys the following rights for children with disabilities:

- Children with disabilities have a substantive right to an education.

- School officials may not unilaterally exclude a student with disabilities from the classroom for dangerous or disruptive conduct for an indiscriminate amount of time when the conduct is a result of a disability.

- School officials may temporarily suspend a student for up to 10 days to protect the safety of others and provide a cooling off period.

- An IEP meeting can be called during the temporary suspension to determine the student's new placement.

Congress had periodically considered the reauthorization of IDEA. When the bill was amended in 1997, major concerns surfaced concerning disciplinary procedures for children with disabilities. This concern was largely the result of the increase in student use of drugs and dangerous weapons. Therefore, the law was amended to allow school personnel to change the placement of children with disabilities in certain situations. This change of placement can be made if the student possesses illegal drugs or brings a weapon to school or to a school function. Under these circumstances, the placement can be changed to

- An appropriate interim alternative setting, another setting, or suspension for not more than 10 days (to the extent such alternatives would be applied to children without disabilities)

- An appropriate interim alternative educational setting for the same amount of time that a child without disabilities would be subject to discipline, but not more than 45 days

An interim alternative should only be considered when

- Maintaining the current placement could cause harm to the student or others

- The current placement is inappropriate

- The school made an effort to minimize the current risk with supplementary aids and other services

A manifestation review is required when it is determined that disciplinary action is required (see Chapter 11).

How are children in nonpublic schools served?   This issue is addressed in IDEA and accompanying regulations. Each state must adopt the following policies and procedures:

- Provision must be made for participation in special education and related services for children with disabilities enrolled in private elementary and secondary schools.

- The local public district of residence must provide equitable opportunity for participation in the program.

- Although service to private schools does not have to be equal, it should be comparable (*K.R. v. Anderson Community School Corporation*, 1996/1997).

- The federal statute refers to two categories of students with disabilities that relate to private schools:

  1. *Children with disabilities attending approved private schools in accordance with an IEP developed by the public school.* These students with disabilities are placed in a private school setting specifically designed to meet their educational needs following an appropriate IEP determination. The placement must be state approved, and the state must pay the cost.

  2. *Children with disabilities attending private schools voluntarily.* For students whose parents or guardians voluntarily place their child in a private school, the law requires only that provisions must be made for participation in the local special education program. IDEA intended to differentiate between children placed in private settings through the IEP process and those voluntarily placed in private schools by parents or guardians. For this category, the state's responsibility is not as extensive as it is for children who attend public school. Yet, the state is held to providing genuine opportunity to learn for children with disabilities in this category (see Chapter 12).

The Burlington Test   In 1985, The U.S. Supreme Court held that the courts had the power to order public schools to reimburse parents with children in private school for expenditures on private special education if the court finds that the public school's IEP was inappropriate (*Burlington School Committee v. Massachusetts Board of Education*, 1985). The principle was reiterated by the U.S. Supreme Court in *Florence County School District Four v. Carter* (1993).

Children With Disabilities in Sectarian Schools and the Establishment Clause   In the landmark case *Zobrest v. Catalina Foothills School District* (1993), the U.S. Supreme Court ruled that using state funds for the education of children with disabilities in a sectarian school was not a violation of the Establishment Clause of the first amendment of the U.S. Constitution, in which the government is prohibited from making any law respecting an establishment of religion. The court held that the Establishment Clause does not prevent school authorities from furnishing a sign language interpreter to a child enrolled in a sectarian school to facilitate their education. Government programs that neutrally provide benefits to a broad range of citizens defined without reference to religion are not subject to an Establishment Clause challenge just because the sectarian institution may also receive an attenuated financial benefit.

What is the definition of the LRE?   IDEA promotes the philosophy that children with disabilities should be educated with children without disabilities in a typical classroom setting whenever possible. This philosophy is based on the belief that children with disabilities benefit from the opportunity to socialize and interact with typically developing children (McCabe et al., 2020). In addition, placing students with disabilities within a general education classroom setting lessens the possibility that they will be stigmatized or pointed out as being different. This legal philosophy assumes that the general education classroom will have satisfactory supplemental aids and services.

IDEA regulations require a "continuum of alternative placements" and mandates that consideration is given to any harmful effect on the child when selecting an LRE. The precise meaning of *LRE* has been an area of significant debate and court action. One clear operational definition is that the continuum of alternative placement is broad, ranging from the general education classroom to a hospital placement to the child's home.

Different federal circuit courts have interpreted the definition of LRE differently in various cases. For example, the Third, Fifth, and 11th Circuit Courts have used what is known as the Daniel R.R. test (*Daniel R.R. v. State Board of Education*, 1989). The Daniel R.R. test is a two-prong test. The first question asks whether learning in the general education classroom can be achieved satisfactorily for a given child when provided with supplemental aids and services. If the answer is no, and the school intends to provide special education or remove the child from the general education setting, then the second question asks whether the school has included the child to the maximum extent possible. The court in *Daniel R.R. v State Board of Education* determined several factors that school authorities should consider when deciding the level of general education classroom placement:

- The child's ability to profit from the general curriculum

- The nonacademic benefits (e.g., social interaction)

- The impact on the general education students in the classroom

The Fourth, Sixth, and Eighth Circuits Courts have applied a test decided in the *Roncker v. Walter* (1983) case. Although the court recognized the strong congressional support for the inclusion of students with disabilities, the opinion pointed out that it is not mandatory in all cases. The Roncker test requires that the school show that a separate placement would offer superior educational services for the student.

- If the school determines that a separate placement is superior to inclusion, then the school must demonstrate why it is superior, and the court must determine if it is possible for the same services to be offered in an inclusive setting.

- If such additional and commensurate services can be offered in the general education classroom, then the court will hold that a separate or segregated placement is not appropriate.

- If, however, the marginal benefits received from inclusion are far outweighed by the benefits gained from services that could not be easily provided in the inclusive setting, then the court will hold that the inclusive setting is not appropriate.

In *Sacramento City School District v. Rachel H.* (1994), the Ninth Circuit Court combined elements from both the Daniel R.R. and Roncker tests in determining its position on inclusion. The court's four-pronged analysis considered

1. The educational benefits of full-time placement in a general education classroom

2. The nonacademic benefits of the placement

3. The effect the student with disabilities had on the teacher and other students in the general education classroom

4. The cost of the inclusive placement

Two significant points need to be made in relation to inclusion that are not integral to the decisions in the three court cases just described. First, the factors discussed in all the cases should not be interpreted as being the exclusive or exhaustive list of factors relevant to the issue of inclusion. Second, the primary responsibility of developing the program for the child with a disability lies with the state and local school agencies with the cooperation of the child's parents or guardians. As to whose position will prevail in issues of conflict, the court in *Lachman v. Illinois State Board of Education* (1988) concluded that parental discretion in the matter of placement must defer to the judgment of the professional educators of the public school district. Parents, no matter how well intended, do not have the right under IDEA to compel a school district to provide a specific program or employ a specific methodology in providing for their child.

In *Oberti v. Board of Education of the Borough of Clementon School District* (1993), the court drew precedent mainly from the Daniel R.R. case in adopting a three-prong process to determine whether a child with disability can be educated satisfactorily in a general education class with supplemental aids and services. The court determined that several factors should be considered, including 1) whether the school district has made reasonable efforts to accommodate the child in the general education classroom; 2) the educational benefits available to the child in a general education class, with appropriate aids and services, compared with the benefits provided in a special education class; and 3) the possible negative effects of the inclusion of the child on the education of the other students in the general education class. It should be noted that cost, among others, is another factor that could be considered.

What are the laws relative to IEPs?   The IEP is the written design of an educational plan for a student with a disability that includes identifying the child's educational needs, annual goals and objectives, specific educational programs, services to be offered, and evaluation procedures for monitoring progress. The IEP is the cornerstone on which instruction will be provided for the child with disability. The IEP is developed by an education team that consists of the child's teacher, parents or guardians, and a person qualified to interpret evaluation results and knows the curriculum. The IEP must be evaluated annually and contain the following components:

- *Present level of performance:* The child's present level of performance must be stated, requiring the school district to specifically indicate how the child's disability affects their involvement and progress in the general curriculum.

- *Goals:* The annual goals must be reasonably challenging while measurable, and the child must progress in the general curriculum. (Some states require benchmarks or objectives in addition to goals for students who do not participate in high-stakes assessments.)

- *Accommodations:* Does the child require accommodations in how the information will be presented or how the child will demonstrate their knowledge to the teacher?

- *Modifications:* Program modifications must be provided that will enable the child to advance appropriately toward attaining annual goals.

- *Assessments:* Provision must be made for the child to participate in state or school district student achievement assessments.

- *Evaluation measures:* Evaluation procedures must relate to IEP goals and measure the child's progress toward annual goals.

- *Parent reports:* Parents must receive periodic report cards indicating the child's progress and the extent to which the progress is sufficient to achieve annual goals.

Section 504 of the Rehabilitation Act of 1973

School personnel are often confused about the difference between the provisions of IDEA and Section 504 of the Rehabilitation Act of 1973. Under Section 504, an individual with a disability is one who 1) has a physical or mental impairment that substantially limits one or more major life activities and 2) has a record of impairment. To receive consideration under Section 504, the person must

- Demonstrate that they suffer from a physical or mental impairment

- Identify the activity claimed to be impaired and establish that it constitutes a major life activity

- Demonstrate that their impairment substantially limits the major life activity previously identified

The major differences between IDEA 2004 and Section 504 are delineated in Table 1.1.

Table 1.1. Major differences between the Individuals with Disabilities Education Improvement Act and Section 504

IDEA	Section 504
Disability code required	Record of impairment required
Need to qualify under regulations	Doctor note required
Requires an individualized education program	Requires a Section 504 plan
Goals are mandated	Only accommodations
School receives federal funding	No funding provided
Requires staffing (special educator, related services)	No staff required
May include related services	Generally no related services
Annual meeting required	Meetings not mandated
Due process protection	Protects from discrimination
Unique educational needs are met	Plan must be followed
Monitored through the Office of Exceptional Children	Monitored through the Office of Civil Rights

Do all children with disabilities receive an extended school year? The issue of whether a child with a disability is entitled to instruction beyond the typical school year is determined by the IEP. Therefore, an extended school year may be required for some students under certain circumstances, depending on the IEP. Legal cases involving this issue surfaced when states passed statutes that set a maximum number of days of instruction for the public school year, including summer. When parents and advocates for children with disabilities requested an extended school year, they did so based on the claim that serious regression occurred in children with disabilities over the summer vacation. The schools' rebuttal was that regression was due to many factors other than disability and, therefore, the schools refused to grant the extended school year to students with disabilities with IEPs. The federal courts ruled that a set school year was contrary to the federal intent of all legislation relating to children with disabilities. Although several cases have been litigated, *Reusch v. Fountain* (1994) ruled that the following factors should be considered by the IEP team when considering extended school year services:

- Regression and recoupment (Is the child likely to lose critical skills or fail to recover these skills within a reasonable time?)

- Degree of progress toward IEP goals and objectives

- Emerging skills/breakthrough opportunities (Will a lengthy summer break cause significant problems for a child who is learning a key skill such as reading?)

- Interfering behavior (Does the child's behavior interfere with their ability to benefit from special education?)

- Nature and/or severity of disability

- Special circumstances that interfere with child's ability to benefit from special education.

Although determining eligibility for an extended school year requires a review of progress monitoring data and an in-depth conversation among all IEP team members, it also requires strong leadership skills to ensure that the student's needs are met.

IEP RUBRIC

The authors of this book have developed a rubric to help determine if IEP documents are following the law. The rubric includes the following key areas as mandated under IDEA 2004:

- The student's present levels, including academic achievement and functional performance

- Measurable annual goals

- Benchmarks and short-term objectives for students who take alternate assessments

- Periodic reports to parents

- Special education and related services

- Supports necessary to provide the LRE

- Accommodations

- Coordinated transition activities and services beginning at the age of 16

- Appropriate technical information

The purpose of the rubric and this text is to support all IEP teams in developing effective IEPs and assist in the evaluation of an IEP. Having a tool to evaluate an IEP's quality enhances the effectiveness of the IEP as a legal document protecting the rights of students. The complete rubric can be found online at the Brookes Download Hub. Although school personnel are required to master this complex and ever-changing critical document, parents may have little or no understanding of the document or the planning process; yet, they are to be equal team members. The rubric is meant to level the playing field and assist parents in becoming equal team members in the development of their child's IEP. The presentation of the IEP rubric will instruct participants in evaluating the effectiveness and accuracy of their IEP with relationship to the law.

SUMMARY

The evolution of special education services continues to unfold as practice is shaped by law, and law is determined by unique challenges to see the future in a new light. Many of our current laws will be reauthorized within the next few years, which will reshape the special education field once again. In subsequent chapters, readers are reminded of current best practices in the development of IEP plans that assist students in achieving their academic dreams.

ACTIVITY

The activity included in this chapter is intended for the reader to gain a deeper understanding of the content covered. The activity associated with this chapter includes the following:

- Activity 1.1. Landmark Court Cases and Implications

Activity 1.1.

Landmark Court Cases and Implications

Supporting chapter: Chapter 1 (Overview of the History and Legal Perspectives of Special Education)

Purpose: The purpose of this activity is to reflect on key court cases and how they have influenced the teaching profession, both at the instructional and institutional levels.

Directions: Use the following table to reflect on the landmark court cases and write one to two sentences on how the court cases have influenced the teaching profession at the instructional (classroom) level and at the district (institutional) level.

Case	Issue	Instructional implications: What are the implications at the classroom level?	Institutional implications: What are the implications at the district level?
Pennsylvania Association for Retarded Children (PARC) v. Commonwealth of Pennsylvania (1971)	Public education for children with intellectual disabilities		
Mills v. Board of Education of the District of Columbia (1972)	Special education for all children with disabilities		
Board of Education of the Hendrick Hudson Central School District v. Amy Rowley (1982)	Free appropriate public education (FAPE)		
Irving Independent School District v. Amber Tatro (1984)	Defining related services		
Burlington School Committee v. Massachusetts Department of Education (1985)	Private school placement		

Case	Issue	Instructional implications: What are the implications at the classroom level?	Institutional implications: What are the implications at the district level?
Honig v. Doe (1988)	Exclusion from school		
Timothy W. v. Rochester School District (1989)	FAPE		
Endrew F. v. Douglas County School District (2017)	FAPE		

2

IEP Considerations for Culturally and Linguistically Diverse Learners

Clarissa E. Rosas

After reading this chapter and engaging in activities related to this chapter, you will be able to meet the following outcomes:

- Explain the importance of culturally responsive IEPs

- Identify the stages of second language acquisition

- Distinguish between social and academic language

- Describe culturally responsive practices that should be considered when developing IEPs

- Summarize best practices when using an interpreter at IEP meetings

As discussed in Chapter 1, the pervasive pattern of discrimination, exclusion, and denial of services for individuals with disabilities resulted in the enactment of the Education for All Handicapped Children Act of 1975 (PL 94-142), which was renamed as the Individuals with Disabilities Education Act (IDEA) of 1990 (PL 101-476). IDEA strengthened two fundamental principles each time it was reauthorized: free appropriate public education (FAPE) and least restrictive environment (LRE). Consequently, the IEP, which has been in existence since the passage of the Education for All Handicapped Children Act, serves to memorialize the educational plan designed to address the individual needs of the student and ensure the fundamental requirements of FAPE in the LRE. Yet, this well-intended IEP has evolved into a legal document that primarily focuses on mandated services more than an instructional tool that addresses the unique learning supports required for individuals with disabilities. When used solely as a legal document, the IEP denies the precise fundamental requirements of FAPE and LRE that it was designed to protect. For students of color, IEPs that are used primarily as legal documents often leads to practices that exclude and deny instructional supports to address the student's unique needs (Baca & Cervantes, 2004).

Many terms are used to refer to individuals who come from nonmainstream culture. Historically, these students fall within one of the following categories: African American (Black), Hispanic (Latino/a/x), Asian/Pacific Islander, and/or American Indian/Alaska Native (U.S. Census Bureau, 2017). These students are often referred to as **culturally and linguistically diverse (CLD)**, students of color, and minorities (even when they represent the majority population). Although CLD is not a disability, students from these backgrounds historically have been and continue to be at risk for over- and underrepresentation in special education. Even when appropriately identified, these students are at risk for not realizing their full potential because their home culture and language are often neglected in the IEP (Baca & Cervantes, 2004). This lack of cultural responsiveness has resulted in poor educational outcomes for students of color with disabilities (National Center for Education Statistics [NCES], 2019). This chapter approaches the IEP as an instructional tool that not only meets legal mandates but also includes the child's home culture and language as solutions to address the unique needs of the child.

IDEA'S KEY COMPONENTS

- **Free appropriate public education (FAPE).** Requires that the student be educated in a manner that meets their educational needs by a public educational agency that is free to the family.
  - *Zero Reject.* Mandates that the school cannot deny a child an education due to the severity of their needs.
- **Least restrictive environment (LRE).** The student is educated in a manner that is most like their typical peers.
- **Procedural safeguards** (due process). The family has the right to disagree with the placement, services, and educational plan for their child and can bring the school district to court.
- **Parental participation** (shared decision making). Parents have the right to participate as part of the education team for their child.
- **Nondiscriminatory evaluation.** Requires schools to utilize a team approach in assessing a student in all suspected areas of a disability using measures that are valid, reliable, culturally relevant, and linguistically appropriate.
- **Individualized education program (IEP).** The IEP team assesses current evaluation information and develops a written document designed to meet the unique educational needs of each student with a disability.

DEMOGRAPHIC TRENDS FOR STUDENTS WHO ARE CULTURALLY AND LINGUISTICALLY DIVERSE

Given the current demographics and trajectory of children from CLD backgrounds, this population will continue to increase more rapidly than other student groups. By 2027, 55% of public school students enrolled in prekindergarten through 12th grade will be students of color, and 25% will be **English language learners (ELLs)** (NCES, 2019). Although most ELLs are heavily concentrated in California, Florida,

Illinois, New York, and Texas, the majority of public schools across the country report ELLs as a subgroup of their student population. The Hispanic/Latinx population is the largest and fastest growing student group, with Spanish as the most common language spoken by ELLs in 46 states and the District of Columbia (U.S. Department of Education, 2019). According to the NCES, 14.7% of the ELL population in public elementary and secondary schools are individuals with a disability.

HISTORICAL DISCRIMINATION

The over- and underrepresentation of students from CLD backgrounds in special education has been a controversial topic for approximately half a century. Two major litigations in the early 1970s influenced federal legislation on inappropriate placements of students who are CLD in special education programs. *Diana v. State Board of Education in California* (1970) focused on nondiscriminatory practices that led to inappropriate placements of students from CLD backgrounds. This case centered on the district's English-only assessment policy, which resulted in misdiagnosis and overrepresentation in special education programs for ELLs. *Larry P. v. Riles* (1971) addressed the issue of IQ assessments as racially and culturally biased against CLD populations, which often led to overrepresentation in special education. These two cases had significant impact in the Education of All Handicapped Children Act of 1975, which specifically addressed the discriminatory practices by requiring students to be assessed in their native language and in a nondiscriminatory manner. Procedural safeguards that specifically protect students who come from CLD backgrounds were included in the reauthorization of Education of All Handicapped Children Act of 1975, later replaced with IDEA. These safeguards require that the child be tested in their native language, free from racial or cultural biases, and the assessment provides accurate information on the child's level of academic achievement and functional performance. Although IDEA 2004 continues to provide safeguards addressing discriminatory practices and accurate assessment and placement of students from CLD backgrounds, most students from CLD backgrounds continue to be mislabeled, and services provided within the context of special education are not culturally responsive and relevant (National Center for Learning Disabilities, 2020; Shealey et al., 2011).

IDEA §1414. Evaluations, eligibility determinations, individualized education programs, and educational placements

(5) Special rule for eligibility determination

In making a determination of eligibility under paragraph (4)(A), a child shall not be determined to be a child with a disability if the determinant factor for such determination is—

(A) lack of appropriate instruction in reading, including in the essential components of reading instruction (as defined in section 6368[3] of this title, as such section was in effect on the day before December 10, 2015);

(B) lack of instruction in math; or

(C) limited English proficiency.

Misidentification

Many issues arise when a child's home culture and language are different from the school's or teacher's culture. Because a child's home culture sets the foundation for the values and beliefs that shape social behavior and norms, it is critical that educators be cognizant of cultural differences and the potential for misperceived problems. Cultural differences are influenced by numerous variables such as home language, country of birth of the student and parents, length of residency in the United States, generation membership in the United States, degree of acculturation to the United States, parents' education level, socioeconomic status, age, and gender of the student. These cultural differences influence cognitive learning styles, which may be at odds with the teaching style or school culture. Although cultural differences are not a disability, these differences have historically been misperceived as problems, resulting in some districts having twice the expected number of students of color identified as having a disability. This disproportionality is exasperated when you consider that many of these students come from homes where English is not the primary spoken language. Given that ELLs are a diverse population representing many languages, cultures, and ethnicities, the process of identifying a disability is complex and difficult because the process of acquiring a second language can easily be mistaken as a disability. Incorrectly labeling these students as having a disability instead of a language difference places these students in jeopardy for not realizing their full potential, which often results in school failure and poor postschool outcomes (Reyes, 2017).

ELLs who are properly identified as having a disability are often not offered an appropriate curriculum to address their disability because their language and culture are not integrated into their IEP. IEP teams that understand how culture and language affects learning can develop IEPs that are responsive to the individual needs of learners who come from CLD backgrounds.

IDEA §1414. (3) Development of IEP

(B) Consideration of special factors

The IEP Team shall—

(ii) in the case of a child with limited English proficiency, consider the language needs of the child as such needs relate to the child's IEP.

Second Language Acquisition

Children develop language that is reflective of the social norms of their community. Therefore, language development should be viewed from the home cultural context, which often deviates from traditional expectations. For example, mainstream cultures expect children to experience high-level verbalization; however, not all cultures have this same expectation. Some cultures value listening more than speaking; hence, children are encouraged to be silent. Children reach language milestones at different ages because of these cultural differences. Like first language acquisition, there are predictable stages that second language learners go through; however, many variables can affect the advancement of language acquisition. When developing IEPs, it is critical for the team to consider the stage of second language acquisition for the student who is CLD. Include supports necessary to promote Vygotsky's (1978) Zone of Proximal Development. Table 2.1 provides an overview of the stages.

IEP teams often focus on deficits or skills not mastered and fail to consider the language and cultural strengths that the child brings to school. For example, some cultures have the eldest child take on a leadership role in the lives of their younger siblings. These students often serve as role models and teachers by helping their younger siblings learn about the world. The IEP team can build on this supportive skill by including collaborative learning group opportunities to address area of needs.

Table 2.1. Stages of second language acquisition

Stages of second language acquisition	Characteristics of second language acquisition
Preproduction	• Individual is typically silent • The younger the child, the longer the silent period • Emphasis on listening—learning the rules of the language and comprehension • Uses gestures such as nodding "yes" and "no" or pointing
Early production	• Limited comprehension • Emerging short words and phrases with many grammatical errors • Uses present tense
Speech emergent	• Spoken language increases • Dependency on context clues • Vocabulary increases • Production of simple sentences with decreased grammatical errors
Beginning fluency	• Fluency in social situations with minor errors • Academic and noncontextual language challenging • Gaps in vocabulary • Difficulty understanding jokes
Intermediate fluency	• Communication fluency stronger in social situations • Fluency noted in academic situations and ability to communicate in higher order cognitive skills • Vocabulary gaps and expressions evident
Advanced fluency	• Uses compound to complex sentences with few grammatical errors • Good comprehension • Fluent in all contexts • Successfully uses academic language • Idiomatic expressions sometimes incorrect • Native-like fluency

Sources: Robertson and Ford (n.d.); Roseberry-McKibbin (2007).

There are many variables to consider about language development. One variable that has important implications for second language acquisition is the extent to which the first language was developed. Several studies support the conclusion that a strong foundation in the first language will result in better outcomes for second language acquisition (Cummins, 1994, 2000; Cunningham & Graham, 2000; Demont, 2001). Information about language structures such as form, use, and content from the first language serves as the foundation that frames second language acquisition. Jim Cummins, world-leading authority on first and second language acquisition, explained this principle in his Dual Iceberg Model in 1981 when he presented the concept of the Common Underlying Proficiency (CUP). Cummins' CUP theory is that there is a relationship between first language proficiency and the learning of a second language. The skills learned during the acquisition of the first language are transferable to the second language. For this reason, children who have first language literacy have better outcomes when learning a second or even a third language. Conversely, students who have limited experience in their first language can be overwhelmed with second language skills needed for academic success. Therefore, the IEP team should encourage and support families who are CLD to maintain their home language so that the student is successful in the development of their second language.

Language Proficiency

Acquiring proficiency in one or more languages is a complex undertaking with significant individual variation and developmental trajectory. According to the American Speech-Language-Hearing Association (2019), *language proficiency* is defined as "effective receptive and expressive language skills in both written and spoken modalities" (p. 2). When considering bilingualism, there is inconsistency as to what level of language proficiency is required for each language. At one end of the spectrum are those that believe native-like fluency in both languages is required to be bilingual. Conversely, others believe that minimum proficiency in one or both languages is sufficient to be considered bilingual. Yet, most believe that bilingual individuals have a variation of proficiency based on the situational context.

Bilingual students with disabilities exhibit a variation of proficiency in each language. The rate of attaining second language proficiency may be slower, however, especially if they exhibit difficulty in their native language acquisition. These students must not only maintain their home language in order to participate in their home and community culture, but also skills learned during the acquisition of their first language that will result in positive outcomes as they develop their second language. In addition to maintaining and developing their home language, it is also important for these students to acquire English to participate in the school environment. Although acquiring English proficiency may take time, this does not mean that students with disabilities cannot become bilingual. Many students with disabilities are born into non-English speaking homes and become bilingual. These students often will require intervention and instruction in their home language for communication to be comprehensible. When developing the IEP, the team needs to consider that students who are CLD may need to use their home language to communicate at school and process new concepts.

Stop and Think!

How can IEP team members support home language development?

Language proficiency includes a level of mastery of receptive and expressive skills according to situational context in social and academic environments. Cummins (1981) differentiated between social and academic language by describing a continuum of language proficiency ranging from **basic interpersonal communication skills (BICS)** to **cognitive academic language proficiency (CALP)**. BICS, also referred to as *social language,* is the ability to communicate in social situations that are cognitively undemanding and contextually embedded. This type of interaction requires participants to remember, understand, and apply language in supported environments. These supported environments allow communication to be comprehensible because the message is supported by interactions that include gestures, intonations, and objects to convey the message, thus providing internal scaffolding. The focus is on comprehensible communication; therefore, this type of communication allows for clarification and repetition when the message is not understood. When provided a supported learning environment, second language learners can achieve this native-like proficiency within 1–3 years.

CALP, also known as *academic language,* is at the opposite end of the continuum. *CALP* refers to the communication skills needed for academic success in cognitive demanding and context-reduced communication (Cummins, 1981). This level of proficiency is essential for school success as it requires a high level of mastery in all components of language (form, content, and use); background knowledge in specific subjects; and its application to high cognitive demanding tasks (analysis, evaluation, and creation) in contextually reduced environments. Unlike BICS, which is learned in nonstructured social settings, CALP is typically learned in more formal settings through interaction with teachers and textbooks that are context reduced, meaning more dependency on formal language and less on visual supports (realia). When provided with a supported environment, this level of language proficiency can be achieved within 5–7 years; however, it can take longer without a support system (Collier, 2011; Cummins, 1980, 1981, 1994). This type of language proficiency serves as the foundation for school success because language is the primary mode of learning. Studies indicate that monolingual English speakers, especially those from low-socioeconomic communities, also struggle with academic language (Adger et al., 2018). "Academic language involves the use of higher-level vocabulary, more complex sentence structures, and more sophisticated forms of expression than is generally found in everyday conversation" (Short & Echevarria, 2016, p. 2). Therefore, IEP teams must be cognizant of the language demands embedded in the curriculum and instruction while including supports and structures necessary for students who are CLD to be successful.

Use of Interpreters

Research supports that parental involvement in their child's education results in positive outcomes for students. Some parents from CLD backgrounds may feel apprehensive about becoming involved in their child's school, including the IEP process, due to their limited English proficiency, unfamiliarity with mainstream school culture, or cultural beliefs that teachers are the experts in their child's education. For these families, teachers must take extra steps to ensure that they are effectively communicating and interacting with parents. To ensure parental involvement, IDEA put procedural safeguards into place that mandate informed consent from parents. Informed consent requires a full understanding of the information provided to make a decision. This informed consent mandate is required by IDEA for initial evaluation, reevaluation, and initiation of services.

IDEA §300.300 Parental consent

(b) Parental consent for services.

(1) A public agency that is responsible for making FAPE available to a child with a disability must obtain informed consent from the parent of the child before the initial provision of special education and related services to the child.

(2) The public agency must make reasonable efforts to obtain informed consent from the parent for the initial provision of special education and related services to the child.

IDEA further holds public agencies (i.e., schools) responsible for providing opportunities for families to attend IEP meetings and ensure that the communication and actions of the IEP meeting be understood by the family.

IDEA §300.322 Parent participation

(e) Use of interpreters or other action, as appropriate. The public agency must take whatever action is necessary to ensure that the parent understands the proceedings of the IEP Team meeting, including arranging for an interpreter for parents with deafness or whose native language is other than English.

The IEP team should secure the services of a competent interpreter to guarantee that the communication is comprehensible to parents so they can make informed decisions. Although most schools use translation services to convert documents such as referral and IEP forms from English to other languages in order to meet IDEA's requirement, they often are incomprehensible because the intent of the message is lost in the translation. Many families who are CLD do not have the literacy skills and/or special education background knowledge needed to fully comprehend the translated documents and will require an interpreter to explain the information provided in the documents before an informed consent can be obtained. Use of a qualified interpreter who has language proficiency in the family's home language and English is a critical first step in meeting the requirements of IDEA. Table 2.2 provides best practices on the use of interpreters for IEP meetings.

Table 2.2. Best practices for using interpreters at IEP meetings

Before the meeting	During the meeting	After the meeting
Secure an interpreter with academic proficiency in English and families' home language who has knowledge of special education.	Introductions include the interpreter and their purpose at the meeting.	Ask parents for feedback and satisfaction with use of an interpreter.
The Interpreter should have knowledge of the family's culture.	Remind members that the interpreter will not be making any decisions and their sole purpose is to interpret the communication exchange.	Seek impressions from the interpreter on any challenges during the meeting.
The case manager schedules a briefing to review the purpose of the meeting, provide relevant background, and present a list of specialized vocabulary to be used.	Inform the group of interpreting etiquette, which includes speaking directly to the family member (not the interpreter), avoiding side conversations, using simple language, avoiding jargon, speaking slowly, and pausing after each communication for interpretation.	
Ask the interpreter to share with IEP team the relevant home culture or language that may affect the meeting.	Periodically check for understanding.	
The interpreter and family decide on interpreting style: consecutive (interpret the message after the speaker pauses) or simultaneous (interprets the message while the speaker is talking).	Be cognizant of body language.	
	If needed, remind members of interpreting etiquette.	
Schedule a meeting with additional time for interpretation.	Summarize key points at the conclusion of meeting.	

Although the use of a qualified interpreter may fulfill the requirement of IDEA, the intent of the law is to include parents as full participants in the decision-making process. Yet, including parents as full participants in the education decision-making process is uncommon and a foreign concept for many cultures. Some cultures have the highest regard for the teaching profession and believe that it is the teachers' role to make the educational decisions for their child. Therefore, the request for full participation in the decision-making process is viewed by some cultures as disrespectful to the educators (Lynch & Hanson, 2011). The communication style of mainstream culture used in these decision-making situations often is substantially different from other cultures. For example, there is a reliance on explicit formal communication at IEP meetings that reflect mainstream culture. This type of communication depends heavily on detailed messages with the expectation that IEP participants will be assertive and verbose to document services on the IEP form, whereas some cultures rely on implicit communication and nonverbal cues. For these cultures, there is more reliance on relationships and body language. School personnel often misinterpret a family's nonassertive and quiet nature as an indicator for a lack of interest in participating in their child's education, which is often not the situation. Therefore, the IEP team must take a slower approach when working with families from CLD backgrounds and utilize an interpreter who is not only proficient in English and the home language but also knowledgeable about the family's culture. The use of a competent interpreter can be extremely helpful in establishing a home–school partnership.

Stop and Think!

The team should consider both the intervention and language of instruction when developing an IEP for a student who is in the process of acquiring English as a second language.

SUMMARY

Given the current demographic realities, students with disabilities who are CLD will continue to need high-quality educational programs that are culturally responsive to their needs. The IEP document must serve as an instructional tool that includes the child's home culture and language as solutions to address the child's unique needs. It must be written in a manner that not only meets the requirements outlined in IDEA but is also comprehensible to all team members. Table 2.3 provides an outline of the elements discussed in this chapter that IEP teams must consider. Failure to not include these elements puts this population at risk for not realizing their full potential. In subsequent chapters, you are reminded of culturally responsive practices in the development of IEPs so that students who are CLD can meet their full potential. The list in Figure 2.1 can be used in preparation for the IEP meeting.

Table 2.3.   Elements to consider in language proficiency

Elements	Social language proficiency	Academic language proficiency
Time line	1–3 years	5–7+ years
Purpose	Daily communication in social situations	Formal academic learning that requires reading, writing, speaking, and listening
Learning domains	Remembering, understanding, and applying	Analyzing, evaluating, and creating
Language components	Learning language to communicate • Pronunciation • Vocabulary • Syntax	Using language to learn • Semantics • Pragmatics
Stages of second language acquisition	Preproduction Early production Speech emergent Beginning fluency	Intermediate–advanced fluency
Communication supports	Multiple supports Gestures, objects, intonations, realia	Few supports Academic tasks requiring analysis and synthesis

PREPARATION FOR THE IEP MEETING:
CONSIDERATIONS FOR LEARNERS WHO ARE CULTURALLY AND LINGUISTICALLY DIVERSE

Prior to the Meeting

- [ ] Identify the language proficiency level for first and second languages.
- [ ] Identify home culture.
- [ ] Consult with family on home language use.
- [ ] Secure a qualified interpreter that matches families' cultural and linguistic backgrounds.
- [ ] Meet with interpreter regarding home culture practices and/or beliefs that may affect meeting.
- [ ] Check with family on their preferred style of interpreting.
- [ ] Schedule meeting with extended time for interpreting.
- [ ] Notify all IEP members that an interpreter will be at the meeting and professional protocol for effective use of an interpreter.

During the Meeting

- [ ] Address how the school will support the child's home and English proficiency development.
- [ ] Introduce all members of the meeting and the purpose of the meeting.
- [ ] Remind all members that all communication should focus on the parents.
- [ ] Strategically encourage parent/family to contribute toward the discussion.
- [ ] Remind group of etiquette of using an interpreter.
- [ ] Periodically check with interpreter for families' understanding.
- [ ] Summarize key points at conclusion of meeting.

After the Meeting

- [ ] Check with parents on the use of an interpreter and if they understood the meeting and key takeaways.

Figure 2.1. Preparation for the IEP meeting: Considerations for learners who are culturally and linguistically diverse.

ACTIVITIES

The activities included in this chapter are intended for the reader to gain a deeper understanding of the content covered. The activities associated with this chapter include the following:

- Activity 2.1. Misinterpretation of a Language Difference Versus a Disability

- Activity 2.2. Alignment of Stages of Second Language Acquisition and Bloom's Taxonomy

- Activity 2.3. Identification of Social and Academic Language

- Activity 2.4. Use of an Interpreter

Activity 2.1.

Misinterpretation of a Language Difference Versus a Disability

Supporting chapter: Chapter 2 (IEP Considerations for Culturally and Linguistically Diverse Learners)

Purpose: The purpose of this activity is to gain an understanding of how the characteristics of second language acquisition can be misinterpreted as a characteristic of a disability.

Directions: Use the following table to identify a disability with similar features as the second language learning characteristics. In the last column, describe the responsibility of the IEP team if they suspect a difference was mistaken as a disability.

Stages of second language acquisition	Characteristics of second language acquisition	Disability with similar features	Responsibilities to correct error if a difference was mistaken as a disability
Preproduction	• Individual is typically silent • The younger the child, the longer the silent period • Emphasis on listening–learning the rules of the language and comprehension • Uses gestures such as nodding "yes" and "no" or pointing		
Early production	• Limited comprehension • Emerging short words and phrases with many grammatical errors • Uses present tense		
Speech emergent	• Spoken language increases • Dependency on context clues • Vocabulary increases • Production of simple sentences with decreased grammatical errors		
Beginning fluency	• Fluency in social situations with minor errors • Academic and noncontextual language is challenging • Gaps in vocabulary • Difficulty understanding jokes		

Stages of second language acquisition	Characteristics of second language acquisition	Disability with similar features	Responsibilities to correct error if a difference was mistaken as a disability
Intermediate fluency	• Communication fluency stronger in social situations • Fluency noted in academic situations and ability to communicate in higher order cognitive skills • Vocabulary gaps and expressions evident		
Advanced fluency	• Uses compound to complex sentences with few grammatical errors • Good comprehension • Fluent in all contexts • Successfully uses academic language • Idiomatic expressions sometimes incorrect • Native-like fluency		

Activity 2.2.

Alignment of Stages of Second Language Acquisition and Bloom's Taxonomy

Supporting chapter: Chapter 2 (IEP Considerations for Culturally and Linguistically Diverse Learners)

Purpose: The purpose of this activity is to acknowledge the level of cognitive complexity in second language acquisition with the stages of Bloom's Taxonomy.

Directions: Align the stages of second language acquisition (see Table 2.1) with Bloom's Taxonomy in the following figure.

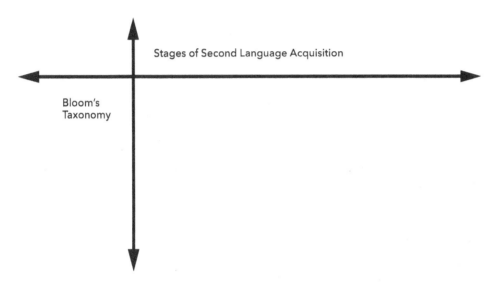

Activity 2.3.

Identification of Social and Academic Language

Supporting chapter: Chapter 2 (IEP Considerations for Culturally and Linguistically Diverse Learners)

Purpose: The purpose of this activity is to understand the difference between social language and academic language.

Directions: Observe and record a child's oral language interaction with a teacher for 5–10 minutes. Next, identify the communication demands of the teacher (basic interpersonal communication skills [BICS] vs. cognitive academic language proficiency [CALP]) and the student's language proficiency. Then answer the following questions:

1. What type of vocabulary did the teacher use in the exchange?
2. Were any contextual supports included in the communication?
   - If so, describe the supports and how they were used to make the communication comprehensible.
   - If not, what supports could have been used to make the communication comprehensible?
3. What type of vocabulary did the student use in the exchange?
4. How does this activity help you understand the needs of students who are culturally and linguistically diverse?

Activity 2.4.

Use of an Interpreter

Supporting chapter: Chapter 2 (IEP Considerations for Culturally and Linguistically Diverse Learners)

Purpose: The purpose of this activity is to research interpreting services available to schools.

Directions: Interview an interpreter who is used by the school for IEP meetings. Then answer the following questions:

1. What is the educational background of the interpreter?
2. How do they prepare for interpreting IEP meetings?
3. What are some of the challenges they encounter when interpreting IEP meetings?
4. What suggestions do they have to make interpreting IEP meetings go smoothly?

3

Collaborative Teaming for Better IEPs

Kathleen G. Winterman

After reading this chapter and engaging in activities related to this chapter, you will be able to meet the following outcomes:

- Explain and analyze the roles parents, teachers (general and intervention specialists), students, related services providers, and administrators play within the IEP meeting.

- Describe the legal mandates that support parent involvement in IEP meetings.

- Identify special factors to address the child's unique needs.

A core principle of the Individuals with Disabilities Education Improvement Act (IDEA) of 2004 (PL 108-446) is the belief that parents are collaborative team members in the development of their child's IEP. IDEA was created for schools and parents to share equal responsibility in the process, ensuring that the child's needs are met (Fish, 2008). IDEA is based on the working relationship between the child's home and school, which fosters an education team with the goal of providing the child with the agreed-on services (Zirkel, 2020). During the IEP meeting, the child's present levels, goals, objectives, placement, evaluation criteria, and duration of services are determined (National Center on Intensive Intervention, n.d.; Yell & Drasgrow, 2010). IDEA empowers parents and school personnel to work together to develop a shared vision of the child's ideal educational programming. This is often not a reality. Unfortunately, due to the need to complete the IEP process, school personnel often choose expediency instead of true shared visioning for a student. With each reauthorization, IDEA has continued to strengthen the parents' role within the team meeting. Parents are to provide informed consent prior to the start of any assessments to determine if the child has a special learning need; however, they cannot truly provide informed consent if they do not understand the process. School teams should provide parents with information regarding the identification process for parents to truly be active participants.

Collaboration between parents and professionals is one of the key elements of special education that is protected by IDEA. *Collaborative teaming* may be defined as two or more people working together toward a common goal in which all members have a role in the decision making (Janney et al., 2013). Collaboration within the school is a method of problem solving the issues of teaching and learning in partnership with others, which requires shared thinking and engagement in interactive teaming by those who have knowledge to meet the needs of all students, whether culturally diverse, academically talented, or in need of special education (Clark, 2000; Tucker & Schwartz, 2013). Collaboration is a complex set of interactions that build on and influence the types of relationships established and is considered an integral component of the IEP team process. Many individuals lack the necessary skills needed to effectively collaborate, and this may be one of the biggest challenges for education teams, particularly when working together to develop effective IEPs.

Collaboration (parental participation) is a legal mandate that embodies best educational practice for the inclusion of children with disabilities; however, barriers still exist that prevent the full implementation of IDEA, and these issues minimize a parent's ability to truly be a collaborative team member at the IEP table (Kurth et al., 2020).

IDEA'S KEY COMPONENTS

- **Free appropriate public education (FAPE).** Requires that the student be educated in a manner that meets their educational needs by public educational agency that is free to the family.
  - *Zero Reject.* Mandates that the school cannot deny a child an education due to the severity of their needs.
- **Least restrictive environment (LRE).** The student is educated in a manner that is most like their typical peers.
- **Procedural safeguards** (due process). The family has the right to disagree with the placement, services, and educational plan for their child and can bring the school district to court.
- **Parental participation** (shared decision making). Parents have the right to participate as part of the education team for their child.
- **Nondiscriminatory evaluation.** Requires schools to utilize a team approach in assessing a student in all suspected areas of a disability using measures that are valid, reliable, culturally relevant, and linguistically appropriate.
- **Individualized education program (IEP).** The IEP team assesses current evaluation information and develops a written document designed to meet the unique educational needs of each student with a disability.

Team success can be enhanced with guidance and direction regarding the common purpose of the IEP meeting. Prior to the IEP meeting, school personnel can contact the student's parents to determine their desires for their child's goals and objectives for the upcoming year and their need for supports, such as an interpreter or parent advocate. The parents' input will help shape the discussion regarding the student's educational needs. Providing parents with updates about their child's goal attainment and academic successes can assist the team in determining the student's academic direction for the school year. True collaboration is a challenging task. To collaborate effectively, teams must be willing to work toward a common goal and acknowledge differing approaches and agendas while incorporating opportunities for input with respectful and reflective listening.

CONNECTION TO LEGAL PERSPECTIVE

Parents have the right to participate in every decision related to the identification, evaluation, and placement of their child and must give consent for any initial evaluation, assessment, or placement decision. As previously mentioned, the letter and the spirit of IDEA encourage a partnership between the parents and the school that promotes collaboration to provide appropriate services for the child (Zirkel, 2020). The exact IDEA mandate is as follows:

(a) General. The public agency must ensure that the IEP Team for each child with a disability includes—
   (1) The parents of the child;
   (2) Not less than one regular education teacher of the child (if the child is, or may be, participating in the regular education environment);
   (3) Not less than one special education teacher of the child, or where appropriate, not less than one special education provider of the child;
   (4) A representative of the public agency who—
       (i) Is qualified to provide, or supervise the provision of, specially designed instruction to meet the unique needs of children with disabilities;
       (ii) Is knowledgeable about the general education curriculum; and
       (iii) Is knowledgeable about the availability of resources of the public agency.
   (5) An individual who can interpret the instructional implications of evaluation results, who may be a member of the team described in paragraphs (a)(2) through (a)(6) of this section;
   (6) At the discretion of the parent or the agency, other individuals who have knowledge or special expertise regarding the child, including related services personnel as appropriate; and
   (7) Whenever appropriate, the child with a disability. (§ 300.321)

Although IDEA mandates that parents are part of the collaborative team, their roles are not clearly defined or elaborated on to give all parties a distinct understanding of how the team should evolve. Many state departments of education provide guidance on collaborative teaming, such as Ohio's *A Guide to Parents' Rights in Special Education* (Ohio Department of Education, 2017), a free guide to understanding IDEA. Parents are to participate in IEP meeting activities by sharing information, assisting with the development of annual goals and objectives, assisting in the determination of related services, and consenting to special education and related services. IDEA clearly recognizes the special role of parents as it clearly defines the essence of parental consent. Specifically, IDEA states

(a) The parent has been fully informed of all information relevant to the activity for which consent is sought, in his or her native language, or through another mode of communication;

(b) The parent understands and agrees in writing to the carrying out of the activity for which his or her consent is sought, and the consent describes that activity and lists the records (if any) that will be released and to whom; and

(c) (1) The parent understands that the granting of consent is voluntary on the part of the parent and may be revoked at any time.

(2) If a parent revokes consent, that revocation is not retroactive (i.e., it does not negate an action that has occurred after the consent was given and before the consent was revoked). (§ 300.9)

Ultimately, IDEA defines who should participate in the meeting, but it does not provide a road map to allow for the collective goals of true *teaming* to benefit the child. To act in the child's best interest, all IEP team members (i.e., parents, students, teachers, special educators, related services providers, interpreters, administrators) must come to the table ready to listen and work together to develop a meaningful IEP.

As the team prepares for the IEP meeting, the lead team member—who is often the special educator (but any person can fulfill this role)—should prompt the team to think about ways in which all members can have an equal voice. One way to do this is to ask each team member ahead of time to share any questions or ideas for potential goals and objectives they may have so everyone has time to reflect prior to the meeting. IDEA clearly states that parents must be meaningfully involved in both program and placement decisions. Procedural safeguards protect parent involvement by requiring informed consent from parents. Therefore, it is critical that extra measures are taken by school personnel to ensure that families not only have a full understanding of the information regarding their child but also be actively involved in all aspects of programing and placement decisions. For those families using an interpreter, school personnel must meet prior to the IEP meeting to engage parents in the process. This also lays a good foundation for future dialogue among team members. (See Chapter 2 for best practices in planning and using an interpreter at IEP meetings.)

The following Challenge Scenario presents an example of collaboration between a parent and a teacher as they prepare for an upcoming IEP meeting and work together to determine the next steps for supporting a young student with a disability. Each comes to the table with their own set of experiences and expectations, leading each to a different approach to work toward the desired outcome.

Challenge Scenario

Parent's Reflection on Previous Meetings

My son's IEP is due again. I have been to IEP meetings for the past 3 years and the results have always been the same—nothing changed. As each year goes by, my son, Jimmy, is still lagging behind his classmates and seems to be getting further behind. I question why I should even bother going to the meetings. The teachers already seemed to know what they were going to do regardless of what I said. We have tried every therapy known to man and have spent thousands of dollars a year on outside support, but the school has never appeared interested in learning more about what we are doing at home or what our goals are for our son.

This has always bothered me because I know that other schools do things differently. I have heard my friends talk about really being included in their child's IEP meetings. I have even heard of the students not only attending the meetings but also actually leading various parts of it. So I was prepared for this upcoming meeting to be the same old thing.

But this time, when the special education teacher called to see if I could be available for an IEP meeting in 2 weeks, she actually asked me what time would be convenient for me. She also sent me an update on all of Jimmy's current goals and objectives, and then she called me again to ask what I thought the priorities should be in Jimmy's IEP. She has even met with Jimmy to review all his current goals and asked him what he wanted to focus on during the next academic year. I have also received updated reports from all the distinct therapists and specialists who are currently working with him. Looks like things might be different this time. I like the change.

Teacher Background Information

A bachelor's degree in the science of education is what it says on my college diploma. I have wanted to be a special educator ever since I started volunteering with children with disabilities at my church. I am a new teacher at this school, and I am excited and nervous about starting to have IEP meetings with my students' parents. My college experiences have prepared me for this, and I have looked forward to it for what seems like my entire life. At my new school, they call it "IEP season". This is the time of year when many students' IEPs need to be reviewed to stay in compliance with the federal law, IDEA, which mandates an annual review of the students' educational programs. Many parents do not seem like they want to be involved in the IEP development, though. This makes me wonder why. My cooperating teacher made it seem so easy when I was student teaching. He set up such an inviting and engaging environment for students and parents to participate. I know that I can do the same if the students and their parents give me a chance, but I know that I need to lay the foundation of trust for this relationship to be established.

The Meeting Begins

"Welcome, Mrs. Bennett, it's so nice to see you again. Jimmy told me this morning that he was looking forward to our meeting. We are so glad that you could come. Jimmy, where would you and your mom like to sit? Mrs. Bennett, have you met everyone here today?"

Scenario Reflection

Based on the Challenge Scenario, document and discuss your initial thoughts regarding the following questions:

- Discuss how you would establish the IEP team. Who would you include?

- Do new members need to be added to this team?

- How would you get the parents involved in the IEP process?

- What information would you send out to parents prior to the meeting?

- How would you encourage the student to be an active team member?

- Why could parents become apathetic to the IEP process?

- How would you involve all team members?

- How would you get the dialogue started?

After all the introductions take place, each team member reviews Jimmy's successes and challenges in achieving his current goals and the supports and services that were necessary to achieve these goals. Jimmy is asked to state his goals for the upcoming year, and he states that he would like to be a police officer when he grows up, so he hopes to improve his reading skills over the next year. He acknowledges that he has struggled to read for years and is embarrassed if he is called on to read at school. He has had a reading goal on his IEP for the past 3 years with limited success.

Stop and Think!

Questions to prompt the IEP team's thinking include

- What motivates this student?

- Knowing that Jimmy wants to be a police officer, how would you incorporate this into his learning?

- How can we blend a student's learning needs with what motivates them as a learner?

- What are some strategies that can be used to help a struggling learner?

- How can we assist a student's learning while keeping their self-esteem intact?

- What options have already been tried, and what level of success did we meet? What has the family tried?

TAKING A LOOK AT WHO IS AT THE IEP TABLE

The education team must remember that there are multiple perspectives that intertwine during the dynamics of the IEP meeting. The following sections present the various team members that typically participate at an IEP meeting. The IEP team represents the student's educational interests and must include the student's parent(s) or guardian(s), a general educator (unless the student is in a self-contained classroom without access or expectation to participate in the general curriculum), an intervention specialist or special educator, a school district representative, a parent advocate, an interpreter, and/or someone who can interpret the testing.

The Student

Students should be involved in the IEP meeting, regardless of age. Students who are very young (preschool through first grade) can share what they like about school, what their strengths are, and one skill they would like to improve. As students get older, their roles can increase to leading discussions related to strategies that have and have not been successful and giving the team a better understanding of their rate of success on current goals and objectives. Older students can help the team with future planning and establishing the skills necessary to meet their personal aspirations. Once the team has the student's voice and motivation in mind, determining their goals and objectives becomes an easier task.

Parents

Parents are equal team members on their child's IEP team. The school is required to make multiple attempts to encourage parent participation. Parents are strongly encouraged to attend the IEP meetings because they are able to share their child's life history and how IEP goals fit in with the family's culture and expectations; therefore, it is critical that the school is cognizant of cultural differences that may impede initial collaboration. To mitigate these differences, it is important that the school understands these differences and works with parents to bridge the cultural divide.

Parents are to provide informed consent prior to the start of any assessments to determine if the child has a special learning need; however, they cannot truly provide informed consent if they do not understand the process and/or the language. Parents share their child's hopes and dreams and help provide the road map to achieve these dreams. They provide a unique perspective of the student's interests and level of functioning at home and within the community. Parents also provide the student's medical and social-emotional history as well as hold knowledge of past strategies and their level of success. They can encourage the team to think creatively about the supports required to meet the student's educational needs, which may lead to discussions of the LRE. Long after a child is finished with the school experience, the parents will be there to support their child into adulthood and throughout their life. Parents carry the burden of living with the results of an effective or ineffective education team.

While examining the shared responsibility of the student's IEP, the team must be cognizant that the services offered, and their implementation, are the responsibility of the school and not the family or student. Some families supplement school services, but they are under no obligation to fund the resources necessary for the child's successful realization of IEP goals, objectives, or services. The family's participation in the process is voluntary but critically valuable. It is mandatory that parents are invited, but it is not mandatory that they participate. The burden of attempting to get the family to participate rests on the school. Accommodating the family's schedule, language needs, and/or communication style must be addressed. After several documented attempts to involve the family in the process, the school can move forward without family participation. To simply attempt to contact parents and then move on is unacceptable because the value that the parents' input can provide is immeasurable. In addition, this violates the spirit of true collaboration. Parents will benefit from coaching to fully understand their role in the IEP meeting.

According to Lo and Xu (2019), the demographics of the U.S. population is becoming increasingly diverse. The U.S. Census Bureau (2017) projected more than half of the U.S. population will belong to a minority group by 2044. Students from diverse backgrounds currently comprise more than 53% of the special education student population. Although their parents are the key decision makers and advocates who ensure that they receive services and support that address their individual needs, Lo and Xu's research indicated that families from diverse backgrounds face many challenges that prevent them from taking on active roles in their child's education.

Systemic parental engagement is essential to ensure that parents are not considered apathetic or unresponsive to their child's education when, in reality, it is a language or cultural difference that is impeding their participation. As the U.S. population continues to become more diverse, school personnel will need to develop more culturally responsive approaches to gain a greater understanding of what constitutes involvement, which may look different depending on the student and family's cultural background (see Chapter 2).

General Education Teachers

When IDEA was reenacted in 1997 and 2004, additional mandates required more specific information regarding the participation of children with disabilities in the general curriculum. The IEP must include a statement with the present level of performance that addresses how the child's disability affects their progress in the general curriculum, along with program modifications. As such, the development of a child's IEP is no longer the exclusive responsibility of the special education teacher. General education teachers are now required to participate in the IEP meeting and bring valuable content knowledge on the student's present level of performance. This requirement provides a clear distinction that general education teachers have responsibility for the learning of all children. General educators with inclusionary students are responsible for implementing the IEP goals and objectives as prescribed. Students with disabilities now must fully participate in state and district testing or in an alternate assessment to monitor their progress in the general curriculum. Academic reporting is mandated to inform parents of children with disabilities on their child's progress at the same intervals as children without disabilities. Pertinent and timely information must be reported regarding the child's IEP goal attainment.

The Every Student Succeeds Act of 2015 (PL 114-94) continues the No Child Left Behind Act of 2001 (PL 107-110) mandate of highly qualified teachers by ensuring that each state achieve high standards. Therefore, general education teachers possess the content knowledge of each subject area they teach, and their role in the IEP team is to share the academic expectations (i.e., standards) for that grade or subject matter. Their professional knowledge assists the team with establishing goals and objectives that are related to the content standards for all students in a particular grade or subject. Therefore, general education teachers play a key role in the development and implementation of the IEP to ensure students' academic success.

Intervention Specialists or Special Education Teachers

An intervention specialist is an educator who is specially trained to work with students who have learning challenges. Intervention specialists are knowledgeable about educational laws and diverse learning strategies, and they are usually charged with implementing the educational programming for students who qualify for special educational services as mandated under IDEA. They are considered the primary source of knowledge for developing accommodations and modifications, monitoring the child's academic programming, and reporting the child's goals attainment. Depending on the student's academic needs, the intervention specialist might be the child's teacher of record, but it is more likely that they will support the child within the child's grade level or a particular subject area. The teacher of record may or may not be the student's primary teacher or general educator, but they are the person who grades the student and must be highly qualified in the areas in which the child is being taught. Most intervention specialists support students in these settings by coteaching and consulting with general education teachers. Like general education teachers, intervention specialists must be highly qualified in the content areas that they teach.

Administrator

The term *administrator* is a bit of a misnomer. The role really represents the person from the public school district that is capable of authorizing district funds to provide the services necessary to meet a child's unique learning needs. This responsibility can be charged to a multitude of personnel from the school district, including directors of special services, building principals, assistant principals, school psychologists, counselors, or other educational staff members. This person should be capable of designing services for the student or supervising these services. The individual should also be knowledgeable about the general education curriculum.

Finally, the IEP team must have someone from the school who is able to interpret the data (i.e., someone who can decipher testing data received from assessments) in attendance as well. Many times, this is a school administrator, but not always. This role could be fulfilled by the general educator, intervention specialist, school psychologist, or related services provider, such as an occupational therapist or speech-language pathologist (SLP).

Related Services Personnel

A variety of related services providers may also be represented on the IEP team, depending on a child's needs. These staff members include, but are not limited to, SLPs, occupational therapists, physical therapists, school nurses, school counselors, mental health professionals, English as a second language (ESL) teachers, bilingual teachers, interpreters, and school psychologists, as well as the child's private services providers. Although these professionals may be included in the IEP meeting, their attendance is not mandatory unless the services they provide are directly related to the goals and objectives discussed. Private services providers can share their opinion of the child's skills within the family and in relation to the outside community. These professionals often have a long-term relationship with the child and family and have seen their growth and struggles over a period of years.

Parent Advocate

Some families seek the assistance and advice of a parent advocate. An advocate may be a school employee or someone from the community who is financially compensated or who serves in a volunteer capacity to advise the child's parents or guardians. This person can often help a child's parents understand what professionals are telling them, or the advocate can speak on the family's behalf. Some families like having someone to support them through the IEP process, especially if they have been disappointed in the outcome of previous meetings. Advocates are not necessary for the meeting to take place.

Stop and Think!

There are many advocacy groups available for parents. Some are local organizations within specific school districts, whereas others support specific disabilities. The following list provides examples of national organizations that are available to provide guidance to families:

- The American Association on Intellectual and Developmental Disabilities is an organization that promotes research for individuals with intellectual disabilities.

- The Autism Society of America advocates for services, access, and opportunities for individuals with autism spectrum disorders.

- The National Alliance on Mental Illness focuses on support for individuals with mental illness and their families.

- The National Association for Down Syndrome provides supports for families and empowers individuals who have with Down syndrome.

- TASH is an international advocacy group that supports the rights of people with significant disabilities.

- Council for Exceptional Children is the largest international professional organization dedicated to improving the success of children and youth with disabilities.

- The Council for Learning Disabilities (CLD), an international organization composed of professionals who represent diverse disciplines, is committed to enhancing the education and quality of life for individuals with learning disabilities across the life span.

- The Arc is the largest national community-based organization advocating for and serving people with intellectual and developmental disabilities.

Active parental involvement in the IEP meeting is the cornerstone of the collaborative team process. Strong parental involvement is reflective of a culture that values individualism, equality, and exercising one's rights (Lo & Xu, 2019). These values are not always shared by the families, however. A family's culture can play a large role in how they perceive their child's needs and the role family members play within the IEP meeting. The IEP team must be respectful of the family's culture and communicate clearly and effectively to enable parents to be active, equal team members. Including interpreters is a foundational component for parents of culturally and linguistically diverse (CLD) backgrounds (see Chapter 2). To curtail the involvement of parents in the educational decisions not only denies parents their rights to full participation, which is protected under legislation, but also sets barriers for them. Such barriers can be even more problematic for families from CLD backgrounds who often have different perceptions of how decisions about their child's education are made.

STUDENT-LED IEP MEETINGS

Student-led IEP meetings are an important way to help improve parent participation and increase student involvement and commitment to the process while creating a more supportive environment for students within general education settings (Davis & Cummings, 2019; Mason et al., 2004; Myers & Eisenman, 2005). Students who actively participate and lead their own IEP meetings learn to demonstrate goal setting, planning, self-evaluation, public speaking, and self-advocacy skills in a setting that is uniquely their own (Biegun et al., 2020; Martin et al., 2006).

In a 3-year study of more than 1,638 IEP meetings, special education teachers did most of the speaking, whereas general education teachers and students did not feel comfortable speaking (Martin et al., 2004). Students often did not understand their role or why the meeting was being held. Students must be directly taught how to participate in these high-stakes meetings. Once they are taught, students learn to advocate for their own learning needs, and their participation levels in all aspects of education increase (Biegun et al., 2020; Martin et al., 2004). Teaching students to be active members in their IEP meetings is one way to foster self-determination (Cavendish et al., 2017).

Preparing students to lead their IEP meetings provides them with an authentic opportunity to learn and practice critical life skills. To assist students in the task of leading their IEP meetings, they must be educated about their disability. Students should be trained over a minimum of four to six sessions in which they share their future plans, discuss their current level of performance, and seek out recommendations for goals from their teachers and parents, as well as develop their own goals and learn their legal rights to an appropriate education (Mason et al., 2004).

Generally, the special education teacher assists in training the students to be prepared for their IEP meetings. Students need to be aware of their strengths and weaknesses to determine the future supports they require. Students learn what will happen at the IEP meeting and what purpose the IEP serves. In preparing for the meeting, students should learn how to determine an agenda by identifying what is important to them and should be given an opportunity to role-play prior to the meeting. Teachers can use practice sessions to prompt students' thinking by offering them potential questions that they may be asked. Mason et al. (2004) suggested that there are three levels of student participation in a student-led IEP meeting. First, students share their future goals or plans. Next, they discuss their strengths and weaknesses and the necessary accommodations for success while also being able to offer potential goals. Finally, students assert the previous information and close the IEP team meeting.

DEVELOPING THE TEAM

In addition to the family's culture, each individual team has its own unique culture. Who and what the team values will have an impact on the team's interactions (Grossman, 2020). Similarly, how the meeting is structured, the environment, and the complexity of the language and written documents all have an impact on the likelihood of parents' involvement within the meeting (Winterman & Rosas, 2016). All these nuances create the dance that becomes the art of collaboration in an IEP meeting.

> ## Stop and Think!
> ### Self-Determination
>
> Individuals with intellectual and developmental disabilities (IDD) have the same right to, and responsibilities that accompany, self-determination as everyone else. They are entitled to opportunities, respectful support, and the authority to exert control in their lives, to direct their services, and to act on their own behalf. (American Association on Intellectual and Developmental Disabilities, 2018)
>
> To provide individuals with disabilities the opportunity to practice self-determination, they must be afforded opportunities to practice these skills with the support of their team so they are prepared to act as responsible members of society in the future.

Throughout the collaboration process, families are dealing with their aspirations for their child while facing a reality that may offer a different picture. These issues, coupled with the complexities of the IEP forms and the emotions surrounding the circumstances of the meeting, can often create barriers that impede a family from fulfilling their role in the IEP team meeting. The goal of every IEP team member is to find a common ground and work together to develop an educationally sound, truly individualized, effective document that can serve as a guiding force for the student's education.

To begin the IEP meeting, team members all must believe that they are there for the student's benefit, and all outside roles and responsibilities should be secondary. Because the student is the main focus of collaboration during an IEP meeting, it is important to honor the perspective of the student by using student-centered planning to promote student empowerment and eventual leadership. Prior to the meeting, the student and family should be prompted to think of their vision for the future. What type of schooling experiences will be necessary to reach those future dreams? Will the student live independently or require assistance? What type of work or career does the student aspire to achieve? The answers to these questions lay the foundation of the discussion within the IEP meeting. For a preschool student who wants to work at a bank, the focus of the IEP could be based on learning how to count and recognize money. For an elementary student with a behavior disorder who wants to grow up to be a firefighter, learning how to get along with others would be a desirable skill. Establishing goals and objectives lays the foundation for the meeting and the services provided for the student in the future.

These future dreams all unfold within the IEP meeting. Team discussions can often get bogged down with only thinking about the present. The collective team must maintain its sights clearly on the future and the larger picture that represents the child's life. As the student grows and develops, the makeup of the team may evolve to reflect its members' strengths, interests, and life goals. The special factors discussed at the end of this chapter will assist the team in exploring questions and areas that are not addressed in other areas of the IEP but can have an impact on the direction the team takes in developing goals and objectives.

Conflict Resolution

The possibility for conflict to arise is inherent within any human interaction. Managing conflict is an essential skill to effective collaboration. Maintaining the meeting's focus on the child's needs will assist in moving the discussion forward. To stimulate these conversations, the special factors component of the IEP is intended to prompt or help initiate the dialogue.

Several steps may be taken if disagreement among the varying parties continues. According to Martin (2017), 10 different strategies can be used to divert conflict, with the primary focus being recentered on the student and their needs, which is the reason for the meeting. In addition, areas of agreement should be restated while seeking clarity for issues of concern. The meeting may be stopped and resumed at another time after additional information is gathered. New or additional resources and personnel can be included to assist with the disagreement. If necessary, mediation might be needed to help determine the best direction for the team. The parent maintains the right to sign the IEP to show their attendance at the IEP meeting, but they may choose to refuse to consent to the services and implementation of the IEP. Maintaining an amiable relationship with all team members is in the best interest of the child.

Developing goals and objectives is a mutual activity in which the collective thinking of the team must be represented—it is a mutual task. The team represents the varying interests that reflect different aspects of the child's life. Each team member shares equally in the responsibility for key decisions as well as accountability for the outcomes of the student's IEP—both its successes and failures. Demonstrating mutual respect for each team member and their perspective allows the team to work to honor the role they represent in the child's life.

SUMMARY

The foundation of the IEP is the collaborative team that supports the student and provides guidance for the services and supports required to assist the student with their academic success. The checklist in Figure 3.1 can be used in preparation for the IEP meeting.

PREPARATION FOR THE IEP MEETING:
COLLABORATIVE TEAMING

Prior to the Meeting

- [ ] Meet and establish a positive relationship with parents/family.
- [ ] Identify student's strengths (i.e., funds of knowledge).
- [ ] Review current IEP goal(s) and identify key collaborators.
- [ ] Identify if you need to add anyone to the team.
- [ ] If using an interpreter, then meet with interpreter to review IEP focus (see Chapter 2).

During the Meeting

- [ ] Introduce all team members and identify their role.
- [ ] Create an atmosphere of open communication.
- [ ] Encourage members to use jargon-free language so all can understand.
- [ ] Ensure all written and oral communication is comprehensible.
- [ ] Monitor the involvement of each member and their emotional level.
- [ ] Check to see if members agree with the present levels, goals, objectives, and the least restrictive environment.
- [ ] If using an interpreter, then be sure to use appropriate interpreter etiquette (see Chapter 2).

After the Meeting

- [ ] Debrief with all team members, including parents, regarding the effectiveness of the meeting.
- [ ] Review with the student how they did as a self-advocate and discuss ways to improve.
- [ ] Send copies of meeting documents to all participants.
- [ ] Follow up on any unresolved issues.
- [ ] Check with parents on the use of an interpreter and if they understood the meeting and key takeaways.

Figure 3.1. Preparation for the IEP meeting: Collaborative teaming.

THE IEP CHECKLIST: SPECIAL FACTORS

What follows is a section of the IEP rubric in which the special factors are considered. These global issues have an impact on the IEP team's dialogue and set the stage for further conversation that shapes the goals and objectives.

Special Instructional Factors	Discussion needed	
	Yes	No
Does the child have behavior that impedes their learning or the learning of others?		
Does the child have limited English proficiency?		
Is the child blind or visually impaired?		
Does the child have communication needs (required for individuals who are deaf or hearing impaired)?		
Does the child need assistive technology devices and/or services?		
Does the child require specially designed physical education?		
Will the child participate in statewide testing?		

ACTIVITIES

The activities included in this chapter are intended for the reader to gain a deeper understanding of the content covered. The activities associated with this chapter include the following:

- Activity 3.1. Collaborative Considerations
- Activity 3.2. Parent Interview

Activity 3.1.

Collaborative Considerations

Supporting chapter: Chapter 3 (Collaborative Teaming for Better IEPs)

Purpose: The purpose of this activity is to develop an appreciation for collaboration when designing an IEP to meet the student's needs.

Directions: Consider a child with a disability. Work with your team to generate factors that should be considered when planning instruction and services for the student.

Factors to consider	Pros	Cons
Level of support needed in the general education classroom		
Physical supports needed (e.g., mobility needs, strength, endurance issues)		
Academic supports needed (e.g., modifications or content changes to the curriculum)		
Academic access (e.g., accommodations such as amount of work to complete, preferential seating)		
Physical access (e.g., adaptive equipment such as weighted pencils, slant boards, specialized seating)		
Teacher beliefs on inclusion		
Teacher supports needed (e.g., curriculum at another level)		

Activity 3.2.

Parent Interview

Supporting chapter: Chapter 3 (Collaborative Teaming for Better IEPs)

Purpose: The purpose of this activity is to gain a better understanding of the parent's perspective of the IEP process and their child's development prior to the IEP meeting.

Directions: Teacher/teacher candidate will interview a parent of a child with a disability. The child must be between the ages of 0–8 years old. You will obtain background information as well as a history of the child's development, including adaptive behavior, social, fine and gross motor, language, and cognitive domains. The interviewer will ask at least five questions of the parent. In your write-up, connect the parent's responses to known theory or information. Please refer to the rubric in Figure 3.1.

	Unprofessional effort	Acceptable	Excellent
Interview report	Directions regarding requirements of observation not followed. Developmental areas and/or theories were omitted. Typed summary not submitted. Verification of observation not provided at end of semester.	Observation conducted according to requirements. Developmental areas were identified as were the theories, but summary is vague as to the results of the observation.	Directions regarding the summary were followed. Developmental areas were clearly identified along with the theories. Summary was well written with clear ties to information from the text. Strong analysis to theories presented from the text.

II

Key Areas of
IEP Development

4

Present Levels of Academic Achievement and Functional Performance

Lisa M. Campbell, Clarissa E. Rosas, and Laura Clarke

After reading this chapter and engaging in activities related to this chapter, you will be able to meet the following outcomes:

- Detail steps to take prior to any formal planning of an IEP.

- Discuss the importance of including student's strengths, home culture, language proficiency, and area of needs in the **Present Levels of Academic Achievement and Functional Performance (PLAAFP)** section of the IEP.

- Explain how quantitative and qualitative information in the IEP allows for construction of meaningful goals.

- Develop meaningful and compliant narratives on the PLAAFP that is culturally responsive to the strengths and needs of a child from a culturally and linguistically diverse (CLD) background.

- Identify the funds of knowledge that teachers may tap into to enhance student's academic progress.

Once it has been determined that a student qualifies for special education, the next step is to develop a plan to outline the supports and services that a student with a disability will require to successfully benefit from their educational program (see Table 4.1). It is essential to clearly establish the student's strengths and areas for improvement prior to beginning any formal planning related to the services that will be outlined in a student's IEP. This information is recorded in the PLAAFP section on the formal IEP and is important because it serves as the foundation on which future instructional plans and educational services for each student are built.

Table 4.1.   Steps leading to special education services

Steps	Summary description
Prereferral	Identification of concerns regarding student's progress in general education and student's response to evidence-based intervention to resolve the concerns. Team reviews student's progress and if teacher needs to continue intervention or if a new intervention is warranted.
Referral	Gather information as to possible reasons for the student's struggle. Team decides if additional information is needed; new strategy should be tried and/or team determines if referral for evaluation is warranted.
Identification	Assessment and review of student's progress is completed to determine if the student has a disability.
Eligibility	Reviews all assessment results and determines if the disability adversely affects the child's educational performance and qualifies for special education services.
Development of IEP	IEP team constructs a written plan that specifies the child's individualized education.

CONNECTION TO LEGAL PERSPECTIVE

The PLAAFP section is one of the most important sections of the IEP because it is essentially the baseline from which progress can be measured. In addition, the PLAAFP provides the framework from which goals will be determined. To better understand the PLAAFP section, it is helpful to review the legal provisions outlined in the Individuals with Disabilities Education Improvement Act (IDEA) of 2004 (PL 108-446). It specifically states that an IEP must contain

(1) A statement of the child's present levels of educational performance, including—
    (i) How the child's disability affects the child's involvement and progress in the general curriculum (i.e., the same curriculum as for nondisabled children); or
    (ii) For preschool children, as appropriate, how the disability affects the child's participation in appropriate activities (§ 300.347[a])

What exactly does this mean? It is important to have a complete and accurate understanding because much of the other information in the IEP will be determined by the PLAAFP statements.

In short, the law requires that a clear description, supported by relevant data, be included in the IEP that outlines what the student can do. This statement is intended to comprehensively address the student's strengths, current performance levels, abilities, and needs. The most important data and information is reflective of the full and individual student evaluation that is conducted in accordance with the evaluation and eligibility provisions of IDEA (§ 300.301 through § 300.311). In addition, the U.S. Department of Education's (2010) Question and Answer Document described the PLAAFP section of an IEP as having a direct relationship with the goals and services outlined in the IEP. Since the ruling of *Endrew F. v. Douglas County School District* (2017), IEP teams are required to provide a clear, persuasive, and responsive explanation of how the IEP was reasonably calculated for the student to make progress. Therefore, the PLAAFP section needs to clearly establish a student's baseline performance relative to their area(s) of eligibility, strengths, and needs (Yell & Bateman, 2020). Consequently, it is critical that IEP teams accurately document the child's academic and functional performance. There are a variety of ways that this critical information is documented in IEPs. Some states require that the PLAAFP is written in one comprehensive summary, whereas others require that the student's performance level is written in several smaller descriptions according to the student's area of needs. Irrespectively of the documentation requirement by individual states, there are fundamental requisites that are noted in IDEA. These fundamental requirements are noted in the checklist found in the appendix to this book (also available from the Brookes Download Hub), which describes the student's current academic and functional performance, the student's strengths and needs, and explains the effect of a student's disability on their education performance.

IDEA'S KEY COMPONENTS

- **Free appropriate public education (FAPE).** Requires that the student be educated in a manner that meets their educational needs by a public educational agency that is free to the family.
  - *Zero Reject.* Mandates that the school cannot deny a child an education due to the severity of their needs.
- **Least restrictive environment (LRE).** The student is educated in a manner that is most like their typical peers.
- **Procedural safeguards** (due process). The family has the right to disagree with the placement, services, and educational plan for their child and can bring the school district to court.
- **Parental participation** (shared decision making). Parents have the right to participate as part of the education team for their child.
- **Nondiscriminatory evaluation.** Requires schools to utilize a team approach in assessing a student in all suspected areas of a disability using measures that are valid, reliable, culturally relevant, and linguistically appropriate.
- **Individualized education program (IEP).** The IEP team assesses current evaluation information and develops a written document designed to meet the unique educational needs of each student with a disability.

ACADEMIC ACHIEVEMENT VERSUS FUNCTIONAL PERFORMANCE

Although the terms *academic achievement* and *functional performance* are referred to in IDEA 2004, they are not specifically defined within the law. Both terms are included in U.S. Department of Education documents, however. The commentary in the *Federal Register* for Assistance to States for the Education of Children With Disabilities and Preschool Grants for Children With Disabilities (U.S. Department of Education, 2006) noted that "academic achievement generally refers to a child's performance in academic areas (e.g., reading or language arts, math, science, and history)" (71 Fed. Reg. at 46662). The student's performance should be documented both qualitatively and quantitatively in order to construct meaningful goal and objective statements that can lead to instruction. The PLAAFP must be descriptive and specific whether an IEP is based on the initial evaluation or annual progress on goals and objectives. The quantitative portion of the PLAAFP uses data to delineate the specific levels of functioning, whereas the qualitative portion describes the student's present levels of performance. Because the PLAAFP drives the development of IEP goals and objectives, documenting the student's level of performance both qualitatively and quantitatively provides the necessary information for constructing meaningful and compliant goals and objectives.

The PLAAFP is not only limited to academic considerations but also includes social, emotional, behavioral, and functional issues. **Functional performance** refers to essential and critical skills needed for students to perform routine activities in daily living, including communication, academic language, mobility, behavior, and social skills. Therefore, it is critical to consider cultural and linguistic characteristics of the student in this section of the IEP. In addition, it is critical that the PLAAFP data reflect nonacademic skills necessary for independent living for all students, but particularly those with more severe cognitive and physical disabilities. The description of a student's PLAAFP should be based on data in the student's area(s) of eligibility that are gathered by members of the IEP team and include the following important components:

- The student's strengths

- English and home language proficiency level

- Language of instruction (home/native language or English with supports)

- Description of the student's academic and/or functional needs

- Areas targeted for improvement

- Supports that help the student learn

- Limitations that prevent the child from learning

- Objective data from valid, reliable, and current evaluations of the child intended for specifically establishing the baseline for goal(s); this baseline is critical to ensure that goals are appropriately ambitious

- How the child's disability affects their ability to be involved in and progress in the general education curriculum (i.e., the curriculum for students without disabilities) or, for preschool children, how the disability affects participation in age-appropriate activities

- Parental input and concerns

Special Considerations for Determining Present Levels of Academic Achievement

In the development of the student's present levels of academic achievement, it is critical for the IEP team to consider not only the student's strengths and needs based on their area of eligibility, but also how the student's behaviors might affect their learning and the learning of others.

Behaviors Related to the Student's Disability   When considering behaviors that might impede a student's learning or that of others, the IEP team should take into account factors such as **externalizing behaviors** that occur due to a student's frustration with their academic challenges. For example, when a student with a specific learning disability in reading fluency is presented with a reading passage above their ability, one student might curse at the teacher and throw their book, whereas another student with the same disability might rip up their paper. **Internalizing behaviors** that occur due to frustration can also affect a student's learning. For example, other students with a specific learning disability in reading fluency might put down their head and refuse to look at a passage above their ability level or might get so overwhelmed with the first sentence that they spend the entire reading time trying to decode one sentence and never move forward or ask for help.

Trauma   In addition to behaviors specifically tied to a student's disability, many students also have some level of trauma in their personal lives that can affect their learning (National Child Traumatic Stress Network [NCTSN], 2012). *Childhood trauma* has been defined as a child experiencing violence (physical, sexual, or psychological), abuse, a threat to their life, or death of another person, among other adverse experiences (Pinderhughes et al., 2015). Because traumatic life events are inherently complex, there is no way to isolate their impact on student learning and behavior (NCTSN, 2012). Students can exhibit a wide range of social, emotional, and behavioral responses to trauma and are likely to have trauma triggers that can affect their ability to engage in classroom learning. Because the impact of childhood trauma can be pervasive, it is crucial to consider if a student has experienced trauma in their lives that might be affecting their learning.

Cultural and Linguistic Backgrounds   It is equally important to consider a student's cultural and linguistic background. As data is collected for the PLAAFP, IEP teams should consider the strengths and needs a student might have based on their cultural heritage and linguistic background. For some students from a bilingual home, their language facility might support a deeper understanding of spoken language, which would be a strength. Other students might have language deficits in their home language and in English, which would be an area of need for which data should be collected and analyzed. For students who come from CLD backgrounds, it is important to include language proficiency in both the home language and English as well as culture qualities. Vygotsky, a renowned psychologist from the Soviet Union, developed the sociocultural theory, which provides a foundational understanding of the connection between a student's home culture and language and the acquisition of a new culture and language. Vygotsky theorized that cognitive development occurs when a student is in their Zone of Proximal Development (ZPD). That is, ZPD is the difference between what a student can do independently and what can be done with guidance and support from a more knowledgeable individual. Language development serves two major roles: 1) as a means to transmit information from an adult to a child and 2) as a tool for intellectual adaptation. Vygotsky further hypothesized that language develops from social interactions for purposeful communication. Therefore, because language is foundational to address a student's needs at the ZPD level, it is critical that the IEP team include the language proficiency level of both the student's home language and English in the PLAAFP.

In addition, the IEP team must also include the home culture in the PLAAFP because integrating the home culture with school-based practices allows for students from CLD backgrounds to tap into their prior knowledge and experiences to gain a deeper level of understanding of new content and concepts. From a cultural relevance perspective, because most school-based practices are grounded in mainstream, middle-class norms, tapping into the student's home culture, also referred to as *funds of knowledge,* increases learning opportunities and allows instruction to be more comprehensible. Therefore, the culturally responsive IEP team should include the student's funds of knowledge in the PLAAFP to address both academic achievement and functional performance. The following Challenge Scenario presents an example of a PLAAFP in reading for a student from a CLD background.

Challenge Scenario

Alex completed the Renaissance Early Literacy measure in April 2020 and received a Scaled Score of 684. This is an increase of 166 from the Scaled Score of 518, which was obtained at the start of this academic year. Scaled Scores relate to three developmental reading stages: Emergent Reader (300-674), Transitional Reader (675-774), and Probable Reader (775-900). A Scaled Score of 684 means that Alex is now at the Transition Reader level. Alex can accurately identify the alphabet and produce letter-sound relationships. He recognizes most beginning and ending consonant sounds and long and short vowel sounds. Alex can blend sounds and word parts to read simple words (CVC and CVCe). He uses a variety of strategies to figure out words, such as pictures, story patterns, and phonics. His estimated oral reading fluency was 24. This means that he can read 24 words per minute; the average second grader can read 86 words per minute. Reading fluency is an important skill to comprehend text efficiently.

His parents report that Alex enjoys being read to in Spanish and often retells these stories to his sister using the pictures in the book. Because he is the eldest child in the family, he assumes the responsibility of overseeing homework for his younger sisters. During this time, he also prefers to work on his homework rather than completing assignments independently. When asked questions from his sisters in Spanish or English, he is slow to respond but usually responds in Spanish. His parents report that Alex enjoys being an older brother and the responsibilities of taking care of his younger sisters.

Alex is at the Beginning Fluency level of second language acquisition, as evident by his ability to communicate in social situations with minor errors. He relies on contextual clues to understand academic vocabulary. Based on the WIDA ACCESS test, Alex has reached an overall English language proficiency at the Emerging (Level 2). Following is his language proficiency for each domain:

- *Listening:* Level 2—Alex understands and participates in oral conversations on familiar topics. He can follow two- to three-step directions with visual supports.

- *Speaking:* Level 2—Alex can share ideas and information in English using short sentences and simple vocabulary.

- *Reading:* Level 2—Alex can follow the sequential events of a story with simple text and pictures.

- *Writing:* Level 1—Alex can communicate concepts through illustration and copying words and phrases.

Scenario Reflection

Based on the Challenge Scenario, document and discuss your thoughts regarding the following:

- Discuss the importance of documenting the cultural background of the child in the PLAAFP.

- Why is it important for the IEP team to know the language proficiency level of the child's home language and English?

When constructing the PLAAFP, providing the level of academic and functional performance and the cultural and language qualities provides important information that can lead to the development of goals that are meaningful for instructional purposes. In the Challenge Scenario example, both the reading level (Transition) and the conditions in which Alex learns best (small group, extended wait time, instruction in Spanish, and visual supports) were provided. This information and Alex's funds of knowledge (responsibility of eldest child) will allow the IEP team to identify goals that address Alex's reading deficit in a culturally responsive manner, which will also inform instruction.

Functional Assessment

Additional regulations note that *functional performance* refers to "skills or activities that are not considered academic or related to a child's academic achievement." This term "is often used in the context of routine activities of everyday living" (71 Fed. Reg. at 46661; p. 46661). In addition, the regulations require that "the evaluation procedures used to measure a child's functional skills must meet the same validity and reliability standards as all other evaluation procedures" (71 Fed. Reg. at 46661). Therefore, the evaluation must be administered by a knowledgeable individual who has the training and expertise to ensure the use of sound practices in assessment measures—which have been shown through research to be effective and consistent—for the identification of a child's functional skills.

Special Considerations for Functional Performance

Two fundamental purposes of special education are for students to develop to their fullest potential and become independent members of society. The functional skills are those competencies that support these two purposes of special education, which may be in conflict with families who may have different goals for their child, however. For example, some cultures may view that the family collectively will care for the child with a disability throughout their life; therefore, functional skills supporting independent living will likely not be viewed or supported by family members. In addition, when considering a student's functional performance, the IEP team must take into consideration the cultural dimensions because cultural norms and values affect functional performance. For example, **high-context cultures** (e.g., traditional Hispanic/Latinx) rely on non-verbal communication more than use of words, whereas **low-context cultures** (e.g., U.S. American culture) rely on verbal communication to covey messages. Therefore, students from high-context cultures who often rely on nonverbal cues may have extended periods of silence, which may be misunderstood as a deficit in functional performance. It is important for the IEP team to consult with families on cultural dimensions to make certain that values and norms included in functional skill are culturally responsive to the families' values and norms. Any relevant cultural and/or linguistic differences should be noted within the context of academic and functional performance assessment.

An Additional Dimension to Present Levels: Considering Student Present Levels in Crisis

As functional data is collected and considered for the PLAAFP section, it is also important to consider the student's ability to respond during a crisis. Crisis can happen in a wide range of circumstances, from fire to natural disasters (e.g., tornados, hurricanes, flooding) to manmade crises (e.g., violence in the community, violence on school grounds).

Many students with disabilities have skill deficits when it comes to responding to a crisis. From challenges in responding to fast-changing circumstances to being able to process and avoid dangerous situations, it is critical that IEP teams consider a student's ability to maintain their personal safety and develop a plan to support the student's acquisition of life-saving safety skills (Clarke et al., 2014). Table 4.2 provides crisis considerations that should be included in the PLAAFP.

Table 4.2.   Present Levels of Academic Achievement and Functional Performance (PLAAFP): Considerations for students in a crisis

PLAAFP area	Strengths and needs considerations
Communication	Can the student understand the language of a crisis, follow multistep directions, and respond to questions that are asked verbally or using a communication device?
Sensory	Does the student have sensory needs that must be met for them to follow directions and shelter in place?
	Does the student have any vision or hearing differences that might affect how they can respond to a crisis? Will they be able to see obstacles in their path, hear sounds of crisis, and so forth?
Behavior	Does the student have any behavioral concerns (e.g., anxiety, depression, oppositional defiance, obsessive-compulsive disorder, autism) that might affect their ability to follow directions or respond to a new routine that is not part of their daily routine or visual schedule?
Medical	Does the student have any medical needs that might be affected by a prolonged sheltering in place (e.g., insulin, oxygen, suctioning)?

Challenge Scenario

In the following scenario, two educators are trying to understand the section of Jarod's IEP that includes his PLAAFP. Review and reflect on the interaction detailed in the vignette.

Mr. Gabriel: Have you had a chance to look at what I wrote up for Jarod's IEP? I have notes on the whole IEP ready for our meeting except for that first part about present levels of performance and functions or functioning. I wasn't really even sure what that meant, so I left it for last. I knew we were meeting today, so I thought we could just put together a few sentences for that part.

Mrs. Castillo: Oh, okay. Yeah, I guess that's a good idea. But how did you suggest any goals or objectives without determining the present levels?

Mr. Gabriel: Um, well, I don't know. I looked at some other IEPs, and I made sure that everything I wrote up for possible goals and objectives were measurable statements. I think they sound really good. Do you want to see them?

Mrs. Castillo: The goals and objectives? Well, sure, but how would they be appropriate for Jarod if we haven't determined his present levels?

Mr. Gabriel: I'm not really sure what you mean. I guess maybe I really don't understand that section. How should we get started then?

Mrs. Castillo: Well, I'm not positive I've always understood this section of the IEP perfectly either, but I do know that the goals and objectives have to come from current observations of what the student can do and from the data that suggests his strengths and weaknesses. I mean, present does mean current, happening right now, doesn't it? So, looking at his current data, assessments, evaluations, classwork, and things like that would be important. Let's start there.

Mr. Gabriel: Oh, this is going to be much more detailed than what I was thinking. I guess that means my suggestions for goals, objectives, and specialized instruction may be way off base depending on a lot of different factors, even including what Jarod is good at. Wow, that is very different than what I thought that section was about.

Mrs. Castillo: I know. The most important thing I've learned is to make sure there is objective information that defines strengths and areas for improvement and how those things will have an impact on the student's ability to make progress in the general curriculum. Also, it will be important to get information from Jarod's family for this section and get their input on how they would like his present levels to be reflected in his educational services.

Mr. Gabriel: That makes a lot of sense, but in the past, I really think I have just written my opinions here based on what I thought I knew about students. And then families always just pretty much went along with my thoughts and plans for their child.

Mrs. Castillo: Yeah, I think a lot of teachers do that. Let's develop Jarod's plan together and work with his parents to complete it. Then we'll both be much better at this process in the future.

Scenario Reflection

Based on the Challenge Scenario, document and discuss your initial thoughts regarding the following questions:

- What kind of information would you need to gather in order to begin writing a student's PLAAFP section of an IEP?

- Why is it important to have clear and measurable present levels established and written prior to completing any other sections of the IEP?

- Why is it important to indicate how the student's disability affects their involvement in the general education curriculum?

- What do you believe are the primary purposes of communicating a student's PLAAFP to others on the team and in writing on the IEP?

Stop and Think!

- How would you use the Present Levels of Academic Achievement and Functional Performance section to plan instruction?

- Would you need to take into account the relationship between functional performance and academic achievement? Explain your answer.

- Explain how culture and language proficiency affect instruction.

- Explain how you would support crisis planning for a student with a significant physical, behavioral, or emotional disability.

AREAS TARGETED FOR IMPROVEMENT

It is critical to have a clear picture of the child's current academic and functional level of performance to plan for the educational needs of the child. This plan begins with identifying the targeted areas for improvement. Reflecting on the child's strengths and documenting culture and language proficiency are essential for being culturally responsive to the needs of children from CLD backgrounds.

Baseline Data

A critical purpose for detailing a student's PLAAFP in the IEP is to adhere to the requirements of IDEA. An equally important purpose of the PLAAFP section of the IEP, however, is to lay the foundation on which the appropriate goals, objectives, services, supports, accommodations, adaptations, and placements are designed for each individual child. The unique needs of the child that will be addressed by special education and related services are presented purposefully at the beginning of this section. Addressing this section as a preliminary step to completing any other sections establishes a baseline of measurable information that will serve as the starting point for developing goals and objectives/benchmarks and, ultimately, other important and legally required components of the IEP. Monitoring the student's progress toward meeting IEP goals is one of these requirements. Therefore, having clear baseline data is critical for progress monitoring. Not only is a summary of the student's evaluation data, including specific subtest performance levels, essential for the academic achievement considerations, but it is also important to consider which standards the student has met and which standards they still need to meet. Since the early 2000s, the IEP has evolved into a critical document that blends the best of special education and standards-based education to ensure that students with disabilities meet academic content standards (Samuels, 2012).

Parent Input

As equal members of the IEP team, the parents and, when possible, the student should assist in identifying details for the PLAAFP section. Not only can the family and the student share insights related to the student's academic and personal strengths and interests, but they can also report on whether the skills being learned at school are transferring to home and life. In addition, they can provide valuable insight on the home culture and language(s). Parents and/or family members are the only individuals with this critical insight; therefore, careful and accurate documentation should include their insight so that the PLAFFP is meaningful. Given the vision and desired outcomes for special education services established by the student and the family, the expectations of the general curriculum, and the PLAAFP section, the IEP team can establish a clear path for accomplishing the goals and objectives in the IEP while proactively planning to address any obstacles that may prevent progress in the general curriculum. Although it is clear that parental involvement is critical in the IEP process, their involvement may appear different than the school's expectations, such as parents not verbalizing their desires, which may be reflective of cultural background and previous school experiences. It is important that school personnel recognize the valuable knowledge that families can bring to the IEP process and encourage them to be engaged in the process. For many families who are CLD, this encouragement and engagement starts with developing a relationship with the family and using their preferred language to communicate important information about their child. Use of an interpreter is critical to ensure that the information discussed at the IEP meeting is comprehensible and understood by all members (see Chapter 2).

> ### Stop and Think!
> Some districts segment the Present Levels of Academic Achievement and Functional Performance (PLAAFP) section into academic area of needs in the IEP. These sections of the present levels must also consider student strengths, parent input, baseline data, cultural dimensions, language proficiency in home and English, communication or assistive technology, and how the student's academic and functional needs have an impact on involvement and progress in the general education curriculum.

(continued)

Stop and Think! *(continued)*

Consider the following example of a segmented PLAAFP section of the IEP. Does it include all of the requirements as discussed in this chapter? Explain your response.

When given a list of basic sight words during fourth quarter of the academic year, Pierre correctly identified 60 out of 100. Pierre successfully identified one-syllable words correctly. When given a 145-word passage from fifth-grade reading material during fourth quarter, Pierre read 60 words correctly compared with an average of 139 words per minute by peers. Pierre uses context clues to gain meaning. He does not independently use the decoding strategy of segmenting words into familiar patterns, which has implications for Pierre's learning in other content areas. Sixth-grade students are expected to monitor their own comprehension by adjusting speed to fit the purpose or by skimming, scanning, reading on, looking back, and taking notes or summarizing what they have read so far in text. Pierre's slow reading pace affects the amount of material he is able to read within an instructional period in all academic areas, and it affects his comprehension. Pierre's parents indicate that he is able to complete work involving reading when the material is supported by visuals and when materials are read to him.

Objective Data

In addition to the important information the students and their families can provide, formal evaluation data must be considered in shaping the PLAAFP section. For students who are CLD and are not proficient in academic English, however, it is important to assess their primary language because their performance in the formal evaluation often is not a true reflection of their academic ability or performance. If the child is new to special education services, then the evaluation data will come from the formal tests and observations administered during the initial evaluation for eligibility, such as tests assessing intelligence, academic achievement, English and home language proficiency, and acuity (e.g., vision, hearing). If the IEP is being reviewed and revised, then the evaluation data can come from any and all formal and informal assessments performed throughout the year.

Assessment information used in writing the IEP should be current, measurable, objective, and functional—from both academic and nonacademic areas—as it serves as a baseline of information for writing goals, short-term objectives, and benchmarks. It also should include the results of the student's most recent evaluation or reevaluation (e.g., formal and informal educational performance data, state and/or district assessments). Assessment results should include test results with quantifiable data from diagnostic tests or other specialized designed testing of a student's academic and behavioral performance levels. Not only must assessment results be detailed, but results should also be discussed in terms of the student's performance level and how the assessment results have instructional relevance. The IEP team must be vigilant in assuring that assessment results of language proficiency are included in the PLAAFP for students who are CLD. This information is not only required to meet IDEA mandates but is also necessary in the development of goals and curriculum that meet the unique needs of the student. Most schools perform two types of assessments to learn about the student's language proficiency. The first type consists of a home language survey/questionnaire that identifies the language or languages spoken at home. It serves to alert the school that the child may be exposed to another language besides English. The second type of assessment is to complete a formal measure of the child's home language and English proficiency. The following is a list of some of the most common language proficiency measures available.

- Basic Inventory of Natural Language (Herbert, 1986)—available in 30 different types

- Ber-Sil Elementary and Secondary Spanish Tests (Beringer, 1976)—available in Spanish, Tagalog, Ilokano, Cantonese, Mandarin, Korean, and Persian

- Bilingual Syntax Measure I and II (Burt et al., 1980)—available in Spanish and English

- Bilingual Verbal Ability Tests–Normative Update (Muñoz-Sandoval et al., 2005)—available in 15 languages

- Boehm Test of Basic Concepts–Third Edition (Boehm, 2001)—available in English and Spanish

- Language Assessment Scales–Oral (DeAvila & Duncan, 1991)—available in Spanish and English

- Prueba de Desarrollo Inicial de Lenguaje (Hresko et al., 1982—available in Spanish

- Screening Test of Spanish Grammar (Toronto, 1973)—available in Spanish

- Test de Vocabulario en Imágenes Peabody (Dunn et al., 1986)—available in Spanish

- Woodcock-Muñoz Language Survey–Third Edition (Woodcock et al., 2017)—available in Spanish and English

Although formal assessments provide important information about language proficiency, it is important to note that informal measures also provide critical information on language development. Because learning a language takes place in a variety of environments, it is important to assess how students are developing their home language and English. Informal measures such as family interviews, home visits, observation of student's interaction with peers in social situations, and use of language in academic setting are valuable. Table 4.3 provides a list of informal language proficiency measures that can be helpful when assessing language proficiency development.

Once home language and English proficiency is determined, it is important to gather even more specific data. Formal test results including criterion-referenced test results, standardized test results, and/or achievement test results are important to review and consider. These types of formal tests, however, will not provide all of the information needed to proceed. There are several other formal and informal assessments that can generate results and contribute to a collection of data that reflects the student's PLAAFP. Assessments that result in the subsequent development of educational services and programs can be categorized into four different types—selected response, extended written response, performance assessment, and personal communication (Stiggins, 2011).

Table 4.3. Informal language proficiency measures

Assessment area	Name (author)
English and Spanish language development	World-Class Instructional Design and Assessment (WIDA)-ACCESS Tests, WIDA Screener and Kindergarten W-APT (Wisconsin Center for Education Research at University of Wisconsin, Madison)
Home language	Home Language Survey (U.S. Department of Education, 2016b)
Oral language-English and home language	Student Oral Language Observation Matrix (San Jose Unified School District, 2019)
Social and academic language-English and home language	Classroom Language Interaction Checklist (Collier, 2016)
Spanish	Brigance Assessment of Basic Skills-Revised, Spanish Edition (Curriculum Associates)

Selected Response   A **selected response assessment** requires a student to produce evidence of learning by selecting a correct response from a number of choices, including multiple choice, true/false, and matching questions. Selected response assessments are effective for measuring knowledge acquisition, and it is easy to set criteria for success (e.g., 17 correct out of 20 is a passing score). Yet, they cannot determine a student's depth of knowledge, their ability to apply or transfer knowledge, or if the student is guessing.

Extended Written Response   An **extended written response** assessment requires a student to produce evidence of learning by constructing a written response to a question or task that is at least several sentences in length. These types of assessments require the student to apply reasoning or problem-solving skills in order to generate their response.

Performance Assessment   A **performance assessment** requires a student to produce evidence of learning by either creating or developing a product or performance. This type of assessment generally requires students to demonstrate something that meets specific criteria. Performance assessments typically illuminate students' skills, conceptual understandings, abilities to apply knowledge and skills, execution abilities, and process abilities. One example of a performance assessment is when asked to count to 30, the student orally rote counts to 30; another example is when asked to purchase a drink in the cafeteria, the student provides the correct amount of money to purchase the drink. Both of these examples require a student to demonstrate a specific criteria.

Personal Communication   **Personal communication assessments** require a student to produce evidence of learning by speaking or writing. The teacher may directly interact with the student either in writing or verbally. Personal communication assessments may extend over a period of time.

Selecting an Assessment Method   Assessments are abundant and readily available in teachers' manuals, school district offices, and by request from a school-based psychologist. To select the appropriate assessment methods and match the learning targets/IEP focus, it is important to know who will use the assessment and how it will be used. Chappuis et al. (2009) stated that "assessment must be for learning, not just of learning" (p. 14). Therefore, acknowledging that the purpose of the assessment is to assist in identifying the student's PLAAFP will assist the IEP team in appropriately communicating the assessment results in a fashion that will guide decisions related to educational services for the student.

It is important not only to use assessments to identify that a student is struggling in a particular academic area but also to discern the exact knowledge, skills, and competencies that students have already mastered. Some of the most commonly used tools for effectively identifying PLAAFP and for monitoring student growth throughout the school year include

- **Curriculum-based assessment/measurement (CBM).** CBMs are beneficial in determining student performance in reading (sight words, comprehension), mathematics (facts, formulas, operations), and writing (mechanics, content, structure, organization). Probes for CBMs often include brief reading passages, short spelling lists, or samples of math items from the curriculum.

- **Short-cycle assessments.** These are frequent or daily formative assessments specific to an instructional goal that provide information in relation to content standard mastery or lack thereof.

- **Checklists.** Teacher observations can be documented through checklists. They are often used most appropriately for monitoring observable skills, when multiple steps are required to perform a task or skill, and/or determining mastery of social-emotional or behavioral competencies.

In addition, benchmark and progress monitoring data generated from a variety of commercial resources can be informative in developing the PLAAFP. Teacher-, school-, or district-created tools are often helpful, but they are not always valid and reliable. Table 4.4 provides a list of available assessment tools/probes.

Additional data may be gathered from running records (reading), portfolios, work samples, inventories, report cards and grades, as well as observational and anecdotal notes. These are less objective sources, however, and should only be used to support conclusions drawn from other data sources or provide additional examples of student levels.

It is also essential to consider functional in addition to academic data in collecting evidence to support the PLAAFP. The following sources can be helpful to determine present levels of functional performance:

- Attendance records

- Physical therapy evaluations

- Occupational therapy evaluations

- Vision evaluations

- Hearing evaluations

- Behavior/discipline records

- Parent input

- Previous IEP, if applicable

Table 4.4. Assessment resources for measuring and monitoring reading/English language arts and math skills

Assessment tools/ probes	Publisher/ author	Details
AIMSweb/ aimswebPlus	Pearson	Reading and math tools available
		Grades K–8 probes provided for short-term skills and end-of-year goals
		Per student or site-based subscription rates apply
easyCBM	Developed by researchers at University of Oregon and available in web-based format	The Lite easyCBM progress monitoring system is available for free online
		Teacher deluxe editions are available online for a subscription fee
		Offers benchmark and progress monitoring tools for both math and reading in grades K–8
FASTearlymath/ FASTearlyreading/ FASTCBMReading	Developed by researchers at the University of Minnesota and exclusively licensed to Fast Bridge Learning	FAST is an acronym for "Formative Assessment System for Teachers"
		Curriculum-based and computer adaptive measurements are available
		Tools available include:
		CBMReading (English and Spanish) (K–6) CBMMath (1–6)
		earlyReading (English and Spanish) (K–1) earlyMath (K–1)
		aReading (adaptive reading) (K–12)
		aMath (adaptive math)
		Social Emotional/Behavior Rating Scales
		Developmental Milestones (kindergarten)
		Per student or site-based subscription rates apply
i-Ready	Curriculum Associates	Offers diagnostic and growth monitoring
		Reading/English language arts and math tools are available
		Brief, computer-delivered, adaptive assessments available for grades K–8
		Growth monitoring reports track skill acquisition toward end-of-year goals
		Per student or site-based subscription rates apply
mClass	Amplify (based on research from the University of Oregon)	Identifies the need for targeted instruction with the only licensed digital version of the research-based DIBELS 8th Edition assessment
		Tools available to measure:
		Phonological awareness
		Alphabetic principle/phonics
		Early literacy measures
		Text and reading comprehension
		Computer based
		Progress monitoring and benchmark tools for grades K–6
		Subscription or licensing fees apply

Assessment tools/ probes	Publisher/ author	Details
STAR	Renaissance	STAR Reading (K–12), STAR Math (1–12), STAR Early Literacy (K–3), and STAR CBM and STAR Custom are available in English and Spanish
		Short-term skills and end-of-year goals can be monitored
		Assessments are computer adaptive
		Per student or site-based subscription fees apply

Stop and Think!

You have read and learned about the importance of including meaningful assessment data in the Present Levels of Academic Achievement and Functional Performance (PLAAFP) section of the IEP. Now reconsider your response to the Jarod scenario. Revise your responses.

- What kind of information would need to be gathered in order to begin writing the PLAAFP section of an IEP?

- Explain the importance of including home culture and language proficiency for students from culturally and linguistically diverse backgrounds.

- Why is it important to have clear and measurable present levels established and written prior to completing any other sections of the IEP?

- What do you believe are the primary purposes of communicating a student's PLAAFP?

SUMMARY

This chapter detailed the important steps to take prior to beginning any formal planning related to educational services outlined in a student's IEP. First, the IEP team must outline and thoroughly discuss the learner's strengths and areas for improvement while also considering the context of home culture and language proficiency for students with CLD backgrounds. These strengths and needs are recorded in the PLAAFP section of the IEP. This section is important because it provides the foundation for developing rigorous supports to create an opportunity for greater student success. In short, it is the basis from which all other IEP components are developed. Each area of need identified in the PLAAFP must be addressed in another appropriate section of the IEP form. In its entirety, this section is used to describe the student's current performance in areas affected by the student's disability. The IEP team is also charged with ensuring that the PLAAFP is culturally responsive to the needs of all students.

In addition to the legal and procedural considerations for writing the PLAAFP section of the IEP, this chapter also addressed the purpose of connecting this section seamlessly to classroom instruction and the importance of engaging families in the process. Finally, it is important to note that provisions for crisis planning and management may be relevant for some students, and the PLAAFP section should be updated and revised as both academic and functional skills increase or diminish. The list in Figure 4.1 can be used in preparation for the IEP meeting.

Culturally Responsive Present Levels of Academic Achievement and Functional Performance

In order to develop Present Levels of Academic Achievement and Functional Performance that are meaningful and responsive to the needs of CLD populations, the following elements must be thoroughly discussed at the IEP meeting and included in the IEP:

- *Home culture strengths/funds of knowledge.* Provide sufficient information on how home culture supports student's learning and progress.

- *Instructionally relevant assessments.* Include assessment results that are meaningful for instruction and note how results relate to the student's performance and instructional needs.

- *Language proficiency level.* Discuss home/native language and English language social and academic level of proficiency.

- *Effective language intervention.* Discuss strategies, approaches, and supports that have successfully been used to support the student's language development (home/native and English).

- *Instructional language.* Include which language (native or English) is required for instruction to be comprehensible.

- *Parent/family goals.* Include long-term and short-term family goals that are specific to the child; keep in mind that some families may have a different view for long-term planning.

PREPARATION FOR THE IEP MEETING:
PRESENT LEVELS OF ACADEMIC ACHIEVEMENT AND FUNCTIONAL SUPPORTS

Prior to the Meeting

☐ Review prior IEP and student progress monitoring data to determine baseline of student's academic achievement and functional performance.

☐ Identify student's strengths and funds of knowledge.

☐ Ascertain the student's home language and/or English language proficiency level.

☐ Pinpoint the student's preferred language of instruction and/or supports.

☐ Characterize the student's ability to respond to a crisis from communication, sensory, behavioral, and medical perspectives.

☐ Prepare a list of questions to ask parents to gain their perspective of the student's present level of performance.

☐ Secure and meet with interpreter as needed (see Chapter 2).

During the Meeting

☐ Communicate (orally and in writing) and document student's present level of performance in a nonjargon comprehensible manner that can serve as baseline data.

☐ Detail student's strengths and funds of knowledge.

☐ Document student's home language and English proficiency level.

☐ Involve parents in identifying the student's present levels of performance and funds of knowledge.

☐ Record assessment results that are instructionally relevant and written in a manner that can be understood by all IEP members.

☐ Read the Present Levels of Academic Achievement and Functional Performance (PLAAFP) section of the IEP aloud to all participants and ask for accuracy and/or corrections.

☐ If using an interpreter, then be sure to use appropriate interpreter etiquette (see Chapter 2).

After the Meeting

☐ Debrief with all team members, including parents. Discuss the effectiveness of the meeting.

☐ Check with parents on the use of an interpreter and if they understood the meeting and key takeaways.

Figure 4.1. Preparation for the IEP meeting: Present levels of academic achievement and functional supports.

THE IEP CHECKLIST: PRESENT LEVELS OF
ACADEMIC ACHIEVEMENT AND FUNCTIONAL PERFORMANCE

The following checklist can be used as an inventory to ensure that the PLAAFP section of the IEP meets IDEA regulations.

Key Area (IEP section): **Student's Present Levels of Academic Achievement and Functional Performance**	Criteria met	
	Yes	No
P1: Present levels are prioritized based on student's needs.		
P2: A statement is included that explains the effect of a student's disability on their educational performance and involvement and progress in the general education curriculum.		
P3: A statement is included that clearly indicates the student's actual performance in academic and functional areas (e.g., behavioral, communication).		
P4: A statement is included that describes the student's strengths and needs (Present Levels of Academic Achievement and Functional Performance).		
P5: Sufficient details are provided on the student's level of functioning to develop goals.		

ACTIVITIES

The activities included in this chapter are intended for the reader to gain a deeper understanding of the content covered. For this chapter, each activity builds on the skills of the previous activity. The activities associated with this chapter include the following:

- Activity 4.1. Check for Understanding: Identification of Strengths and Weaknesses in Present Levels of Academic Achievement and Functional Performance Sections: Part I

- Activity 4.2. Check for Understanding: Writing Measurable Present Levels of Academic Achievement and Functional Performance Sections: Part II

- Activity 4.3. Identification of Quality Present Levels of Academic Achievement and Functional Performance Sections

- Activity 4.4. Recording Student's Funds of Knowledge

- Activity 4.5. Funds of Knowledge Photo Essay

Activity 4.1.

Landmark Check for Understanding: Identification of Strengths and Weaknesses in Present Levels of Academic Achievement and Functional Performance Sections: Part I

Supporting chapter: Chapter 4 (Present Levels of Academic Achievement and Functional Performance)

Purpose: The purpose of this activity is to develop the skill of writing a meaningful Present Levels of Academic Achievement and Functional Performance (PLAAFP) section in a student's IEP.

Directions: Consider the content discussed in Chapter 4 to evaluate the examples of information in the following table to be considered for the PLAAFP section in a student's IEP. Discuss the strengths and weaknesses of each example and determine if it is a strong or weak contribution and what, if any, critical information is missing. Indicate the portion of the statement that is missing, if appropriate. Please note that none of the examples present a complete PLAAFP section, but they do suggest the range of detail and information that must be considered in constructing this section of the IEP for one area (e.g., reading, math, functional performance).

Present Levels of Academic Achievement and Functional Performance contribution	Circle what is missing	Strengths/ weaknesses
Lauren, a fourth-grade student, can read at a first-grade level as measured by the placement tests within the district-adopted reading series. She uses picture and context clues to help understand what she is reading. Lauren's parents have shared that she communicates primarily in Spanish at home and enjoys selecting her own books and reading to others. Results of standardized testing using the Woodcock-Johnson–IV (WJ IV) indicate a total reading quotient of 75 (below average range). Lauren's basic writing skills are at a 1.2 grade level as documented by the WJR Writing subtest. Lauren does not require any communication or assistive technology devices to successfully participate in language arts courses.	Strengths Parent input Language proficiency Home culture Baseline data Communication/assistive technology needs Nothing missing	
Jake is often tardy or absent from school. He hardly ever completes or turns in his homework. As a result, his grades in almost all classes are at a failing level. He seems willing to complete in-class assignments, but he lacks the organizational skills to accurately complete these tasks on a consistent basis. Jake's mother stated that he dislikes school and often pretends to be sick, and he very rarely brings any books or assignments home.	Strengths Parent input Language proficiency Home culture Baseline data Communication/assistive technology needs Nothing missing	

Present Levels of Academic Achievement and Functional Performance contribution	Circle what is missing	Strengths/ weaknesses
Cierra is a 6-year-old kindergarten student. Her parents noted that she enjoys school, follows simple directions well, and shows strengths in interacting with family members and friends outside of school. In class, Cierra shows strengths in her ability to match pictures with words. She communicates with a DynaVox device and can consistently produce two- and three-word phrases based on data collected by the intervention specialist. According to a visual motor integration test administered last month, Cierra scored in the 15th percentile for her age. Her difficulty with expressive vocabulary makes it difficult for Cierra to participate in general education kindergarten classes during core content subjects. With assistive technology devices, however, she is able to fully participate in nonacademic subjects and specials with her same-age peers.	Strengths Parent input Language proficiency Home culture Baseline data Communication/assistive technology needs Nothing missing	
Caleb is able to add and subtract double digits without regrouping. He can tell time to the hour and half hour, count money, and make change with minimal support. Caleb can stay on task for academic lessons for periods up to 45 minutes. Visual aids and manipulatives help Caleb attend to mathematical performance tasks. Although below grade level, he is progressing in all math domains represented in the Common Core State Standards. Caleb scored a 77% on a curriculum-based measurement including mixed math probes at the sixth-grade level given at the beginning of this grading period. Caleb also lacks the prerequisite skills to grasp the level of content peers are learning. Therefore, he needs a calculator and consistent teacher and peer support to succeed in general curriculum math courses. In addition, Caleb benefits from participating in math intervention sessions for 30 minutes each session three times per week.	Strengths Parent input Language proficiency Home culture Baseline data Communication/assistive technology needs Nothing missing	

Present Levels of Academic Achievement and Functional Performance contribution	Circle what is missing	Strengths/ weaknesses
Chrissy, a sixth-grade student, has a reading level of a mid–third-grade student, as evidenced on the Brigance Inventory of Basic Skills. She knows all of her letters and sounds and has a sight word vocabulary of 28 words. She reads third-grade passages orally with a fluency rate of 88 words per minute with five to seven errors. Chrissy's parents observe that she is able to read environmental print in order to function safely at home and in the community. They are concerned that she is not able to recall or retell details of what she reads orally. Based on informal observation, Chrissy's teacher notes that Chrissy demonstrates weakness in comprehension and attention. She appears to be a good oral reader, however. Her difficulty in sequencing and comprehension will likely cause Chrissy frustration in the general education setting, particularly when reading for information in the content areas.	Strengths Parent input Language proficiency Home culture Baseline data Communication/assistive technology needs Nothing missing	

Activity 4.2.

Check for Understanding: Writing Measurable Present Levels of Academic Achievement and Functional Performance Sections: Part II

Supporting chapter: Chapter 4 (Present Levels of Academic Achievement and Functional Performance)

Purpose: The purpose of this activity is to develop the skill of writing a meaningful Present Levels of Academic Achievement and Functional Performance (PLAAFP) section in a student's IEP.

Directions: Consider the PLAAFP section of the IEP as noted in the table in Activity 4.1. Match statements from that activity to the following scripts, revising if necessary, for clarification. Following are additional considerations when writing the performance of children in the PLAAFP section of the IEP:

For documenting student strengths, consider these scripts:

_____(child's name) can _____ as evidenced by _____.

_____(child's name) can _____ at _____ grade level as measured by _____.

_____(child's name) communicates in _____ as evidenced by _____

_____(child's name) proficiency in _____ (language) is _____ (level) as evidenced by _____.

For documenting parental observations and concerns, consider these scripts:

_____(child's name)'s parents report that they can _____.

_____(child's name)'s parents report that they are concerned about _____.

_____(child's name)'s parents report that at home they prefers to use _____ (language).

_____(child's name)'s parents report that at home and in the community they use _____ (language[s]) effectively or ineffectively (select one) to communicate.

For documenting baseline data, consider these scripts:

_____(child's name) can _____ at _____ (level), as formally measured by _____.

_____(child's name) can _____ at _____ (level), as informally measured by _____.

For documenting language proficiency, consider this script:

_____(child's name) can communicate _____ at (level), as informally measured by _____.

_____(child's name) can communicate _____ at (level), as formally measured by _____.

For documenting communication and/or assistive technology needs, consider this script:

_____ (child's name) benefits from _____ when _____.

For documenting impact statements, which refer to how the disability manifests itself and affects the child's performance, consider these scripts:

In order to progress in the general education curriculum activities, _____(child's name) needs _____.

As a result of their difficulty in _____, _____(child's name) is unable to participate in the general education curriculum during _____ and needs _____.

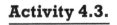

Activity 4.3.

Identification of Quality Present Levels of Academic Achievement and Functional Performance Sections

Supporting chapter: Chapter 4 (Present Levels of Academic Achievement and Functional Performance)

Purpose: The purpose of this activity is to identify quality Present Levels of Academic Achievement and Functional Performance (PLAAFP) sections that are both meaningful and measurable.

Directions: Use an IEP to inventory the PLAAFP section and indicate the quality of the information provided. Then, rank the quality of the goals and provide evidence to support your ranking.

Rubric scale: Use the following scale and circle the number that best ranks the IEP area reviewed in the table that follows.

1 = Standard not met	2 = Standard partially met	3 = Standard met	4 = Standard exceeds
• IEP document fails to provide evidence of meeting the IDEA 2004 requirements. • IEP does not address the IDEA 2004 requirements.	• Performance provides evidence of partially meeting IDEA 2004 requirements. • Performance addresses some of the IDEA 2004 requirements.	• Performance provides evidence of meeting most/all of the IDEA 2004 requirements. • Performance addresses most/ all of the IDEA 2004 requirements.	• Performance provides evidence of exceeding all IDEA 2004 requirements. • All indicators are addressed in the IEP and go beyond expectations.

Key Area (IEP Section): Student's Present Levels of Academic Achievement and Functional Performance	Ranking	Rationale for Ranking
P1: Present levels are prioritized based on student's needs.	1 2 3 4	
P2: A statement is included that explains the effect of a student's disability on their educational performance and involvement and progress in the general education curriculum.	1 2 3 4	
P3: A statement is included that clearly indicates the student's actual performance in academic and functional areas (e.g., behavioral, communication).	1 2 3 4	
P4: A statement is included that describes the student's strengths and needs (Present Levels of Academic Achievement and Functional Performance [PLAAFP]).	1 2 3 4	
P5: Sufficient details are provided on the student's level of functioning to develop goals.	1 2 3 4	

Rewritten PLAAFP statement:

_____

_____

_____

_____

Activity 4.4.

Recording Student's Funds of Knowledge

Supporting chapter: Chapter 4 (Present Levels of Academic Achievement and Functional Performance)

Purpose: The purpose of this activity is to apply a student's funds of knowledge to inform culturally relevant instructional practices.

Directions: Use the form provided to record a student's interests, activities, and skills outside of the school environment as reported by parents and/or your observation. This will require a home visit and/or having an informal conversation with your student's parent or family. Next, fill in the funds of knowledge for each category and consider how you can apply them to instructional practices. Skip the categories that do not apply to the student's family, and add new categories based on the culture of the student.

Categories	Cultural funds of knowledge	Application to classroom instruction
Caregiving		
Cooking		
Educational activities		
Family outings		
Family values/traditions		
Health practices		
Household chores		
Language		
Religion		
Responsibilities		

Activity 4.5.

Funds of Knowledge Photo Essay

Supporting chapter: Chapter 4 (Present Levels of Academic Achievement and Functional Performance)

Purpose: The purpose of this activity is to identify a student's funds of knowledge in order to apply to culturally relevant instructional practices.

Directions: Instruct students to create a photo essay of a typical day or weekend in their home family life. Next, identify the funds of knowledge presented in the essay. Consider how you will apply this information to instructional practices.

5

Goals

Clarissa E. Rosas

After reading this chapter and engaging in activities related to this chapter, you will be able to meet the following outcomes:

- Construct meaningful and measurable IEP goal statements.

- Create culturally responsive IEP goal statements.

Since the establishment of mandatory public education, the responsibility for educating children has shifted from parents and caregivers to the public sector. The enactment of the No Child Left Behind Act (NCLB) of 2001 (PL 107-110), coupled with the reauthorization of Individuals with Disabilities Education Improvement Act (IDEA) of 2004 (PL 108-446), laid the foundation for public schools to be held accountable for the education of children. The replacement of NCLB with Every Student Succeeds Act (ESSA) of 2015 (PL 114-95) strengthened this accountability and bolstered the importance of writing meaningful goals for students with disabilities. Writing clear, meaningful goals is critical because they serve as the foundation from which supports and services are determined. In addition, teachers are held accountable for the instruction, supports, and services they deliver to meet the goals as outlined in the IEP. It is imperative, then, that those responsible for generating IEPs have the background knowledge and expertise to write measurable and meaningful goals. To fully understand what this means, it is important to review the legal provisions related to the development of IEP goals as outlined in IDEA 2004.

CONNECTION TO LEGAL PERSPECTIVE

The student's goals are at the heart of the IEP. Goals are statements that describe the achievements that a child will strive to accomplish as a result of specific intervention(s).

These goals are derived from the Present Levels of Academic Achievement and Functional Performance (PLAAFP) section of the IEP (see Chapter 4). In essence, the goals determine the intervention(s) for the student, which may include specialized services, adaptations, and/or modifications. According to IDEA 2004, IEPs must include the following:

> (2)(i) A statement of measurable annual goals, including academic and functional goals designed to—
> (A) Meet the child's needs that result from the child's disability to enable the child to be involved in and make progress in the general education curriculum; and
> (B) Meet each of the child's other educational needs that result from the child's disability (§ 300.320[a][2][i][A] and [B])

In short, the law requires that goals are written using concrete, sensory language that describes the intended results based on 1) the child's PLAAFP and 2) where the team believes the child should be functioning as a result of the intervention. The instructional approach, assessment, services, and any adaptations or modifications that will be available to the child are linked directly to the goals outlined in the IEP. Therefore, it is essential that the Goals section of the IEP include the following:

- Target statements that clearly reflect the needs of the student as noted in the IEP's PLAAFP section

- Statements that aim at addressing key academic and functional needs specific to the student

- Statements that include sensory language, which are specific, observable, and measurable

- Statements that describe robust skills that the student can realistically achieve within 1 year

Goals also must be listed in the IEP in the order of priority as noted in the PLAAFP section.

Although goals must include the criteria previously listed, they also must be meaningful. Meaningful goals serve as a critical guide to the team in the development of an IEP that includes interventions to achieve a specific set of outcomes. Historically, the most challenging aspect for IEP teams is writing goals that are both measurable and meaningful (Rosas & Winterman, 2012). When abstract, ambiguous, and vague words, such as "appropriate," "efficient," or "effective," are used to describe the desired outcome, they often result in assessment measures that are not meaningful. Goal statements that use concrete, sensory-specific language to describe the intended outcome lead to meaningful performance measures that specifically assess if the intended behavior or outcome was achieved.

IEP goal statements serve as leading indicators of performance that are precursors of future success. Therefore, IEP teams must carefully construct goal statements that not only address the needs of the student but are also reasonably ambitious to support potential growth. Although IDEA mandates the IEP process include writing meaningful goal statements, litigation provides clarity on how to implement legislative mandates. The *Endrew F. v. Douglas County School District* (2017) court decision provided clarity on writing goals that promote growth when it stated, "IEP teams are required to 'provide meaningful opportunities for appropriate academic and functional advancements and to enable the child to make progress'" (U.S. Department of Education, p. 6). Because IEP goal statements lead to supports and services to meet the goal, the landmark Endrew case clarified that goal statements must be written in a reasonably robust manner to ensure that the student advances toward their potential.

Stop and Think!

- What is the purpose of IEP goals?

- How are IEP goals used to plan instruction at the classroom level?

- Why must IEP goals be both measurable and meaningful?

Challenge Scenario

In the following scenario, Christina Rose, a general education teacher, describes her experience reviewing an IEP for the purpose of planning instruction for Mario, a new child in her third-grade classroom. Review and reflect on the challenges detailed in the scenario.

When I learned that Mario would be joining our third-grade class, I wanted to learn as much as I could on how to help Mario be successful in school. The intervention specialist (special education teacher) at our school suggested that I read Mario's educational file to learn how I could help him. I had heard about these working files at a workshop and was happy to learn that one was available for Mario. As I reviewed the work samples included in the file, it became evident that Mario had some difficulties with spelling, grammar, and perhaps comprehension and was an English language learner (ELL). As I reviewed the work samples, I noticed that some of his errors were characteristic of ELLs that I have worked with in the past. I began to wonder if the difficulties noted were more of a reflection of Mario learning English rather than a written language deficit.

In order to learn exactly what I needed to do to help Mario, I read his IEP. We learned at a staff development workshop that the IEP is the blueprint to help students be successful in school. Wow, was I ever in for a surprise when I read Mario's IEP! One of his goals indicated that by the end of third grade, he would be able to spell words with 80% accuracy. I have no idea what this means. Does this mean he only needs to spell 80% of a word correctly, or does it mean he should get 80% correct on spelling tests? Eighty percent correct on a spelling test would mean he earned a B. I would like all the children in my class to earn a B in spelling, so what is so special about Mario, and what do they mean by 80%? I also wondered if the issue with spelling could be that Mario was being asked to spell words he did not understand. Because the working file indicated that Mario was an ELL, why wasn't there a goal that focused on academic proficiency?

As I read the next goal, it became even more confusing. The goal stated that Mario would comprehend 75% of a passage. I don't know what it means to comprehend 75% of a passage. How would I ever keep a record of this? Does this mean he is not required to understand an entire passage? Surely, we want him to comprehend all the content covered in social studies and science textbooks. How is he going to pass any mandated standardized tests if we only expect him to comprehend 75% of what he is reading? Because he is in special education, does this mean he should be assigned reading materials below a third-grade level? I also wondered if his comprehension issues were related to being an ELL? At one of our culturally responsive professional development sessions, the presenter indicated that home language proficiency affects English language acquisition. So now I am wondering if the IEP goals are more reflective of normal English language development than a true language disability?

I was very confused about what to do to help Mario. So much for an IEP being a blueprint—Mario's IEP was more like a maze. Maybe I need to meet with the intervention specialist at our school so that she can interpret the IEP for me. Or, maybe I do not even need to worry about all this IEP stuff after all. Mario is in special education, so the special education teacher is really the person responsible for his learning.

Scenario Reflection

Based on the Challenge Scenario, document and discuss your initial thoughts regarding the following questions:

- Who is responsible for implementing Mario's IEP?

- If you were Ms. Rose, what would you do if you thought the IEP goals were more reflective of normal second language acquisition than a disability?

- How would you modify the goals so that they can be meaningful and useful in designing instruction to meet Mario's needs?

- Why is it important for the general education teacher to have a good understanding of the goals for Mario?

ARE GENERAL EDUCATION TEACHERS RESPONSIBLE FOR THE IMPLEMENTATION OF IEP GOALS?

General education teachers have a moral and legal responsibility for the development and implementation of the IEP. IDEA 2004 clearly mandates that the responsibility for the development and implementation of the IEP must include general education teachers. This inclusion of the general education teacher is based on the recognition that the general education teacher is knowledgeable about the general education curriculum and what will be taught and expected for a specific grade level. The general education teacher's expertise provides valuable information on supplementary aids and services that a child with a disability may need to be successful in the general education setting. Specifically, IDEA states that students with disabilities must "be involved and progress in the general curriculum" (§ 300.347[a][3][ii]). Similar to the NCLB legislation, which was replaced by ESSA, IDEA 2004 mandates that goals for students with disabilities be closely aligned with the goals for students without disabilities. By virtue of requiring this alignment, general education teachers have a more pronounced role in the education of children with disabilities. This pronounced role is reinforced by ESSA's requirement that public schools report on the academic progress of *all* students, including those with disabilities, in meeting state-adopted academic standards. Thus, both general and special education teachers are equally responsible for the education of students with disabilities and must take an active role in the planning and implementation of IEPs.

IDEA'S KEY COMPONENTS

- **Free appropriate public education (FAPE).** Requires that the student be educated in a manner that meets their educational needs by public educational agency that is free to the family.
  - *Zero Reject.* Mandates that the school cannot deny a child an education due to the severity of their needs.
- **Least restrictive environment (LRE).** The student is educated in a manner that is most like their typical peers.
- **Procedural safeguards** (due process). The family has the right to disagree with the placement, services, and educational plan for their child and can bring the school district to court.
- **Parental participation** (shared decision making). Parents have the right to participate as part of the education team for their child.
- **Nondiscriminatory evaluation.** Requires schools to utilize a team approach in assessing a student in all suspected areas of a disability using measures that are valid, reliable culturally relevant, and linguistically appropriate.
- **Individualized education program (IEP).** The IEP team assesses current evaluation information and develops a written document designed to meet the unique educational needs of each student with a disability.

Stop and Think!

- Based on the information provided on the responsibilities of general education teachers, how would you respond to Ms. Rose's comment from the Challenge Scenario that the special education teacher is responsible for Mario's education?

- When general education teachers are part of the IEP process, what kind of information do they provide to the team that is critical in the decision process?

- What information is needed in the Challenge Scenario to address Ms. Rose's concern that the IEP goals are more reflective of normal second language acquisition than a true disability?

The intention of ESSA is to increase the academic performance of all students, including those served within special education. To accomplish this, ESSA requires that states identify academic content standards that all students must know and annually assess students in reading and mathematics once a year in Grades 3–8 and once in high school. In addition, science must be assessed annually in elementary, middle, and high school to ensure that students are learning the identified content standards.

States also have the option of adding a school quality factor to their annual report card. These reports hold districts and schools accountable to ensure that all students, including those with disabilities, not only have access to the general education curriculum but also make progress in meeting standards set forth by each state. Although there are regulations on reporting students' achievement toward standards, states have the flexibility to design their own accountability system and plans for improvement for those schools identified as low performing. This type of accountability strengthens the role of general education teachers in the IEP process. General education teachers bring content area expertise and knowledge about what is most important to know within the academic content area. Therefore, general education teachers have a critical role to play in how goals are formulated and implemented for an individual with learning needs. Thus, the involvement of general education teachers in the development of the student's IEP goals is paramount. For students with disabilities who are in the process of acquiring English as second language, coordinating services that addresses their disability and language needs begins with the development of the IEP. These teachers, also referred to as *English as a second language (ESL)* or *English for speakers of other languages (ESOL)* teachers, are knowledgeable about language acquisition and can provide valuable insights on language proficiency as IEP goals are identified.

In addition to the legal requirements, there are three pedagogical reasons that general education and teachers of ELLs need to be involved in the development of goals. First, goals provide a clear focus for instruction that promotes positive outcomes for students. Second, goals serve as points of reference in monitoring and reporting student progress. Third, goals provide a common expectation of skills that a student should acquire as a result of the intervention provided by all service providers (e.g., general education teachers, special education teachers, therapists).

HOW TO WRITE MEASURABLE, OBSERVABLE, AND MEANINGFUL GOALS

Writing measurable goals and objectives is not a new phenomenon. Mager (1962) published a book titled *Preparing Instructional Objectives*, in which he stated that lesson plans were required to include behavioral objectives that were specific and measurable. During the 1970s, the Mager model of writing objectives became popular. This method had three critical components for objectives: 1) they should include measurable action verbs, 2) they should specify what is given to the learner, and 3) they should specify the criteria for success (Mager, 1975). These specific and measurable components are still referred to in the development of objectives as well as IEP goals.

Although the concept of writing measurable goals and objectives is not new, educators are often perplexed about how to write measurable goals that are meaningful. Part of the confusion is due to the terms—*goals*, *objectives*, and *benchmarks*—that are mistakenly used interchangeably. *Goals* are statements based on the needs of an individual student that specify the change that is expected as a result of a prescribed intervention. *Objectives* are the interim steps students would take to reach their goals, and those objectives serve as *benchmarks* to determine if a student is making sufficient progress toward the goal. Because IDEA 2004 requires that schools provide parents with periodic reports on the progress their child is making toward meeting the annual goal(s), it is critical that the goals are not only written in measurable terms but also are meaningful so the student's progress toward meeting the goal can easily be assessed. When IEP goals are not written in measurable terms, then, as Christle and Yell noted, "the IEP will be inadequate" (2010, p. 112).

When writing goals, the IEP team must start with what they currently know about the student, which is documented in the PLAAFP section of the IEP (see Chapter 4). The PLAAFP section provides the IEP team with the background information on the student in order to determine the focus of the IEP goal(s). Once the team has a good understanding of the student's strengths and current academic and functional abilities, the next step is to determine what would be challenging and reasonable to expect the student to achieve within 1 year with appropriate instruction and supports (i.e., intervention). The gap between the student's current abilities and what would be reasonable to expect the student to do within 1 year leads to the development of the student's goals. Reasonable expectations to close the gap require that the team consider the student's potential for growth and any challenges that may impede closing the gap.

Because goals are statements that describe what students will be able to do as a result of interventions (i.e., instruction, supports), it is critical that they be written with reasonably challenging expectations so that students benefit from their educational experiences. When goals are well written, teachers can design instructional experiences to achieve them and can evaluate the effectiveness of the experience according to whether the goals were achieved. In addition, when goals are clearly written, teachers can easily communicate to other teachers, administrators, and parents precisely what has been taught, what will be taught, and how the student is progressing to meet the goals.

Writing standards-based goals requires that the IEP team consider the student's strengths and needs, the content standards that all students must achieve in their district, and the gap between the student's levels of functioning and where they should be performing. Table 5.1 can serve as a guide in the construction of measurable and meaningful goals. The acronym BEST (behavior, evaluation, specific, timely) can be used to remember the questions that guide the IEP team in the development of meaningful and measurable goals.

Stop and Think!

Culturally relevant IEP goals tap into a student's funds of knowledge to create a bridge between prior experiences and knowledge while addressing new learning.

- How can you include a student's strengths while addressing a deficit area in an IEP goal?

Table 5.1. Guide for constructing BEST goals

Critical elements	Guiding questions	Suggestions
B: Behavior	What is the observable act or desired behavior that the student is to perform?	Describe the intended behavior using concrete sensory-specific language that can be seen or heard.
		Examples:
		• Write
		• Read
		• Construct
		• Say
E: Evaluation	What assessment measure and performance indicator will let the IEP team know that the desired behavior was met?	Indicate the assessment measure and specify the key quantifiable performance (i.e., criteria) indicator that will determine if the desired behavior was met.
		Examples:
		• Curriculum-based assessment
		• Observations
		• Rubric
		• Checklists
		Specify the key quantifiable performance indicator that will determine if the desired behavior was met.
		Examples:
		• 80% accuracy
		• 3 out of 5 opportunities
		• Rate of 80 words per minute
S: Specific	What is the specific context or condition when the desired behavior will occur?	Use precise language that describes the condition(s) in which the student will demonstrate the desired behavior.
		Example:
		• When asked to read a passage
		• Given a second-grade textbook
		• During sustained silent reading
T: Timely	When will the desired behavior be accomplished?	State the time line or date.
		Example:
		• By June 20XX
		• At the end of the academic year

Once the IEP team has written the PLAAFP section of the IEP document, they are now ready to construct the annual goal(s) to close the gap between the student's current functional level and the expected functional level. When constructing standard-based IEP goals, the general education teacher provides critical information on grade-level academic standards so that the team can identify the gap between the student's current academic level and the expected level of performance.

Using the Challenge Scenario as an example, the IEP team begins constructing the goal after writing Mario's PLAAFP section. Next, the team considers the academic standards for third graders and the gap between Mario's current performance and what is expected for students in third grade. For the purpose of this example, it is assumed that Mario needs to work on spelling because a goal on spelling was included in his previous IEP, and the third-grade standards indicate mastery of Writing Conventions. Following is the IEP goal constructed by the team:

> By the next annual review, when asked to write an essay, Mario will spell all third-grade words correctly (100%) with the use of an editing device in three consecutive attempts as measured by the teacher's anecdotal records.

Because the IEP team identified a time line, the goal will be reviewed annually to determine if the intended observable behavior—to "write" the measurable product of an "essay"—was met. The IEP team will also be able to determine the achievement of the goal because the evaluation measurement of the "teacher's anecdotal records" and the criteria to demonstrate mastery, "spell all third-grade words correctly", were included. In addition, the IEP team knows the context and condition in which Mario is to perform the correct spelling behavior because the goal specifies "when asked to write an essay . . . with the use of an editing device." The IEP team can use the BEST strategy to make sure that the goal is meaningful and measurable.

Using Bloom's Taxonomy to Craft Measurable Goals

Bloom's taxonomy is a conceptual framework often used by educators to classify the variety of activities designed to promote learning. In 1956, Benjamin Bloom and a group of university professors developed three domains to categorize educational activities—cognitive, affective, and psychomotor (Clark, 2013). The *cognitive domain* refers to the knowledge and intellectual abilities and skills necessary to complete learning activities. This domain classifies six levels of cognitive activities, starting with the simplest and progressing to the more complex. Each level is considered to be more difficult than the previous level. Because writing measurable goals requires using observable and meaningful terms, Bloom's taxonomy in the cognitive domain provides an excellent resource to determine the level of difficulty required and possible terms to articulate the skills or concepts that are included in IEP goals and objectives (see Figure 5.1).

Stop and Think!

- Describe at least one scenario in which you can apply one of the more complex levels of Bloom's cognitive domains.

- How might an IEP team use the progression of the six cognitive domains in Bloom's taxonomy to develop goals that not only address the student's unique challenges but is also meaningfully ambitious to the student (Mario) in the Challenge Scenario?

Figure 5.1.   Verbs from Bloom's old and new taxonomy. *Note:* The arrow indicates the complexity of the cognitive domain. (*Sources:* Anderson & Krathwohl, 2001; Bloom et al., 1956; Clark, 2013.)

CULTURALLY RESPONSIVE GOALS

Because IEP goals are statements derived from the PLAAFP to determine services and are used as indicators to determine a child's progress toward a specific aim, it is essential that all stakeholders support and value the goal(s). Research indicates that most families perceive their participation in IEP meetings as more of a physical presence to sign documents rather than a partner in the decision-making process (Childre & Chambers 2005; Mueller, 2017; Mueller & Buckley, 2014; Williams, 2007). This perception may be even more profound when families come from a culture different than the majority of the individuals at the IEP meeting. As discussed in Chapter 2, the communication style of culturally and linguistically diverse (CLD) family members is often drastically different from the other members of the IEP meeting, resulting in misinterpreting the family's desire to be part of the decision-making process. Therefore, IEP members must be cognizant of cultural differences and take steps to be responsive to the home culture.

IEP goals for students who are CLD must not only reflect the needs of the child but must also align with the priorities of the family and the home culture. For example, a goal that focuses on the functional skill of self-feeding by using a fork or spoon may not match the family's priority or culture of using chopsticks.

Goals are adjusted in these situations to match the family's priority and home culture.

The IEP team must also address language proficiency in the goal statements for ELLs. Because academic language proficiency is required for school success, it is important that IEP goals reflect the advancement of academic language within the context of addressing the child's disability. What follows is an example of an IEP goal that embeds academic language and home culture to address a deficit area:

> By next annual review, after codeveloping a graphic organizer with a Spanish-speaking peer, when asked to write an essay in English language arts, Mario will write a three-paragraph essay that includes an introduction, body paragraph, and conclusion with 80% accuracy as measured by the teacher's rubric/checklist.

In order to be culturally responsive to the unique needs of Mario, a dually identified student in need of special education and ELL services, the IEP team considered Mario's home culture and his language proficiency level. Because Mario is an ELL, the strategy of codeveloping a graphic organizer with a Spanish-speaking peer allows Mario the opportunity to use an evidence-based strategy (i.e., graphic organizer) in a cooperative setting (i.e., with a Spanish speaking peer) that aligns with his home culture and advances academic language proficiency in both English and Spanish. The IEP team will be able to determine if the goal was achieved because the behavior to be performed is to "write" and the measurable product is a "three-paragraph essay". The IEP team will also know if Mario performed the desired behavior as they identified the assessment measure (i.e., rubric/checklist) and the performance indicator (80% accuracy) as part of the evaluation. The specific condition of writing the essay during English language arts allows the team to know when desired behavior will occur. Last, the time line, "by next annual review," allows the IEP team to know when the desired behavior will be met. Using the BEST acronym to develop the IEP goal, along with including the home culture and advancing the language proficiency of an ELL, will result in the development of culturally responsive goals that are meaningful and measurable.

When constructing goals, the IEP team must be mindful to set high expectations that are reasonably ambitious and culturally responsive to the child's home culture and language proficiency. Current educational data indicate that academic outcome and graduation rates for most CLD populations in both general and special education are lower than other subgroups. It is important to set reasonably robust goals for students with mild to moderate levels of disabilities who are CLD to close the achievement gap between students with and without disabilities Continuing the practice of writing IEP goals that reflect only 1-year academic skill level of growth within an academic year will merely maintain the current achievement gap. An ambitious reasonable growth mindset is needed to close the gap (i.e., allowing goals to be written to allow more than one level of growth within an academic year). This growth mindset is aligned with the landmark Endrew case in which the court ruled that goal statements must be written in a reasonably robust manner to advance a student's potential. Constructing IEP goals with a growth mindset that are reasonably calculated, culturally responsive, and clearly stated will enable progress monitoring with the opportunity to make adjustments as needed so the student achieves the goals and makes the necessary progress to close the achievement gap. Figure 5.2 includes a meeting preparation checklist for IEP goals.

PREPARATION FOR THE IEP MEETING:
IEP GOALS

Prior to the Meeting

- [ ] Review prior IEP and student progress monitoring data to determine baseline of student's academic achievement and functional performance.

- [ ] Identify student's strengths and funds of knowledge.

- [ ] Ascertain the student's home language and/or English language proficiency level.

During the Meeting

- [ ] Review the Present Levels of Academic Achievement and Functional Performance (PLAAFP) section and prioritize area of need to construct goal(s).

- [ ] Consider language proficiency and the student's funds of knowledge as strengths while constructing IEP goals.

- [ ] Using BEST, check to make sure that goal(s) are meaningful and compliant.

- [ ] If using an interpreter, be sure to use appropriate interpreter etiquette (see Chapter 2).

After the Meeting

- [ ] Prepare progress monitoring to reflect IEP goal.

- [ ] Debrief with all team members, including parents, on the effectiveness of the meeting.

- [ ] Check with parents on the use of an interpreter and if they understood the meeting and key takeaways.

Figure 5.2. Preparation for the IEP meeting: IEP goals.

SUMMARY

This chapter detailed the importance of writing meaningful IEP goals that can be measured and are culturally responsive for the needs of students who are CLD. The IEP team must first record the learner's strengths and areas for improvement in the PLAAFP section of the IEP. Next, the IEP team must prioritize the needs of the student and construct goals that will address those priorities. As noted in this chapter, goals form the basis from which interventions and services are formed. Therefore, it is critical to ensure that goals address the specific needs, states, or conditions that will be changed as a result of the intervention(s). In this age of accountability, IEP teams must develop meaningful and compliant IEPs that can be easily measured and communicated to *all* stakeholders.

THE IEP CHECKLIST: GOALS

The following checklist can be used as an inventory to ensure that the Goals section of the IEP meets IDEA 2004 regulations.

Key Area (IEP section): **Goal(s)**	Criteria met	
	Yes	No
G1: Goals are listed in the order that reflects the priority of the student's needs in the Present Levels of Academic Achievement and Functional Performance (PLAAFP) section.		
G2: Measurable annual goals are included in academic and/or functional areas.		
G3: Goals are written using specific, observable, and measurable terms.		
G4: Goals describe skills that can realistically be achieved within 1 year.		
G5: Goals are clearly connected to the statement(s) in the PLAAFP section of the student's IEP.		
G6: All goals reflect the criteria listed here.		

ACTIVITIES

The activities included in this chapter are intended for the reader to gain a deeper understanding of the content covered. For this chapter, each activity builds on the skills of the previous activity. The activities associated with this chapter include the following:

- Activity 5.1. Writing the BEST Goal Statement

- Activity 5.2. IEP Goal Sentence Frame

- Activity 5.3. Identification of Quality IEP Goals

- Activity 5.4. Writing Quality IEP Goals

Activity 5.1.

Writing the BEST Goal Statement

Supporting chapter: Chapter 5 (Goals)

Purpose: The purpose of this activity is to develop the skill of writing meaningful and measurable goals.

Direction: Practice writing a goal by considering a child with a disability and answering each question that follows.

Critical Elements of Meaningful and Compliant Goals

Behavior: Describe the intended behavior using concrete sensory-specific language that can be seen or heard.

Evaluation: Indicate the assessment measure and specify the key quantifiable performance indicator (i.e., criteria) that will determine if the desired behavior was met.

Specific: Use precise language that describes the condition for when the student will demonstrate the desired behavior.

Timely: State the time line or date.

Behavior:

- What is the observable act or desired behavior that the student is to perform (e.g., write, construct, name)? _____

Evaluation:

- What assessment measure will be used to determine if the desired behavior was achieved?
_____

- What quantifiable performance indicator will be used to determine if the desired behavior was met? _____

Specific:

- What is the specific context or condition when the desired behavior will occur?

Timely:

- When will the desired behavior be accomplished? (Reminder: Goals are typically written annually.)
_____

Using your responses to these questions, write a goal statement that includes all four BEST elements. _____

Activity 5.2.
IEP Goal Sentence Frame

Supporting chapter: Chapter 5 (Goals)

Purpose: The purpose of this activity is to develop the skill of writing meaningful and measurable goals.

Direction: Practice writing a goal by completing the sentence frame, writing the full goal statement, and checking to see that all BEST elements were included.

By _____

State the *time line* or date when the desired behavior will be accomplished

_____**(Student's name) will** _____**(behavior)**

Specifically state the name of the student and the desired *behavior* that he/she will be able to do that they currently cannot do. Use concrete sensory specific language.

in _____**(condition/context)**

Use *specific* language that describes the condition (example: in a conversation) and the context (example, when asked) for when the student will demonstrate the desired behavior.

with _____**supports**

List any supports that the student may need to meet the goal. (Example: Use of a Spanish-English Dictionary, use of a computer)

with _____ **accuracy as measured by** _____

Evaluate if the desired behavior was achieved by indicating the assessment measure (Example: rubric, checklist) and the quantifiable performance indicator (Example: 80%, 3 out of 5 opportunities)

Using the previous information, write a goal statement.

By _____(time line) _____(student) will _____(behavior) in _____(condition/context) with _____ supports as measured by _____ with _____ accuracy as measured by _____.

Note: Rearrange the sentence so it makes logical sense and then check that it is your BEST goal statement.

By _____

State the **time line** or date when the desired behavior will be accomplished

_____(student's name) will _____(behavior)

Specifically state the name of the student and the desired **behavior** that they will be able to do that they currently cannot do. Use concrete, sensory-specific language.

In _____(condition/context)

Use specific language that describes the condition (e.g., in a conversation) and the context (e.g., when asked) for when the student will demonstrate desired behavior.

With _____ supports

List any supports that the student may need to meet the goal (e.g., using a Spanish-English diction-ary, using a computer).

With _____ accuracy as measured by _____

Evaluate if the desired behavior was achieved by indicating the assessment measure (e.g., rubric, checklist) and the quantifiable performance indicator (e.g., 80%, 3 out of 5 opportunities).

Activity 5.3.

Identification of Quality IEP Goals

Supporting chapter: Chapter 5 (Goals)

Purpose: The purpose of this activity is to identify quality goals that are both meaningful and measurable.

Directions: Use an IEP to inventory the Goals section and indicate the quality of the information provided. Then, rank the quality of the goal and provide evidence to support your ranking.

Rubric scale: Use the following scale and circle the number that best ranks the IEP area reviewed in the table that follows.

1 = Standard not met	2 = Standard partially met	3 = Standard met	4 = Standard exceeds
• IEP fails to provide evidence of meeting the IDEA 2004 requirements. • IEP does not address the IDEA 2004 requirements.	• Performance provides evidence of partially meeting IDEA 2004 requirements. • Performance addresses some of the IDEA 2004 requirements.	• Performance provides evidence of meeting most/all of the IDEA 2004 requirements. • Performance addresses most/all of the IDEA 2004 requirements.	• Performance provides evidence of exceeding all IDEA 2004 requirements. • All indicators are addressed in the IEP and go beyond expectations.

Key Area (IEP Section): *Goals* (complete for each goal)	Ranking	Rationale for Ranking
G1: Goals are listed in the order that reflects the priority of the student's needs in the Present Levels of Academic Achievement and Functional Performance (PLAAFP) section.	1 2 3 4	
G2: Measurable annual goals are included in academic and/or functional areas.	1 2 3 4	
G3: Goals are written using specific, observable, and measurable terms.	1 2 3 4	

Key Area (IEP Section): *Goals* (complete for each goal)	Ranking	Rationale for Ranking
G4: Goals describe skills that can realistically be achieved within 1 year.	1 2 3 4	
G5: Goals are clearly connected to the statement(s) in the PLAAFP section of the student's IEP.	1 2 3 4	
G6: All goals reflect the criteria listed here.	1 2 3 4	

Activity 5.4.

Writing Quality IEP Goals

Supporting chapter: Chapter 5 (Goals)

Purpose: The purpose of this activity is to write quality goals that are both meaningful and measurable.

Directions: Use an IEP to inventory the Goals section, rank the quality of the information provided, and provide rationale as supporting evidence of ranking. For key areas (G1–G6), rewrite any goal with a ranking below a 4 in the space provided so that it exceeds the standard (ranking of 4). Copies of this activity will be required for each goal inventoried and rewritten.

Rubric scale: Using the following scale and circle the number that best ranks the IEP area reviewed.

1 = Standard not met	2 = Standard partially met	3 = Standard met	4 = Standard exceeds
• IEP document fails to provide evidence of meeting the IDEA 2004 requirements. • IEP does not address the IDEA 2004 requirements.	• Performance provides evidence of partially meeting IDEA 2004 requirements. • Performance addresses some of the IDEA 2004 requirements.	• Performance provides evidence of meeting most/all of the IDEA 2004 requirements. • Performance addresses most/all of the IDEA 2004 requirements.	• Performance provides evidence of exceeding all IDEA 2004 requirements. • All indicators are addressed and go beyond expectations.

Key Area Standard (IEP Section): *Goal(s)* (complete for each goal)	Ranking	Rationale for Ranking
G1: Goals are listed in the order that reflects the priority of the student's needs in the Present Levels of Academic Achievement and Functional Performance (PLAAFP) section.	1 2 3 4	
G2: Measurable annual goals are included in academic and/or functional areas.	1 2 3 4	
G3: Goals are written using specific, observable, and measurable terms.	1 2 3 4	
G4: Goals describe skills that can realistically be achieved within 1 year.	1 2 3 4	

Key Area Standard (IEP Section): *Goal(s)* (complete for each goal)	Ranking	Rationale for Ranking
G5: Goals are clearly connected to the statement(s) in the PLAAFP section of the student's IEP.	1 2 3 4	
G6: All the goals reflect the criteria listed here.	1 2 3 4	

Rewritten goal statement(s):

_____

_____

_____

_____

_____

_____

6

Short-Term Objectives

Clarissa E. Rosas

After reading this chapter and engaging in activities related to this chapter, you will be able to meet the following outcomes:

- Construct meaningful and measurable IEP objectives statements that provide the subskills necessary to accomplish the IEP goal.

- Develop culturally responsive objectives to support IEP goal attainment.

Writing goals and short-term objectives are important parts of any IEP development. As discussed in Chapter 5, goals are statements that describe the achievements that a child will strive to accomplish within an academic year because of specific interventions, such as instruction. Short-term objectives serve as indicators to determine if the child is making sufficient progress toward their annual goal(s). Together, the goals and short-term objectives guide the IEP team in determining the type of intervention and services needed.

CONNECTION TO LEGAL PERSPECTIVE

Although writing goals and short-term objectives has been a consistent function of IEP development, the Individuals with Disabilities Education Improvement Act (IDEA) of 2004 (PL 108-446) changed this function by only requiring that short-term objectives be written for those children who take alternate assessments. The legal provisions for including short-term objectives in IEPs are as follows:

> (ii) For children with disabilities who take alternate assessments aligned to alternate achievement standards, a description of benchmarks or short-term objectives:
> (3) A description of—
> (i) How the child's progress toward meeting the annual goals described in paragraph (2) of this section will be measured; and
> (ii) When periodic reports on the progress the child is making toward meeting the annual goals (such as through the use of quarterly or other periodic reports, concurrent with the issuance of report cards) will be provided (§ 300.320[a][2][ii]–§ 300.320[a][3][ii])

IDEA'S KEY COMPONENTS

- **Free appropriate public education (FAPE).** Requires that the student be educated in a manner that meets their educational needs by a public educational agency that is free to the family.
    - *Zero Reject.* Mandates that the school cannot deny a child an education due to the severity of their needs.
- **Least restrictive environment (LRE).** The student is educated in a manner that is most like their typical peers.
- **Procedural safeguards** (due process). The family has the right to disagree with the placement, services, and educational plan for their child and can bring the school district to court.
- **Parental participation** (shared decision making). Parents have the right to participate as part of the education team for their child.
- **Nondiscriminatory evaluation.** Requires schools to utilize a team approach in assessing a student in all suspected areas of a disability using measures that are valid, reliable, culturally relevant, and linguistically appropriate.
- **Individualized education program (IEP).** The IEP team assesses current evaluation information and develops a written document designed to meet the unique educational needs of each student with a disability.

Statewide Assessment

It is important to examine the achievement standard required in general education to understand the provision regarding short-term objectives. As noted in Chapter 5, in an effort to raise the achievement for all students, the No Child Left Behind Act (NCLB) of 2001 (PL 107-110) and the Every Student Succeeds Act (ESSA) of 2015 (PL 114-95) requires each state to identify academic content standards that all students must know and annually assess and report students' progress in meeting the standards. Although ESSA replaced NCLB in 2015, it continued to hold states accountable for the achievement of all students, including those with IEPs.

ESSA now requires states to set achievement standards along with ambitious goals to close the gap between those students who are further behind other students (i.e., special education and historically marginalized populations). As a result, school districts are compelled to develop a plan to improve academic achievement for struggling students to receive federal funding. Consequently, schools are required to publicly report test results and other measures used to assess student achievement along with funding received. These reports are referred to as *State and School District's Report Cards* and include disaggregate test results according to student subgroups. The subgroup student populations include race/ethnicity, gender, socioeconomic status, disability, and English language learners (ELLs).

Although IDEA requires IEP teams to write short-term objectives only for those students who participate in alternative assessment, many school districts have continued the practice of writing short-term objectives for all IEPs. Given

ESSA's focus on closing the achievement gap for struggling students, it is critical that IEP teams construct objectives that are both meaningful and compliant to monitor the progress of students

Alternate Assessments

Although IDEA and ESSA require that students with disabilities be included in all state and district assessments, the regulations also include a provision that allows the IEP team the discretion of substituting the statewide assessment for an alternate measure when the statewide assessment is deemed inappropriate for a particular child (National Center on Educational Outcomes, 2013). IDEA was the first federal legislation to identify an alternative measure to assess students with significant disabilities. NCLB reinforced alternative assessments when it required states, districts, and schools to report the achievement of all students, including those with disabilities. Later, ESSA capped the number of students who can be assessed through alternative measure to 1% of the total student population tested. This cap was an effort to ensure that only those students with significant disabilities would have access to an alternative assessment. According to IDEA, if the IEP team determines that a child cannot participate in the state- or districtwide assessment, then the team must document their rationale for excluding the child in the state- or districtwide assessment and must provide a statement as to why the child needs an alternate assessment. As noted in IDEA 2004, the IEP must contain

> (6)(i) A statement of any individual appropriate accommodations that are necessary to measure the academic achievement and functional performance of the child on State and district wide assessments consistent with § 612(a)(16) of the Act; and
>
> (ii) If the IEP Team determines that the child must take an alternate assessment instead of a particular regular State or district wide assessment of student achievement, a statement of why—
> (A) The child cannot participate in the regular assessment; and
> (B) The particular alternate assessment selected is appropriate for the child (§ 300.320[a][6])

The alternate assessment is essential to measure the performance of a student who is unable to participate in state assessments, especially students with the most significant disabilities. The alternate assessment not only allows students to be included in the educational accountability system—as mandated by federal legislation—but also allows them to have access to assessment measures. Data collected from the alternate assessments are critical to the IEP team as they develop goals and short-term objectives to address individual student needs.

SHORT-TERM OBJECTIVES

If an IEP team determines that a child will not participate in a state- or districtwide assessment and will participate in an alternate assessment, then the team must include goals and short-term objectives or benchmarks in the IEP to comply with IDEA's requirements. IDEA refers to the objectives as short term to emphasize that the objectives should be written as interim steps that a child will take to reach their goal(s). As previously noted, these short-term objectives and benchmarks determine if the child is making sufficient progress toward meeting their annual goal(s) and, therefore, are closely monitored by the child's teachers.

Although IDEA requires that goals and short-term objectives or benchmarks be included in the IEP documents for individual students who require alternate assessments, the U.S. Department of Education (2006) allowed states the discretion to include short-term objectives in IEPs for students who do not require alternate assessments.

> Benchmarks and short-term objectives were specifically removed from . . . the Act. However, because benchmarks and short-term objectives were originally intended to assist parents in monitoring their child's progress toward meeting the child's annual goals, we believe a State could, if it chose to do so, determine the extent to which short-term objectives and benchmarks would be used. However . . . a State that chooses to require benchmarks or short-term objectives in IEPs in that State would have to identify in writing to the LEAs [local education agencies] located in the State and to the Secretary that such rule, regulation, or policy is a State-imposed requirement, which is not required by Part B of the Act or the Federal regulations. (71 Fed. Reg. at 46663)

Because states may choose to continue the practice of using benchmark and/or short-term objectives to gauge a student's progress toward meeting the IEP goal, it is important to note that there is a small difference between the two terms. *Short-term objectives* refer to the intermediate knowledge, skills, and behaviors that a student must achieve prior to an annual goal. *Benchmarks* describe the necessary key milestones that a student must demonstrate to achieve the IEP goal. When constructing short-term objectives, the IEP team breaks down the goal into discrete skills that the student must achieve to master the IEP goal. For example, using the information provided in the Present Levels of Academic Achievement and Functional Performance (PLAAFP) section of the IEP, the team developed the following reading goal for Mario:

> Goal: By the next annual review, when asked to write an essay, Mario will spell all third-grade words correctly (100%) with the use of an editing device in three consecutive attempts as measured by the teacher's anecdotal records.

The IEP team then identified the following interim skills that Mario will need to master in order to master the IEP goal.

- Comprehension of words
- Use of structure analysis to decode words
- Use of a spell checker

Using the identified discrete skills, the IEP team then constructs individual objectives for each skill that must be learned to master the IEP goal. Following is an example of the first short-term objective that Mario will need to achieve to master the IEP goal.

> Objective: By [first quarter date], prior to being asked to spell a series of words at the third-grade level in English language arts, Mario will demonstrate comprehension of the words by orally stating the meaning of the word in English or Spanish 12 out of 15 words as measured by teacher's observation.

As previously stated, short-term objectives and benchmarks were originally intended to assist in monitoring a student's progress toward meeting IEP goal(s). Monitoring a student's progress is necessary to determine if the services noted in the IEP are providing the necessary educational supports. Benchmarks serve as a measurement gauge to determine if the student is progressing adequately toward achieving the goal. In the previous objective example, the benchmark for the first quarter is the milestone of word comprehension in 12 out of 15 words. Word comprehension will be monitored during the first quarter to ensure that the services provided are supporting Mario's progress of comprehending 12 out of 15 words.

Because benchmarks are precursor steps toward a goal, they often serve as performance indicators toward a student's progress in achieving an annual goal. Although IEP teams are only required to include short-term objectives or benchmarks for students who will take alternative assessments as noted in IDEA, most states have continued the practice of including both goals and short-term objectives in IEP documents because IDEA requires periodic reports to parents on their child's progress toward meeting IEP goals. Therefore, it is critical that IEP members be knowledgeable in writing measurable and meaningful short-term objectives that are directly aligned with goals.

Challenge Scenario

In Chapter 5, you met Christina Rose, a third-grade teacher who was welcoming a new student, Mario, into her class. As she was reviewing Mario's IEP, Ms. Rose was confused as to what each of the IEP goals meant and how she could help Mario be successful in her class, especially in passing mandated state assessments. She also wondered if the IEP goal's focus on English spelling was more reflective of the fact that Mario was in the process of learning English more than a written language deficit. In the following scenario, Ms. Rose is consulting with the special education teacher at her school to help understand the Goals and Short-Term Objectives sections of the IEP. Review and reflect on the interaction detailed in the scenario.

Ms. Rose:	Hi! I have been reviewing Mario's IEP and am very confused about the goals stated in the IEP and hope that you can help me.
Special education teacher:	Sure, I would be happy to help you.
Ms. Rose:	I just do not understand what the goals mean. Last month, I attended the IEP workshop and learned that the IEP is like a blueprint in planning instruction for a student with a disability. The presenter said that special attention should be given to the IEP goals and short-term objectives because it will help in planning instruction and also be the focus for monitoring progress toward meeting the goals. I cannot even figure out what Mario's goals mean, and I cannot find any short-term objectives in the IEP. I have no idea how to plan instruction for this child and monitor his success in achieving the goals. Can you help me?
Special education teacher:	Well, let's start off with reading the PLAAFP section first to see how he is doing academically. Umm, I see that he is a third grader reading at a first-grade level and has difficulty with decoding words. It also states that Mario is an ELL and is at the speech emergent level, which means his oral English level

has increased, but he depends on context clues. Not a great surprise that he would have difficulty reading grade-level materials. Let's see how he is doing in his home language. I see that the IEP required an interpreter, so his parents are more comfortable in communicating in their home language. The parents report that the home language is Spanish, and even though Mario's primary language is Spanish, the parents report that at times he appears to not understand what is being communicated. According to the PLAAFP, the diagnostician administered the Woodcock-Muñoz Language Survey (Woodcock et al., 2017) and found that he had some difficulty with processing receptive language in both Spanish and English. I see that he enjoys school, is a hard worker, and is very helpful at home with taking care of his younger siblings; these are strengths we want to tap into and encourage. Now let us look at the IEP goals. It says here that by the end of third grade, Mario will spell words with 80% accuracy and comprehend a passage with 75% accuracy.

Oh my, I see why you are so confused. Seems like some important components of the goals are missing, and objectives are not even included in the IEP. I wonder if the IEP team was unaware that our state has adopted short-term objectives for all IEPs. As I review this IEP, I think there are some real problems with the Goals section of the IEP, so it is not a surprise that you are having difficulty.

Ms. Rose: Yes, I have no idea what the percentages mean. Does 80% mean that Mario only needs to spell 80% of a word correctly? This does not even make sense. I am not sure what 75% means either. Does this mean he is to read any passage with 75% accuracy? What grade level will he be expected to read in a year? What can we do about these goals and the missing short-term objectives? Are objectives the same as goals? I sure don't want to be accountable for something I cannot understand.

Special education teacher: Short-term objectives are incremental steps toward achieving the annual goals. I can see why you are concerned about the Goals and Objectives sections of the IEP because we both are held accountable for Mario's progress in meeting his goals as outlined in the IEP.

Ms. Rose: Because Mario has an IEP, does this mean that he does not need to meet the Common Core State Standards (CCSS)?

Special education teacher: As I am reviewing his IEP, there does not seem to be any provision for alternate assessments, so he still needs to meet the standards as required for all students. We need to make sure that the goals and short-term objectives are written so that Mario has the prerequisite skills to meet the standards and that we address his needs. I think the first thing we should do is correct the goals so that they are meaningful and compliant, and then we can add the short-term objectives. We can address language proficiency when we write the short-term goals. I will contact the parents and let them know that we will be updating the goals and short-term objectives so that they are compliant and meaningful as well as written in a way that can easily be assessed and reported to them regularly.

Ms. Rose: Okay—can we get started right away? I want to be prepared for when Mario joins our class next week.

Scenario Reflection

Based on the Challenge Scenario, document and discuss your initial thoughts regarding the following questions:

- How does a meaningful and measurable goal help in writing short-term objectives in IEPs?

- How would you rewrite the goals to meet the IDEA requirements?

- How could you tap into Mario's funds of knowledge when writing short-term objectives?

- What discrete components or subskills does Mario need to meet the annual goal?

- List the key milestones that Mario will need to demonstrate that he is making progress toward his IEP goal.

Stop and Think!
- Even though the goals in the Challenge Scenario need to be refined, what are some prerequisite skills needed to meet Mario's IEP goal that is focused on spelling?

- How can language proficiency be part of a prerequisite skill for spelling?

- How can short-term objectives be used as target points for progress monitoring?

- What is the advantage of including short-term objectives in IEPs?

Writing Measurable and Meaningful Short-Term Objectives

The criteria for writing short-term objectives are like those of writing goals—they must be meaningful and measurable. Short-term objectives, however, provide statements of incremental steps that the student must accomplish to achieve the annual goals. The BEST (behavior, evaluation, specific, timely) strategy for writing measurable goals can be easily applied to writing short-term objectives, provided the IEP teams write incremental statements that lead to achievement of the goal (see Chapter 5). These statements must provide tiered subskills that the child should accomplish to achieve their annual goals. These tiered steps then serve as benchmarks to monitor a child's progress in meeting annual goals. When the short-term objectives are meaningful and measurable, teachers can easily design instruction to meet the child's needs and effectively monitor the child's progress in meeting the goals set forth in the IEP. In addition, when goals are well written (i.e., meaningful and measurable), appropriate data collection can easily be implemented to monitor the student's progress, thus meeting the requirements of IDEA (Christle & Yell, 2010).

Critical Elements of Meaningful and Compliant Objectives

Behavior: Describe the intended behavior using concrete, sensory-specific language that can be seen or heard.

Evaluation: Indicate the assessment measure and specify the key quantifiable performance (i.e., criteria) indicator that will determine if the desired behavior was met.

Specific: Use precise language that describes the condition for when the student will demonstrate the desired behavior.

Timely: State the time line or date. The time line for short-term objectives and benchmarks is prior to the annual goal.

To write meaningful goals for Mario, the team must know Mario's strengths and needs in addition to the state standards for third graders (see the Challenge Scenario introduced in Chapter 5 and continued in this chapter). For example, it is assumed that Mario needs to work on spelling because a goal on spelling was included in his IEP. In addition, because Mario is a third grader and his state has adopted the CCSS, he is required to master the following Language Strand:

- CCSS.ELA-Literacy.L.3.2: Demonstrate command of the conventions of Standard English capitalization, punctuation, and spelling when writing.

- CCSS.ELA-Literacy.L.3.2e: Use conventional spelling for high-frequency and other studied words and for adding suffixes to base words (e.g., sitting, smiled, cries, happiness).

- CCSS.ELA-Literacy.L.3.2f: Use spelling patterns and generalizations (e.g., word families, position-based spellings, syllable patterns, ending rules, meaningful word parts) in writing words.

- CCSS.ELA-Literacy.L.3.2g: Consult reference materials, including beginning dictionaries, as needed to check and correct spellings.

An example of a meaningful and measurable standard-based goal for Mario is

> By next annual review, when asked to write an essay, Mario will spell all third-grade words correctly (100%) with the use of an editing device in three consecutive attempts as measured by the teacher's anecdotal records

Because the IEP team identified a time line, the goal will be reviewed annually to determine if the intended observable behavior to "write" the measurable product of an "essay" was met. The IEP team will also be able to determine the achievement of the goal because the evaluation measurement of the "teacher's anecdotal records" and the criteria to demonstrate mastery, "spell all third-grade words correctly," were included. In addition, the IEP team knows the context and condition for when Mario is to perform the correct spelling behavior because the goal specifies that "when asked to write an essay . . . with the use of an editing device." The IEP team can use the BEST strategy to make sure that the goal is meaningful and measurable.

Although Mario does not require alternative assessment, if his school district still requires short-term objectives to be included on his IEP, then the IEP team can analyze the skills or subskills needed to meet the annual goal and then construct short-term objectives. The short-term objectives not only serve as extensions of the standard-based goal but also as indicators to gauge Mario's progress throughout the academic year to ensure he will meet the IEP goal. Following are examples of meaningful and measurable short-term objectives that include subskills that support the IEP goal.

Short-Term Objective 1: By [first quarter date], prior to being asked to spell a series of words at the third-grade level in English language arts, Mario will demonstrate comprehension of the words by orally stating the meaning of the word in English or Spanish 12 out of 15 words as measured by teacher's observation.

Short-Term Objective 2: By [second quarter date], when asked to spell a series of words at the third-grade level in English language arts, Mario will demonstrate letter–sound correspondence knowledge and structure analysis by writing 12 out of 15 words correctly on weekly spelling tests.

Short-Term Objective 3: By [third quarter date], when asked to write an essay in English language arts, Mario will use resources to check spelling (e.g., a dictionary, spell check) to ensure that the words in the essay are spelled correctly in 4 of 5 trials as measured by teacher's observation.

These three short-term objectives are the interim subskills needed for Mario to meet the goal of spelling third-grade words with 80% accuracy. His teachers and parents can use the short-term objectives to gauge if he is making progress toward meeting his annual IEP goal. Based on the short-term objectives, Mario's teachers would know that they are to design instruction to teach the use of references as tools for checking spelling and phonology as a skill in decoding. In addition, the short-term objectives would serve as indicators in the selection and/or design of assessment to measure and communicate Mario's progress in correctly spelling third-grade words, which is part of the third-grade standards for his state. The short-term objectives also would serve as a common reference point for language proficiency for all service providers.

Culturally Responsive Short-Term Objectives

When writing short-term objectives that correspond to an IEP goal, the team must be sure that the objectives reflect the home culture and address the language proficiency level of the child. One of the priorities for ELLs is that they develop academic English language proficiency so they may successfully achieve grade-level standards and be prepared for college and/or the workplace. Academic English proficiency is a school-learned skill acquired through interacting with teachers and textbooks that requires instructional intervention and supports (see Chapter 2). IEP teams must develop goals and objectives that bolster language proficiency levels while addressing the academic and functional needs of students who are culturally and linguistically diverse. For example, the focus of Mario's IEP goal was on improving his deficit in writing; however, if Mario is an ELL, then the objectives need to include interventions and supports that strengthen his academic language proficiency while addressing his deficit area. Following are examples of culturally responsive objectives that address Mario's deficit area while also strengthening academic language proficiency.

Goal 1: By next IEP date, when asked to write a three-paragraph essay in English language arts, Mario will spell third-grade words 100% correctly on three consecutive trials as measured by a teacher's observation and anecdotal record.

Short-Term Objective 1: By first quarter (date) and after discussing a social studies topic of his choice with a peer, Mario will develop a graphic organizer that summarizes the social studies topic with 80% accuracy as measured by teacher's observation and checklist.

Short-Term Objective 2: By second quarter (date), Mario will use a graphic organizer and sentence starters to create a paragraph that includes a topic, three details, and a conclusion with 80% accuracy as measured by teacher's observation and checklist.

Short-Term Objective 3: By third quarter (date) and after developing a graphic organizer on a social studies topic of his choice with the use of an English-Spanish dictionary, Mario will write a paragraph that contains a topic, three details, and a conclusion using correctly spelled words with 80% accuracy as measured by teacher's observation and checklist.

These short-term objectives address Mario's writing deficit while concentrating on the development of academic language proficiency. The social studies topic provides the academic subject focus. The instructional supports of using a graphic organizer, sentence starters, and a English-Spanish dictionary provide the supports needed to advance academic language proficiency. All three of the objectives are incremental steps needed to meet the IEP goal while also being culturally responsive to the language needs of the child.

Stop and Think!

Funds of knowledge are the strengths that students acquire through their experiences and knowledge of cultural practices within their family and community. Tapping into the student's prior knowledge and experiences deepens the student's understanding of new concepts.

- How does tapping into a student's prior knowledge and experience deepen a student's understanding of new concepts?

For students with significant disabilities who are ELLs, the emphasis may be on functional skills, which require a certain social language proficiency level rather than academic language proficiency. The school representatives on the IEP team must work closely with the family to determine priorities and language preference (i.e., home language or English). The parameters outlined in the PLAAFP will determine the appropriate type (academic, functional, or behavioral) of goals and language proficiency needs.

SUMMARY

This chapter detailed the importance of writing meaningful and measurable short-term objectives that are aligned with the IEP's goals. Short-term objectives are incremental steps that serve as benchmarks toward achieving annual goals. Although IDEA only requires short-term objectives for students who take alternate assessments, states have the option of continuing the practice of including short-term objectives in IEPs. Most states have continued the practice because short-term objectives not only serve as interim steps toward a goal, but they also can be used to monitor a child's progress and report if sufficient progress is being made to reach the annual goal. See Figure 6.1 for a checklist on preparing short-term objectives ahead of the IEP meeting.

Stop and Think!

Consider the example goal and related short-term objectives written for Mario, and answer the following questions:

- What additional objective(s) could you add to Mario's IEP?

- If you were Mario's teacher, what information provided in the IEP would help you design instruction for him?

- How could the objectives provided serve as a benchmark to monitor Mario's progress toward meeting his annual goal?

PREPARATION FOR THE IEP MEETING:
IEP SHORT-TERM OBJECTIVES

Prior to the Meeting

☐ Identify student's strengths and funds of knowledge.

☐ Review possible IEP goal(s) and identify the prerequisite skills or behaviors that the student needs to meet the goal.

During the Meeting

☐ Share the prerequisite skills or behaviors that are required to meet the IEP goal.

☐ Determine the prerequisite skills or behaviors that the learner has mastered.

☐ Construct short-term objectives that address the prerequisite skill(s) that the learner has not mastered.

☐ Consider language proficiency and the student's funds of knowledge as strengths while constructing the objective.

☐ Use BEST to make sure that the objectives are meaningful and compliant.

☐ If using an interpreter, be sure to use appropriate interpreter etiquette (see Chapter 2).

After the Meeting

☐ Prepare progress monitoring to reflect the IEP short-term objective.

☐ Debrief with all team members, including parents, about the effectiveness of the meeting.

☐ Check with parents on the use of an interpreter and if they understood the meeting and key takeaways.

Figure 6.1. Preparation for the IEP meeting: IEP short-term objectives.

THE IEP CHECKLIST: SHORT-TERM OBJECTIVES

It is critical that IEP team members have the background knowledge and skills to write meaningful and measurable short-term objectives. The following checklist can be used as an inventory to ensure that the Objectives section meets IDEA regulations.

Key Area (IEP section):	Criteria met	
Short-Term Objectives and Benchmarks	Yes	No
O1: Objectives/benchmarks are listed in the order that reflects the priority of the student's needs in the Present Levels of Academic Achievement and Functional Performance (PLAAFP) section.		
O2: At least two objectives are written for each goal.		
O3: Each objective includes a condition and measurable behavior.		
O4: Specific criteria that match the skills being measured are written for each objective.		
O5: Objectives are clearly connected to the student's PLAAFP and address the student's abilities and needs.		

ACTIVITIES

The activities included in this chapter are intended for the reader to gain a deeper understanding of the content covered. For this chapter, each activity builds on the skills of the previous activity. The activities associated with this chapter include the following:

- Activity 6.1. The BEST Objectives

- Activity 6.2. Constructing a Functional Objective

- Activity 6.3. Constructing the BEST Objectives That Lead to a Goal

- Activity 6.4. Identification of Quality IEP Objectives

- Activity 6.5. Writing Quality IEP Objectives

Activity 6.1.

The BEST Objectives

Supporting chapter: Chapter 6 (Short-Term Objectives)

Purpose: The purpose of this activity is to develop the skill of writing meaningful and measurable objectives.

Directions: Practice writing objectives by considering a child with a disability and answering each question that follows.

Critical Elements of Meaningful and Compliant Goals and Objectives

Behavior: Describe the intended behavior using concrete, sensory-specific language that can be seen or heard.

Evaluation: Indicate the assessment measure and specify the key quantifiable performance indicator (i.e., criteria) that will determine if the desired behavior was met.

Specific: Use precise language that describes the condition for when the student will demonstrate the desired behavior.

Timely: State the time line or date.

---

1. **Behavior:** What is the observable act or behavior the student is to perform?

_____

_____

_____

_____

2. **Evaluation:** What assessment measure and performance indicator (i.e., criteria) will let us know that the desired behavior was met?

_____

_____

_____

_____

3. **Specific:** What is the specific context or condition when the desired behavior will occur?

_____

_____

_____

_____

4. **Timely:** When will the desired behavior be accomplished? (Reminder: Objectives are written with due dates prior to the due date of annual goals.)

_____

_____

_____

_____

5. Using your responses to these questions, write one complete objective that includes all four BEST elements.

_____

_____

_____

_____

Activity 6.2.

Constructing a Functional Objective

Supporting chapter: Chapter 6 (Short-Term Objectives)

Purpose: The purpose of this activity is to develop the skill of writing meaningful and measurable functional objectives.

Directions: Practice constructing a functional objective by completing the following table.

Functional	B: Behavior	E: Evaluation	S: Specific	T: Timely
IEP goal	Marco will arrive at the correct classroom location per his schedule within 5 minutes of the bell ringing	As measured by teacher's observation and anecdotal record	Given a visual schedule and one verbal prompt that it is time to transition	By (academic year)
Short-Term Objective 1				
Short-Term Objective 2				

Using the previous table, write full goal and objective statements.

IEP goal statement:

Short-Term Objective 1:

Short-Term Objective 2:

Activity 6.3.

Constructing the BEST Objectives That Lead to a Goal

Supporting chapter: Chapter 6 (Short-Term Objectives)

Purpose: The purpose of this activity is to construct short-term objectives that are intermediate steps leading to an IEP goal.

Directions: Use the BEST strategy to write an IEP goal statement. Next, write the corresponding first and second short-term objective statements that will support the student in meeting the IEP goal.

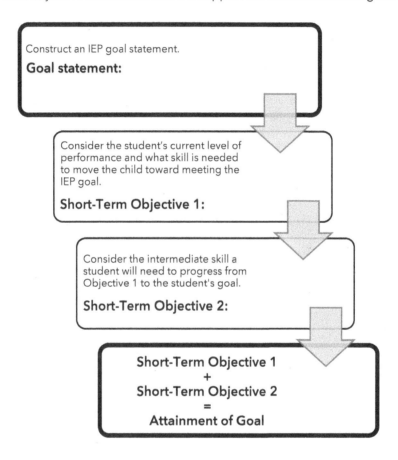

Construct an IEP goal statement.

Goal statement:

Consider the student's current level of performance and what skill is needed to move the child toward meeting the IEP goal.

Short-Term Objective 1:

Consider the intermediate skill a student will need to progress from Objective 1 to the student's goal.

Short-Term Objective 2:

Short-Term Objective 1
+
Short-Term Objective 2
=
Attainment of Goal

Activity 6.4.

Identification of Quality IEP Objectives

Supporting chapter: Chapter 6 (Short-Term Objectives)

Purpose: The purpose of this activity is to identify quality objectives that are meaningful and measurable.

Directions: Use an IEP to inventory the Objectives section and indicate the quality of the information provided. Then, rank the quality of the objective and provide evidence to support your ranking.

Rubric scale: Use the following scale and circle the number that best ranks the IEP area reviewed in the table that follows.

1 = Standard not met	2 = Standard partially met	3 = Standard met	4 = Standard exceeds
• IEP fails to provide evidence of meeting the IDEA 2004 requirements. • IEP does not address the IDEA 2004 requirements.	• Performance provides evidence of partially meeting IDEA 2004 requirements. • Performance addresses some of the IDEA 2004 requirements.	• Performance provides evidence of meeting most/all of the IDEA 2004 requirements. • Performance addresses most/all of the IDEA 2004 requirements.	• Performance provides evidence of exceeding all IDEA 2004 requirements. • All indicators are addressed in the IEP and go beyond expectations.

Key Area (IEP Section): *Short-Term Objectives and Benchmarks* **(complete for each short-term objective or benchmark)**	**Ranking**	**Rationale for Ranking**
O1: Objectives/benchmarks are listed in the order that reflects the priority of the student's needs in the Present Levels of Academic Achievement and Functional Performance (PLAAFP) section.	1 2 3 4	
O2: At least two objectives are written for each goal.	1 2 3 4	
O3: Each objective includes a condition and measurable behavior.	1 2 3 4	
O4: Specific criteria that match the skills being measured are written for each objective.	1 2 3 4	
O5: Objectives are clearly connected to the student's PLAAFP and address the student's abilities and needs.	1 2 3 4	

Activity 6.5.

Writing Quality IEP Objectives

Supporting chapter: Chapter 6 (Short-Term Objectives)

Purpose: The purpose of this activity is to write quality objectives that are meaningful and measurable.

Directions: Use an IEP to inventory the Objectives section, rank the quality of the information provided, and provide rationale as supporting evidence of ranking for each objective. For key areas (O1–O6), rewrite any objective with a ranking below a 4 in the space provided so that it exceeds the standard (ranking of 4). Copies of this activity will be required for each objective inventoried and rewritten.

Rubric scale: Use the following scale and circle the number that best ranks the IEP area reviewed.

1 = Standard not met	2 = Standard partially met	3 = Standard met	4 = Standard exceeds
• IEP fails to provide evidence of meeting the IDEA 2004 requirements. • IEP does not address the IDEA 2004 requirements.	• Performance provides evidence of partially meeting IDEA 2004 requirements. • Performance addresses some of the IDEA 2004 requirements.	• Performance provides evidence of meeting most/all of the IDEA 2004 requirements. • Performance addresses most/all of the IDEA 2004 requirements.	• Performance provides evidence of exceeding all IDEA 2004 requirements. • All indicators are addressed and go beyond expectations.

Key Area (IEP Section): *Short-Term Objectives and Benchmarks* (complete for each short-term objective or benchmark)	Ranking	Rationale for Ranking
O1: Objectives/benchmarks are listed in the order that reflects the priority of the student's needs in the Present Levels of Academic Achievement and Functional Performance (PLAAFP) section.	1 2 3 4	
O2: At least two objectives are written for each goal.	1 2 3 4	
O3: Each objective includes a condition and measurable behavior.	1 2 3 4	
O4: Specific criteria that match the skills being measured are written for each objective.	1 2 3 4	
O5: Objectives are clearly connected to the student's PLAAFP and address the student's abilities and needs.	1 2 3 4	

Rewritten objective statement(s):

_____

_____

_____

_____

_____

_____

7

Measuring and Reporting Progress

Lisa M. Campbell and Clarissa E. Rosas

After reading this chapter and engaging in activities related to this chapter, you will be able to meet the following outcomes:

- Summarize the importance of progress monitoring.

- Explain special considerations of progress monitoring for populations that are culturally and linguistically diverse (CLD).

- Construct a progress monitoring chart that includes goal line and record of progress.

The Every Student Succeeds Act (ESSA) of 2015 (PL 114-95), which replaced the No Child Left Behind (NCLB) Act of 2001 (PL 107-110), and the Individuals with Disabilities Education Improvement Act (IDEA) of 2004 (PL 108-446) require that all students, including those with disabilities, receive high-quality education and hold schools accountable for student achievement. This focus on high-quality education and the requirement that students with IEPs make progress toward meeting reasonably challenging goals requires teachers to frequently monitor the progress of students who may be struggling for the purpose of using the data to guide instructional decision making. The process of progress monitoring with successively more intense instruction is referred to as *response to intervention* (RTI). When IDEA was reauthorized in 2004, progress monitoring through RTI was added in an effort to provide early intervention to struggling students in order to reduce the need of referrals to special education. RTI provides a more intentional approach for referring children to special education by identifying students who do not respond to instruction and providing systematic, intensive intervention (Compton et al., 2010; Fuchs et al., 2012; Fuchs & Vaughn, 2012).

The importance of assessing the progress of students with disabilities is outlined in IDEA and in the ruling in *Endrew F. v. Douglas County School District* (2017). As a result of this ruling, the IEP team is charged with writing reasonable ambitious goals that will allow the student to ". . . make progress appropriate in light of the child's circumstances" (*Endrew F. v. Douglas County School District*, 2017, 0.15). The ruling reinforces the importance of periodic review to ensure that the student is making sufficient progress to meet the goals. Therefore, priority is given to monitoring student progress based on data collection to determine the achievement, or lack thereof, of determined goals and objectives from the student's IEP. This focus requires teachers to become more proficient in assessing student progress and use the data to determine if any educational adjustments are needed for the student to meet goals outlined in their IEP. Although measuring annual goals has always been a function of IEP teams, teacher accountability has increased, requiring teachers to be diligent in their use of ongoing, relevant progress monitoring data.

Finally, it is particularly important for educators to ensure that when measuring and reporting progress, cultural and linguistic considerations are in place for all students, particularly for English language learners (ELLs). The interaction between exceptionality and diversity should be embraced in the context of all formal and informal assessments. In addition, student goals and objectives within their language should be a critical consideration within the context of measuring and reporting progress.

CONNECTION TO LEGAL PERSPECTIVE

Once the student's present levels of academic achievement and functional performance are determined, goals and objectives are identified. Since the ruling of *Endrew F. v. Douglas County School District* (2017), these goals and objectives must meet a higher standard to ensure that students are receiving a quality education (Waterstone, 2017). Progress toward these goals and objectives is measured daily, weekly, monthly, or quarterly based on the intensity of the instruction and intervention provided. Progress toward meeting the identified goals and objectives is measured by comparing expected and actual rates of learning. Instructional programming or adjustments are based on progress monitoring data (i.e., information).

According to IDEA, every student's IEP must detail how progress toward annual goals will be documented and communicated. This communication must provide information on whether the student is making sufficient progress toward the achievement of their annual goals and how the progress will be periodically reported to the student's parents. IDEA 2004 states that each child's IEP must contain

> (3) A description of—
> (i) How the child's progress toward meeting the annual goals will be measured.
> (ii) When periodic reports on the progress the child is making toward meeting the annual goals will be provided such as through the use of quarterly or other periodic reports, concurrent with the issuance of report cards. (34 CFR § 300.320[a][3][I,ii])

Stop and Think!

Academic English proficiency is essential for students to succeed in school, especially in content areas such as English language arts, mathematics, science, and social studies.

- Why is it important to assess student progress in language proficiency (English and home language) for English language learners?

In order to meet the legal requirements of IDEA, teams must consider not only when and how the student's progress will be measured, but also *how well*, or to what specific criteria, the student needs to perform in order to achieve their stated IEP goal(s) (and, for some children, benchmarks or objectives; see Chapter 6). When reporting progress, it is important to indicate what change in services will occur should it come to the attention of the teacher, parent, or other members of the IEP team that the student is not making adequate progress. Sometimes the lack of progress can be addressed by altering instructional approaches or making revisions to the intervention that account for students' cultural and/or linguistic characteristics. If this is not the case, then additional assessment must be completed prior to adding or significantly altering services. It is the IEP team's responsibility to address issues regarding lack of progress in order to adjust the student's educational program and ensure the student is receiving a quality education.

IDEA'S KEY COMPONENTS

- **Free appropriate public education (FAPE).** Requires that the student be educated in a manner that meets their educational needs by a public educational agency that is free to the family.
  - *Zero Reject.* Mandates that the school cannot deny a child an education due to the severity of their needs.
- **Least restrictive environment (LRE).** The student is educated in a manner that is most like their typical peers.
- **Procedural safeguards** (due process). The family has the right to disagree with the placement, services, and educational plan for their child and can bring the school district to court.
- **Parental participation** (shared decision making). Parents have the right to participate as part of the education team for their child.
- **Nondiscriminatory evaluation.** Requires schools to utilize a team approach in assessing a student in all suspected areas of a disability using measures that are valid, reliable, culturally relevant, and linguistically appropriate.
- **Individualized education program (IEP).** The IEP team assesses current evaluation information and develops a written document designed to meet the unique educational needs of each student with a disability.

Progress monitoring has gained greater importance because IDEA and ESSA hold educators accountable for meeting IEP goals. One of the hallmarks of progress monitoring is the practice of assessing students on a regular basis, typically monthly, in order to determine if a student is making adequate progress toward their IEP goals. Students from CLD backgrounds frequently demonstrate skills through one type of performance assessment and other skills through another type of performance assessment. Therefore, it is important that teachers consider different progress monitoring practices to ensure they are recording accurate results. If a student is not making progress as expected, then the teacher can adjust or alter instruction in response to the individual needs to ensure that the student will meet the IEP goals. Commercial progress monitoring assessments are available, as well as those that are teacher created. An effective progress monitoring assessment needs to accurately measure the focus of the IEP goal and be quick and easy to administer so that information (i.e., data) collected can easily be analyzed to determine if the student is responding effectively to instruction. This type of assessment not only provides useful information for instructional decision making but also allows for regular reports on a student's progress in meeting IEP goals.

PROGRESS MONITORING ASSESSMENTS

The requirements outlined in IDEA associated with measuring and reporting progress are set forth to identify when students are not making adequate progress toward annual goals and implement necessary changes before failure becomes eminent. This allows educators to revise and adjust instruction to appropriately support the student. It is important to monitor progress of all students with IEPs throughout the year to ensure that they are on track for meeting benchmarks. Students not making progress, or those at risk for not progressing, are simply monitored more often, and instruction is adjusted as needed. Information on required progress reports must document student progress on each IEP goal and/or objective, not just a chosen one or few. The information provided in the reports must be impartial and include numerical data whenever possible. In addition, the stated criterion established for the goal/objective(s) should be included. The information included in the progress report should be specific and descriptive. General information such as "minimal progress" or "no progress made" should be avoided, as well as details not related to the goals and objectives.

The implications for using the data gathered in regard to student progress (or lack of progress) is the most important factor. Average citizens make decisions based on data daily, but teachers and administrators often make decisions based on opinions and intuition. The underlying premise of measuring and reporting student progress is that student learning will increase over time if changes in instructional interventions, support services, and specialized instruction are based on data. Data can provide educators and members of the IEP team with a snapshot of what students can do and any areas of difficulty. Effective interpretation of the data and decision making based on data will surely have a positive impact on student outcomes. In regard to improving instruction and services for students with disabilities, it is not only the quantity or the quality of the data that is important, but also how the information is used to affect instructional decisions.

Because progress monitoring affects instructional decisions, the ongoing collection of evidence also can be used to evaluate effectiveness of instruction.

Because language affects the progress of students who are CLD in meeting IEP goals and objectives, it is important to include language development and cultural responsiveness related to supports in the progress monitoring. Therefore, multiple progress monitoring measures and practices are often necessary to accurately assess a student's growth toward meeting an IEP goal. Frequency is the primary difference between the formal measurement and reporting of progress required by IDEA and the act of progress monitoring.

Stop and Think!

Using one type of progress monitoring measure and practice does not always yield an accurate assessment of a student's progress toward their IEP goals.

- Why is it essential to use multiple progress monitoring assessment and practices for students who come from culturally and/or linguistically diverse backgrounds?

Benefits of Progress Monitoring

When implemented effectively, the benefits of progress monitoring include the following:

- Additional progress toward goals and objectives because students are receiving the most appropriate instruction

- Informed instructional decisions regarding academic and functional performance

- Documentation of student progress for communicating to families and adhering to legal requirements set forth by IDEA

- Better communication with other educators regarding students' needs

- More timely attainment of goals and objectives, as well as standards

Challenge Scenario

Following are descriptions of progress monitoring assessments that are discussed in the scenario:

- *Maze:* This assessment is available commercially and can be teacher created. The maze assessment requires the student to read a passage silently for 2.5 minutes. Every seventh word is deleted in the passage, and three possible choices are offered. The student circles the word that best fits the meaning of the phrase or sentence in the passage. The student's score is the number of correct replacements they make.

- *Oral reading fluency:* This assessment is also available commercially and can be teacher created. The student reads aloud from a reading passage for 1 minute. As the student reads the text, the examiner records any errors. Reading fluency is calculated by first determining the total words attempted within the timed reading probe and then deducting the number of words read incorrectly from that total.

- **Peer-Assisted Learning Strategies (PALS):** PALS is a structured peer tutoring program in which students work together on reading and mathematics. Visit the web site for more information: https://ies.ed.gov/ncee/wwc/Docs/InterventionReports/wwc_pals_060512.pdf

In the following scenario, Ms. Lawrence, the intervention specialist in a public elementary school, and her coteachers are presenting progress monitoring data for a fourth-grade student named Maria. They are meeting with two general education teachers, an English language arts (ELA) teacher and a social studies (SS) teacher, to discuss Maria's progress toward her IEP goals. Review and reflect on the interaction detailed in the scenario.

Ms. Lawrence:	As you are all aware, Maria scored below the benchmark on the universal screening at the beginning of the year. I have been continuing to gather progress monitoring data on her oral reading fluency rates. I have data points for every week for 6 weeks, and she has made significant progress while she has been receiving reading intervention focused on fluency for 35 minutes each day. I am hoping you are also seeing similar progress in her reading in your classes.
ELA teacher:	I am still very concerned about Maria's reading skills. Sure, she might be fluent, but she is still failing in class quizzes and tests, and her grades on assignments and homework are not improving.
SS teacher:	She does seem to be more confident about reading, but that's really about it. I don't think she comprehends much of what she reads, especially in the content areas such as social studies. I was wondering why we only are monitoring fluency?
Ms. Lawrence:	Well, there is a connection between fluency and comprehension. The more fluent a student, the more they are likely to comprehend. But it seems like we need to revise our focus with Maria.
ELA teacher:	Yes, I think so. Because her IEP goals and objectives are related to reading, comprehending, and answering literal and inferential questions, I think specific intervention and progress monitoring in those areas will be much more beneficial.
Ms. Lawrence:	That is good input. Some of the options we have for comprehension interventions are the paragraph shrinking and prediction relay components from PALS. She should be familiar with these strategies because she is already participating in PALS in other academic areas. I can redesign her intervention sessions to include systematic instruction in multiple content areas using these same strategies. Then we can use a weekly maze assessment to monitor her progress. The maze is a good measure of sentence comprehension, not necessarily passage comprehension. But, based on the difficulties you both report, I think sentence comprehension will be a great place to start with Maria.

SS teacher: That sounds great. I could also give Maria a short content passage and three comprehension questions to answer each week. I know it won't be as valid as the maze assessment, but I think it would be interesting to see if her progress on the maze carries over into content reading.

ELA teacher: If you get me the passages each week, then I can create the questions. I think these plans will provide some comprehension focus and monitoring for Maria. For optimal comprehension, it will also be important to assure that the passages are culturally relevant for Maria.

Scenario Reflection

Based on the Challenge Scenario, document and discuss your initial thoughts regarding the following questions:

- What is the purpose of measuring and reporting progress in relation to IEP goals, and why is it important?

- What are the implications of data collected through progress monitoring?

- What should be done with progress monitoring data, and who should take these actions?

- What are some challenges associated with measuring and communicating a student's progress in relation to IEP goals and objectives?

Consider a final question related to the Challenge Scenario based on the interaction among the educators: What are some considerations educators need to discuss in preparation for implementing progress monitoring or revising data collection plans?

DATA COLLECTION

Although progress monitoring has multiple benefits and has proven to result in improved outcomes for students, there are challenges associated with selecting the most appropriate tools for monitoring progress. It is critical to distinguish progress monitoring tools from screening and diagnostic assessments.

Screening Assessments

Universal screening assessments are used for early identification of students who are on target, students who are in need of some support, or students who are in need of intensive support. Screening assessments test grade-level skills, are brief in length, and are designed to be administered to students with and without disabilities.

Diagnostic Assessments

Diagnostic assessments provide more in-depth information regarding a student's particular strengths and impairments. Typically, only students who have been identified by the screening assessment as performing below standard/ grade level or students who are not responding well to instruction need to participate in a diagnostic assessment. The results are often used to determine appropriate interventions or supports. For students who are CLD and ELLs, special consideration must be given to how a student's English proficiency level affects the results of the assessment tool used. The tools used often lack validity and reliability for CLD populations, resulting in lower scores and inaccurate results.

Progress Monitoring Tools

Unlike screening or diagnostic assessments, progress monitoring tools are ongoing and serve the purpose of providing continuous feedback to teachers, students, parents, and others. They provide formative information needed to modify instruction for individual students. Progress monitoring tools are used to determine a student's rate of progress toward goals and objectives and/or grade-level standards. Effective progress monitoring data are used to heavily influence instructional decisions.

A variety of progress monitoring tools are needed for students who are CLD and ELLs in order to mitigate issues with validity and reliability. Using a variety of progress monitoring tools provides for a more accurate account of the academic and functioning level of CLD and ELL populations.

Formal and informal assessments can be used for measuring and reporting progress, but for ongoing progress monitoring, the following types of assessments most adequately provide the formative data needed for instructional decision making:

- Curriculum-based measurements

- Classroom assessments (commercially and teacher created)

- Adaptive assessments (assessments tailored specifically to an individual based on their performance on previous items on an assessment)

- Large-scale assessments used during the year to monitor growth of individuals and groups of students

- Language samples (oral and written) in both home/native and English language

Progress monitoring tools should be used by any and all members of the IEP team as a way of focusing more intentionally on instruction and support. The responsibility for collecting data does not lie with one specific person but, depending on the information being gathered, may be appropriate for multiple team members or at varying degrees of frequency across multiple measures. However, for CLD students who are also ELLs, it is important to include professionals from the field of bilingual education and/or English as a second language. These professionals will add to the selection of progress monitoring tools and interpretation of results. As previously addressed, the time line for the collection of evidence also varies depending on purpose and intent. For students with specific behavioral goals and objectives, it is equally important to measure and report progress in this area.

Stop and Think!

Social language proficiency is needed for shared communication, whereas academic language proficiency is necessary for language used in the classroom in various content areas (see Chapter 2).

- Given these two distinct language proficiency levels (social and academic), why is it important to progress monitor ELLs' proficiency level for English and the home language?

If a student's IEP includes multiple content areas, functional performance, and/or behavioral goals and objectives, then the provisions for collecting evidence to measure and report progress should be varied and inclusive of multiple measures that reflect the range of goals and objectives.

Tools for progress monitoring can be purchased commercially or created by educators and implemented with varying degrees of fidelity. The reliability and validity of these measures also varies. Although the characteristics may differ slightly, many of the commercial tools for progress monitoring and teacher-created measures include the following areas for measurement:

- Math computation

- Math concepts and applications

- Early numeracy

- Language proficiency

- Quantity discrimination

- Oral reading fluency

- Letter naming

- Sound fluency

- Phoneme segmentation

- Word identification

- Word use

- Reading comprehension

- Appropriate social-emotional interactions

- Functional skills

Measuring and Charting Student Progress

Steps for measuring and charting student progress to inform ongoing progress monitoring includes making a variety of data collection decisions and gathering data over time. Prior to ongoing data collection, a baseline and aim line must be established and charted. It is important to obtain baseline data first. To gather this initial data, a probe representing the skill to be measured is administered and will determine the level at which the student is currently performing. In addition to baseline data, teachers must identify the acceptable level of performance; in other words, the anticipated level of performance expected as a result of instruction. Next, teachers will identify the discrepancy between the student's current performance and desired performance in the form of a goal. The desired performance must be reasonably robust to ensure that the student receives high-quality instruction. Connecting the baseline data and goals will provide an aim line. On any graph, the aim line should reach from the first data point (representing baseline data) to the ultimate goal (representing the expected or desired level of performance) over a designated period of time. The aim line is critical in being able to objectively monitor student performance over time—to determine if satisfactory progress is being made or if instructional interventions should be modified or added to improve outcomes.

The first step in selecting the tool for progress monitoring is choosing the type of measurement that will be used to display the student's progress toward the IEP goal. When goal statements are well written, educators not only can design instructional experiences, but they can also report the student's progress toward meeting the goal. Once the measure for assessing a student's progress toward the IEP goal is selected, the next step is to construct a graph. There are several commerical graphing options available; however, teachers can also create their own graph and have students record and monitor their own progress. Figure 7.1 is an example of a teacher-developed chart that students may use to to progress monitor their growth.

Although Figure 7.1 provides an opportunity for students to graph their progress, it is also important that the graph be analyzed regularly to determine if the student is making sufficient progress to meet their IEP goal. This regular analysis allows for any needed intervention adjustments to ensure that the student meets the goal within the time line outlined in the IEP. Establishing an aim line, also referred to as a *goal line,* is an effective method to determine if the student is on target to meet the IEP goal. The authors prefer to use the term *aim line* because the points along the line represent the target for both goals and objectives. Therefore, the aim line provides educators and parents with a reference to determine if the the student is making the necessary progress to meet the goal or objective by the date noted in the IEP. Baseline data must be collected and averaged to establish an aim line. Baseline data is the academic, behavioral, or functional performance prior to an intervention. Data is typically collected for 3–7 days, and the average score is determined. In Figure 7.2, the baseline of 19% was calculated by reviewing five of Mario's essays prior to the intervention to determine the percentage of third-grade words spelled correctly (example: 20% + 22% + 18% + 14% + 21% = 95%/5 = 19%). The aim line represents the target that Mario should meet by the end of the first semester to ensure that he meets the IEP goal. During the second semester, the aim line would increase to reflect the 100% criteria as noted in the IEP. The aim line provides information on the amount of progress a child needs to make on a weekly basis to reach the IEP goal.

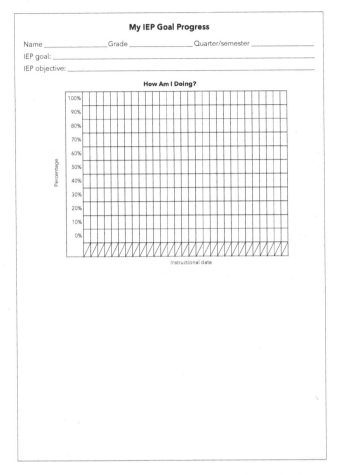

Figure 7.1. Progress monitoring chart.

Once the average data point prior to intervention (i.e., baseline) and aim line are established and noted on the graph, regular plotting of the student's achievement during intervention will allow for parents and the teacher to determine if the student is making sufficient progress to meet the IEP Goal. Figure 7.3 provides an example of Mario's performance on a weekly basis.

The general rule for adequate progress toward the IEP goal is when the student's data points are following the aim line. Approximatley 70% of the student's data points should be at or above the aim line. If the student is not making adequate progress, then a new intervention should be implemented. In Figure 7.3, Mario scored 82% above the aim line, which indicates that he is making sufficient progress toward the aim line, and if he continues the same rate of growth, he will meet his IEP goal by the date indicated in his IEP. If Mario had not made progress toward his aim line, then another intervention is required. Figure 7.4 provides an example of how to graph with a second intervention when a student is

My IEP Goal Tracking

Name: _Mario_   Grade: _3_   Quarter/semester: _First semester_

IEP goal: _By the next annual review, when asked to write an essay, Mario will spell all third-grade words correctly (100%) with the use of an editing device in three consecutive attempts as measured by the teacher's anecdotal records._

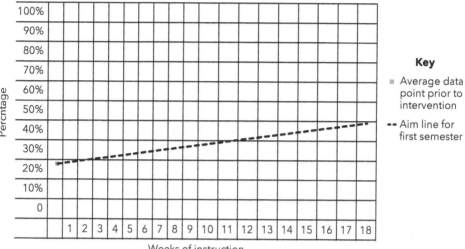

Figure 7.2. Aim line graph.

My IEP Goal Tracking

Name: _Mario_   Grade: _3_   Quarter/semester: _First semester_

IEP goal: _By the next annual review, when asked to write an essay, Mario will spell all third-grade words correctly (100%) with the use of an editing device in three consecutive attempts as measured by the teacher's anecdotal records._

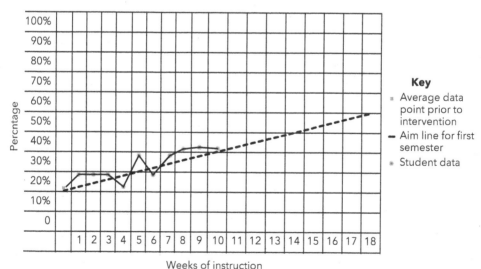

Figure 7.3. Graph of student's performance.

My IEP Goal Tracking

Name: _Mario_   Grade: _3_   Quarter/semester: _First semester_

IEP goal: _By the next annual review, when asked to write an essay, Mario will spell all third-grade words correctly (100%) with the use of an editing device in three consecutive attempts as measured by the teacher's anecdotal records._

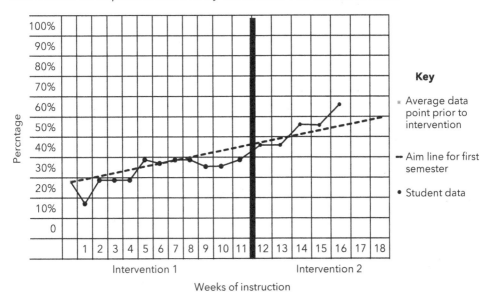

Figure 7.4.   Graph of student's performance requiring a different intervention.

not progressing toward the aim line. In Figure 7.4, notice that the last three data points (weeks 9, 10, and 11) are below the aim line, and the average score of 24 is also below the aim line. These scores indicate that Mario is not making adequate progress toward his aim line; therefore, a different intervention is needed. Using the same graph, a solid dark line is applied to designate when a second intervention was implemented. Because the last three probes (weeks 14, 15, and 16) are above the aim line and the average score of 55 is also above the aim line, Mario is now making sufficient progress to meet the aim line. In the scenario in Figure 7.4, the growth noted during the last 3 weeks (weeks 14, 15, and 16) also indicate that an effective intervention (Intervention 2) was effective in supporting Mario's academic needs in writing essays with correct third-grade spelling. Once Mario completes the first semester, a graph representing the second semester of progress monitoring with an aim line to 100 is needed to ensure that Mario meets his IEP goal by the annual date noted in his IEP.

Important considerations when measuring and charting student progress include the following:

- Set up a graph by finding or creating an appropriate hard copy or digital graph or utilizing an appropriate online chart or graph generator.

- Establish baselines for the skill(s) representing the student's skill deficits or the skills needing to be monitored.

- Set goal(s) by reviewing the current and expected or desired levels of performance. The level of performance must be reasonably robust.

- Draw the aim line by connecting the baseline (data point) to the determined goal (data point). The aim line is sometimes referred to as the *goal line.*

- Plot student performance by gathering and charting data to represent a minimum of six data points over time (data analysis).

- Analyze data and apply predetermined decision rules for making instructional and intervention decisions or changes.

Decision rules may include quantitative data windows and/or may be descriptive and include a review of the slope of the trendline or the discrepancy between the trendline and goal and/or trendline and aim line.

Data-driven instructional decisions are based on the systematic collection and analysis of data. This collection of data may include quantitative and/or qualitative information on the student's academic and/or functional level. Graphing the data with an aim line allows the educator to gauge if the student is on track to meet their IEP goal. Changes in instruction may be warranted if the data reveals a pattern or trend that does not indicate that the student is on track to meet their IEP goal.

Best Practice for Progress Monitoring:

- Select an area/skill to be monitored that is necessary for the student to meet the IEP goal.

- Select an assessment measure that directly assess the student's progress toward meeting the IEP goal.

- Determine the student's current level of performance, also known as the *baseline*.

- Identify a visual representation (e.g., graph) of the student's progress toward the IEP goal.

- Set an aim line/goal line to determine if the student is on track to attain the IEP goal.

- Predetermine the schedule for collecting data and recording the results.

- Regularly collect, analyze, and review the data to determine if the student is on track to attain the IEP goal and the effectiveness of the intervention. Adjust the intervention as needed.

- Report the student's progress to parents and other intervention specialists on a regular basis.

REPORTING PROGRESS

IDEA 2004 requires ". . . periodic reports on the progress the child is making toward meeting the annual goals . . . through the use of quarterly or other periodic reports, concurrent with the issuance of report cards" (34 CFR § 300.320[a][3][I,ii]). The intent of these reports is to track the student's progress toward the IEP goal and refine the intervention, as needed, to ensure that the student is making sufficient progress to achieve the annual goal. The IEP team is charged with identifying the measure to track the student's progress and how it will be communicated to parents. Although progress monitoring is an evidence-based strategy, in practice, some educators do not effectively communicate the student's growth toward the IEP goal or use the data to make instruction decisions (Winterman & Rosas, 2016). Therefore, once the IEP team has identified the framework for progress monitoring, it is incumbent on educators and support specialists, who are required to implement the IEP, to select a systematic approach that allows for meaningful collection and analysis of data that can easily be communicated to parents. To this end, graphs with goal lines and systematic charting of the student's performance provide a visual representation of the student's progress that can quickly and clearly be used to make instructional decisions that ensure that IEP goal(s) are met. Using these types of graphs allows parents to actually see and determine if their child is making progress, rather than just receiving a list of scores without any context for their child's progress. When reporting the progress of a student toward meeting the IEP goals, it is important that the report is both meaningful and all encompassing. The checklist in Figure 7.5 provides key areas that should be included in progress monitoring reports.

SUMMARY

This chapter focused on the practice of measuring and reporting student progress in relation to goals and objectives from the IEP, using data to make instructional decisions, and collecting data for academic and behavioral goals. The process of planning for progress monitoring and using data to make instructional decisions is critical to ensuring the success of the student. Because there are different purposes of progress monitoring, appropriate progress monitoring tools will vary. The responsibility for data collection, frequency of reporting, and use of multiple measures and time lines for collection processes does not lie with just one person, but it can be shared by all members of the IEP team. Different types of progress monitoring tools are available to allow for transition of the information in this chapter into classroom and school practices. The checklist in Figure 7.6 may be used to prepare for IEP meetings.

Key area Progress monitoring report should include the following key areas.	Information provided Check box(es) to confirm that information regarding key area was included in the report.
IEP goal: The IEP goal is included in the report.	☐ Yes ☐ No
Progress report indicates IEP goal(s) were met: Did your report indicate that the student met *all, some,* or *none* of the IEP goal(s)?	☐ Met *all* IEP goals ☐ Met *some* of the IEP goals ☐ Did *not* meet any of the IEP goals
Progress report indicates growth: Did your report indicate that your student made progress toward *all, some,* or *none* of the IEP goal(s)?	☐ Made progress toward *all* the IEP goals ☐ Made progress toward *some* of the IEP goals ☐ Did *not* make any progress toward the IEP goals
Data to support IEP goal met or progress: List the data (e.g., chart, graph, test scores) that supports the student met their IEP goal(s) or made progress. If no information/data is available, then indicate by stating *no data provided.*	☐ Charts ☐ Graphs ☐ Narrative ☐ Percentage ☐ Test scores ☐ No data provided ☐ Other _____
Who gathered the data: Select the individuals who were involved in the data collection.	☐ Counselor ☐ Education assistant ☐ General education teacher ☐ Interpreter ☐ Nurse ☐ Occupational therapist ☐ Parent ☐ Psychologist ☐ Physical therapist ☐ Special education teacher ☐ Student ☐ Speech-language pathologist ☐ Other _____
How often was the IEP data collected?	☐ Daily ☐ Weekly ☐ Monthly ☐ Quarterly ☐ Other _____
Terms defined: Was a key provided in the progress report to define terms or acronyms used to rank your student's progress (e.g., AP: adequate progress; LP: limited progress)?	☐ Yes ☐ No
Instructional strategies changed: Is there any indication in the progress report that the instructional strategies were changed due to the student's progress or lack thereof?	☐ Yes ☐ No

Figure 7.5.   Progress Monitoring Reporting Checklist.

Figure 7.5. *(continued)*

Special interventions or accommodations: List any specialized intervention(s) or accommodation that were included in the original IEP.	☐ Presentations (interpreters, audio books, visual cues) ☐ Response (scribe, speech to text, assistive technology) ☐ Setting (preferential seating, separate room) ☐ Timing (extended breaks)
Progress in the use of special intervention: Did your progress report indicate how your student was progressing with these special interventions?	☐ Yes ☐ No
Special intervention data: List the data (e.g., chart, graph) that support the progress or lack of progress with these special interventions.	☐ Charts ☐ Graphs ☐ Narrative ☐ Percentage ☐ Test scores ☐ Other _____
Frequency of progress report: Select the frequency in which information was provided to the parent on the student's progress report.	☐ Daily ☐ Weekly ☐ Monthly ☐ Quarterly ☐ Interim ☐ Annually ☐ Other _____
Progress report delivery: Select how the report is or was delivered.	☐ Face-to-face meeting ☐ Mail home ☐ E-mail ☐ Send home with child ☐ Pick up at school ☐ Other _____

PREPARATION FOR THE IEP MEETING:
PROGRESS MONITORING

Prior to the Meeting

☐ Ensure that progress monitoring measures are culturally and linguistically responsive to the needs of the students to provide valid and accurate results.

☐ Include home and English proficiency growth as part of progress monitoring for students who are English language learners.

☐ Complete Progress Monitoring Reporting Checklist from Figure 7.5.

☐ Ensure that the student's progress toward the IEP goal is documented and charted/graphed. Best practice includes baseline data at the beginning of the year, middle of the year, and end of the year prior to the IEP meeting.

☐ Confirm that the student's progress monitoring data was communicated with parents at the frequency and delivery mode as outlined in the IEP.

☐ Share progress monitoring data with other staff responsible for services.

☐ Organize data and be prepared to share how the student's progress monitoring data was used to inform teaching practices and daily instruction.

During the Meeting

☐ Share progress monitoring data with IEP team and how the data was used to inform instructional practices.

☐ Include the area that will be monitored for each IEP goal.

☐ If using an interpreter, be sure to use appropriate interpreter etiquette (see Chapter 2).

After the Meeting

☐ Debrief with all team members, including parents, about the effectiveness of the meeting.

☐ Check with parents on the use of an interpreter and if they understood the meeting and key takeaways.

Figure 7.6.   Preparation for the IEP meeting: Progress monitoring.

THE IEP CHECKLIST: MEASURING AND REPORTING PROGRESS

The following checklist can be used as an inventory to ensure that measuring and reporting progress of goals and objectives in the IEP meet IDEA regulations.

Key Area (IEP section): **Measuring and Reporting Progress**		Criteria met	
		Yes	No
M1: A statement is included that describes how a student's progress toward meeting their annual goals will be measured. (Select all measures identified below.)			
☐ Curriculum-based assessment	☐ Portfolios		
☐ Observations	☐ Rubric		
☐ Anecdotal records	☐ Checklists		
☐ Running records	☐ Inventories		
☐ Short-cycle assessments	☐ Work samples		
☐ Performance assessments	☐ Other		
M2: A statement is included describing when and how periodic reports will be provided to the student's parents. (Select all measures identified below.)			
How:	*When:*		
☐ Written report	☐ Each time report cards are issued		
☐ Journal	☐ Reported every ___ weeks		
☐ E-mail	☐ Other:		
☐ Phone calls			
☐ Other:			
M3: A statement is included that informs the reader that the reports are issued as frequently as students in general education receive their report cards.			

ACTIVITIES

The activities included in this chapter are intended for the reader to gain a deeper understanding of the content covered. For this chapter, each activity builds on the skills of the previous activity. The activities associated with this chapter include the following:

- Activity 7.1. Gathering and Documenting Data

- Activity 7.2. Measuring and Charting Progress Section

- Activity 7.3. Writing a Quality Measuring and Reporting Progress Section

Activity 7.1.
Gathering and Documenting Data

Supporting chapter: Chapter 7 (Measuring and Reporting Progress)

Purpose: The purpose of this activity is to practice gathering and documenting data that can be used to guide instruction, measure progress, and ultimately inform the IEP.

Directions: Apply your knowledge of progress monitoring as you engage in the opportunities to practice gathering and documenting student data in oral reading fluency and mathematical computation.

Part 1: Gather Oral Reading Fluency Progress Monitoring Data

After establishing the student's reading level and documenting initial baseline fluency data, have the student read and practice one passage per week for several weeks. On the first day of the week, graph the fluency scores for the first reading of the passage (a "cold" read), or have the student do this if they are able. A simple bar graph is appropriate, and boxes are filled in up to the correct number of words per minute read by the student. Facilitate practice throughout the week with the same passage by using fluency strategies such as choral reading, taped-assisted reading, partner reading, echo reading, and repeated reading. At the end of the week, instruct the student to read the same passage (a "hot" read). Record the fluency scores on the graph as well, or instruct the student to do this if they are able. Cold and hot reads are recorded on separate graphs (see the following example graph). The simple difference between a cold and hot read is that a cold read is a passage the student has never read, and a hot read is a passage that they have practiced throughout the week multiple times. It is important to graph these separately because they provide information relative to the student's experience with the text.

Oral Reading Fluency Graph

Name: _____ Partner/teacher: _____

	M	T	W	T	F		M	T	W	T	F		M	T	W	T	F		M	T	W	T	F
130																							
125																							
120																							
115																							
110																							
105																							
100																							
95																							
90																							
85																							
80																							
75																							
70																							
65																							
60																							
55																							
50																							
45																							
40																							
35																							
30																							
25																							
20																							
15																							
10																							
5																							
0																							
	M	T	W	T	F		M	T	W	T	F		M	T	W	T	F		M	T	W	T	F
	Date:						Date:						Date:						Date:				

Part 2: Gather Math Computation Progress Monitoring Data

Select one or more computation problem types on which the student needs to improve. Using that set of problem types as a guide, find or create several standardized sets of problems with similar items to be used across multiple instructional days. Give the student one of the math computation sets previously created, along with an answer key. Have the student consult their progress monitoring chart and note the baseline score or most recent progress monitoring score. When the assessment session starts, give the student a preselected amount of time to complete as many problems as possible. Have the student set a timer for the allocated time and work on the computation sheet until the timer rings. Then, instruct the student to use the answer key to check their work, with support if needed. Document the student's computational fluency score on the progress monitoring chart (see the following example chart), or ask the student to do this if they are able. Instruction throughout the week is targeted toward the same types of problems, and each week a new data point is gathered using the same procedure.

Progress monitoring				
	Title			
	Student			
	Grade			
	Teacher			
	Benchmark			
	Goal			
	Date	**Number correct**	**Errors**	
1				
2				
3				
4				
5				
6				

Note:
1. It is important to input the **date** and the total **number correct.**
2. You may wish to fill in and graph the errors. The chart with **errors** will graph your errors.

Number correct	Errors

Activity 7.2.

Measuring and Charting Progress Section

Supporting chapter: Chapter 7 (Measuring and Reporting Progress)

Purpose: The purpose of this activity is to practice charting data to measure progress. This data can then be used to guide instruction, plan appropriate interventions, modify interventions, and ultimately inform the IEP.

Directions: Apply your knowledge of charting student data as you engage in creating an aim line, charting or plotting data points for a fictional student, and reflecting on the data represented.

Student Background Information

Dillon is a second-grade student at Willowcrest Elementary School. Dillon's teacher administered the universal screening measure, and his score did not meet the benchmark. Because of this, his teacher began to monitor Dillon's progress in reading over the next 8 weeks. At the end of that period, Dillon's teachers and support staff met to discuss his data. He was referred for Tier 2 instruction. Eight weeks have passed since Dillon started Tier 2 instruction.

Dillon's short-term goal is 50 words per minute for Week 16. Use this information to create a goal line. (The goal line is established using Tier 1 data points.) This step is usually completed after the third data point is collected in order to account for an outlier data point and establish a pattern of performance.

Next, create a graph similar to the one in Figure 7.7—either a hard copy, in digital form, or using a chart or graphing program. Plot Dillon's eight data points for Tier 2.

Week 9	36
Week 10	38
Week 11	40
Week 12	42
Week 13	44
Week 14	47
Week 15	48
Week 16	49

After plotting and reviewing the data, including the position of the trendline in relation to the aim line and designated goal, brainstorm questions and suggest decisions for teachers to discuss in relation to Dillon's progress in their next meeting.

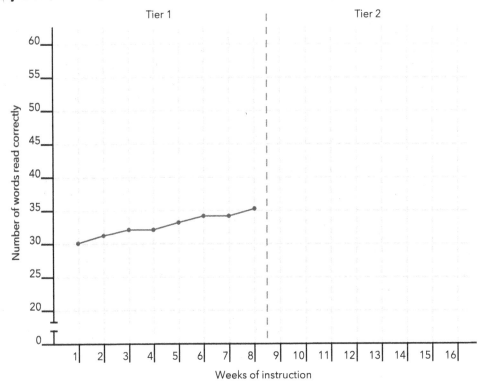

Figure 7.7. Tiered instruction sample graph.

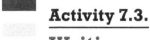

Activity 7.3.

Writing a Quality Measuring and Reporting Progress Section

Supporting chapter: Chapter 7 (Measuring and Reporting Progress)

Purpose: The purpose of this activity is to write quality documentation of the measurement for reporting progress in meeting the IEP's goal and objectives.

Directions: Use an IEP to inventory the Measurement and Reporting Progress section and indicate the quality of the information provided. Then, rank the quality of the Measurement and Reporting Progress section and provide evidence to support your ranking. Rewrite any documentation of the measurement for reporting progress in meeting the IEP's goal and objectives with a ranking below a 4 in the space provided so that it exceeds the standard (ranking of 4).

Rubric scale: Use the following scale and circle the number that best ranks the IEP area reviewed.

1 = Standard not met	2 = Standard partially met	3 = Standard met	4 = Standard exceeds
• IEP fails to provide evidence of meeting the IDEA 2004 requirements. • IEP does not address the IDEA 2004 requirements.	• Performance provides evidence of partially meeting IDEA 2004 requirements. • Performance addresses some of the IDEA 2004 requirements.	• Performance provides evidence of meeting most/all of the IDEA 2004 requirements. • Performance addresses most/all of the IDEA 2004 requirements.	• Performance provides evidence of exceeding all IDEA 2004 requirements. • All indicators are addressed and go beyond expectations.

Key Area (IEP Section): Measuring and Reporting Progress	Ranking	Rationale for Ranking
M1: A statement is included that describes how a student's progress toward meeting their annual goals will be **measured.** (Select all measures identified next.) ☐ Curriculum-based assessment ☐ Portfolios ☐ Observations ☐ Rubric ☐ Anecdotal records ☐ Checklists ☐ Running records ☐ Inventories ☐ Short-cycle assessments ☐ Work samples ☐ Performance assessments ☐ Other	1 2 3 4	

M2: A statement is included describing when and how **periodic reports** will be provided to the student's parents. (Select all measures identified next.) *How:* ☐ Written report ☐ Journal ☐ E-mail ☐ Phone calls ☐ Other: _____ *When:* ☐ Each time report cards are issued ☐ Reported every ___ weeks ☐ Other: _____	1 2 3 4
M3: A statement is included that informs the reader that the reports are issued as frequently as students in general education receive their report cards.	1 2 3 4

Rewritten documentation for the Measuring and Reporting Progress section:

_____

_____

_____

_____

_____

_____

III

Supporting Information

8

Least Restrictive Environment

Clarissa E. Rosas, Laura Clarke,
Kathleen G. Winterman, and Melissa M. Jones

After reading this chapter and engaging in activities related to this chapter, you will be able to meet the following outcomes:

- Explain the importance of the least restrictive environment (LRE).

- Describe the supplementary aids and services that must be considered for special populations.

- Summarize the decision-making factors for LRE.

- Encapsulate the supports needed for culturally and linguistically diverse (CLD) populations that address their disability and language proficiency needs.

IEP teams are charged with ensuring that students with disabilities are afforded the opportunity to receive their instruction and intervention in the LRE (Yell et al., 2020). *LRE* refers to the setting in which instruction and intervention occur in order for a student with a disability to benefit from their education alongside their peers without disabilities to the maximum extent appropriate. In this provision, the IEP team determines the extent to which the student will be educated with their typically developing peers. Determining a student's LRE is not only an educational issue or a legal issue, but it is also an issue of social justice (Sapon-Shevin, 2003; Wright & Wright, 2011). Schools, as a microcosm of society, mimic and help create the attitudes and perceptions of society as a whole. As such, when education teams discuss LRE decisions, their attitudes mirror and either preserve or challenge the attitudes prevalent in society. Given this reality, IEP teams have the potential to dispute preconceived notions and traditions related to ability, exclusion, and segregation and engage in meaningful dialogue about possibilities and perceptions. The Individuals with Disabilities Education Improvement Act (IDEA) of 2004 (PL 108-446) provides the impetus for this dialogue, and conversations about LRE create the space in which such important issues can be addressed.

CONNECTION TO LEGAL PERSPECTIVE

According to Section 504 of the Rehabilitation Act of 1973 (PL 93-112) and IDEA, school districts must provide a free appropriate public education (FAPE) to students with disabilities, and the education provided must be in the LRE. FAPE simply means that school districts cannot charge families for the education provided to their children (*free*), the education must fit the needs and abilities of the student (*appropriate*), and this free and appropriate schooling must be provided by the local school system in order for that system to receive federal and state money (*public education*). A critical component of this law is providing FAPE in the setting that is the least restrictive to the student and most like the setting in which peers without disabilities learn. Specifically, IDEA 2004 describes LRE as follows:

(i) To the maximum extent appropriate, children with disabilities, including children in public or private institutions or other care facilities, are educated with children who are nondisabled; and

(ii) Special classes, separate schooling, or other removal of children with disabilities from the regular educational environment occurs only if the nature or severity of the disability is such that education in regular classes with the use of supplementary aids and services cannot be achieved satisfactorily. (§ 300.114[a])

The LRE is the environment most like that of children without disabilities in which the child with a disability can make progress in the curriculum and on their specific IEP goals. Historically, court rulings have further clarified LRE by 1) requiring school districts and IEP team members to first consider the use of supplementary aids and services in the general education setting before concluding that a student with a disability be educated in a self-contained classroom

IDEA'S KEY COMPONENTS

- **Free appropriate public education (FAPE).** Requires that the student be educated in a manner that meets their educational needs by a public educational agency that is free to the family.
  - *Zero Reject.* Mandates that the school cannot deny a child an education due to the severity of their needs.
- **Least restrictive environment (LRE).** The student is educated in a manner that is most like their typical peers.
- **Procedural safeguards** (due process). The family has the right to disagree with the placement, services, and educational plan for their child and can bring the school district to court.
- **Parental participation** (shared decision making). Parents have the right to participate as part of the education team for their child.
- **Nondiscriminatory evaluation.** Requires schools to utilize a team approach in assessing a student in all suspected areas of a disability using measures that are valid, reliable, culturally relevant, and linguistically appropriate.
- **Individualized education program (IEP).** The IEP team assesses current evaluation information and develops a written document designed to meet the unique educational needs of each student with a disability.

environment (*Greer v. Rome City School District*, 1992; *Oberti v. Board of Education of the Borough of Clementon School District*, 1993); 2) establishing factors for districts and IEP teams to consider to determine the benefits for the student when included in a general education setting (*Oberti v. Board of Education of the Borough of Clementon School District*, 1993; *Sacramento City Unified School District v. Holland*, 1994); and 3) adding extracurricular activities to the list of opportunities students with disabilities should be afforded as a means for addressing various social and educational goals on a student's IEP (*Daniel R.R. v. State Board of Education*, 1989). For students who are CLD, it is important that the LRE provides opportunities for English language proficiency development and opportunities to interact with peers who have similar English language proficiency and cultural experiences. Determining the most appropriate setting in which a student is to receive educational services is made at the IEP team level, with each participant contributing to the conversation.

Stop and Think!

Social justice is generally thought of as affording individuals and groups fair treatment and an impartial share of the benefits of society.

- Have you ever witnessed a situation in which social justice was not evident?

- What did Sapon-Shevin (2003) mean when she wrote, "When one person is oppressed, no one is free" (p. 24)?

- Consider a situation in which you felt unjustly treated. What were your feelings? What actions were you able to take?

- If the situation you considered happened to someone you knew today, what would be your response?

THE INDIVIDUALS WITH DISABILITIES EDUCATION IMPROVEMENT ACT OF 2004 AND LEAST RESTRICTIVE ENVIRONMENT

The legal requirements of LRE come down to three basic components: 1) students with disabilities should have access to and be involved in the general education curriculum, 2) students with disabilities should be educated with their peers without disabilities, and 3) a continuum of services and environments should be provided to meet the needs of individual students (DeMonte, 2010; Karger & Hitchcock, 2004; McLeskey et al., 2010; Sze & Cowden, 2012).

LRE guarantees a student's right to be educated in settings most like the settings provided to students without disabilities, providing the student can be successful when given the appropriate supports (Burstein et al., 2004; Friend & Bursuck, 2011; Karger & Hitchcock, 2004; Palley, 2006). In fact, the law requires IEP teams to consider the general education classroom first when discussing where special education services will be provided, and special classes, separate schools, or other forms of educational segregation from the general education classroom environment should only be used when evidence suggests a student cannot succeed in the general education setting, even with supplementary aids and services. Materials used in the general or special education settings must reflect the student's cultural background and the strategies used should be evidence-based practices to meet the unique needs of the student. Such services could include a modified or alternative set of materials or curriculum, assistance from a paraprofessional or intervention specialist, adaptive equipment, or technology (Friend & Bursuck, 2011). Deciding on a more restrictive environment for a student is a serious matter and requires IEP teams to document the evidence reviewed that demonstrates the need for a more restrictive setting.

Stop and Think!

The U.S. Department of Education's Office of Special Education (2015) published a *Dear Colleague Letter* to state and local educational agencies to confirm that the development of the IEP safeguards free appropriate public education by including statements that ". . . ensure access of the child to the general curriculum . . ." (p. 2).

- How can the IEP team ensure that English language learners with disabilities who have not reached academic language proficiency have access to the general education curriculum?

- What LRE provisions must be included in the IEP to safeguard that classroom materials and services are provided to reflect the cultural background and needs of the student?

When considering LRE, the IEP team must first look at the general education environment and what supplementary aids and services can be provided. This conversation seems to be easier for the IEP team when focusing on issues, such as the need for a reader or scribe, but sometimes the IEP team has a difficult time determining appropriate supplementary aids and services when considering behavioral supports. Some IEP teams have historically chosen more restrictive environments for students with trauma in their background and students from different cultural backgrounds instead of fully considering the possible supplementary aids and services that could be employed to support a student in the general education classroom a greater percentage of the time (Yell et al., 2020). It is important for IEP teams to fully consider the evidence-based interventions currently available and use tools such as the implementation checklists available through the Comprehensive, Integrated, Three-Tiered Model of Prevention, an online resource dedicated to supporting educators in the development and integration of academic, behavioral, and social supports for all students. Among key questions for the IEP team to consider are

- What behavior(s) does the student exhibit that is different than same-age peers without a disability from the same cultural background?

- When is the student most likely to exhibit this behavior?

- What function(s) does this behavior serve for the student?

- What skill or strategy deficits might the student have that impede their ability to display a more appropriate behavior?

- What instruction/intervention(s) would help the student develop a more appropriate behavior?

- What supports might help the student change, control, or modify their behaviors to be able to engage in instruction in the general education classroom?

- Can these skills and strategies be taught in the general education classroom?

- Can supports be put in place that allow the student to be able to tolerate instruction in the general education classroom? (Kentucky Department of Education, 2019)

Challenge Scenario

The following conversation takes place at an IEP meeting. Around the table are seated James Davis; his mother, Ms. Davis; the intervention specialist, Mr. Atkins; a general education teacher, Ms. Bonner; and the assistant principal, Ms. Lopez.

Mr. Atkins: Now that we have determined James's goals and the services that he needs to make progress toward those goals, let's discuss where these services are going to be provided. We want to consider each of the goals separately as we discuss the least restrictive environment for making progress toward these goals.

James: I just want to say right up front that I don't want to go to the special ed class this year.

Ms. Davis: James, it sounds like your goal is to spend as much time as possible in the general education classroom—this is also our goal. We do want to make sure that you are successful in each class, so let's hear what Mr. Atkins suggests.

James: I'm just saying, I don't want to go to that room.

Ms. Davis: Okay, I hear you, but let's wait to hear what Mr. Atkins has to say.

Mr. Atkins: James, nobody wants to make you do something you don't want to do. We just want you to be successful in every class. Let's look at all of the options and see how we can support you. The first goal we decided on was to help you with your auditory processing. You said that was important to you, so we wrote: "Given a written one-step direction for an unfamiliar task, James will independently initiate and complete the direction correctly in 8 of 10 opportunities." We decided that to help you with that goal, I would consult with your teachers to identify the tasks you would be asked to complete in class and then come up with some specific direction words to teach you so that you would better understand the directions given in class.

James: Yeah, I remember that.

Mr. Atkins: Then we said that you and I would practice these words for 10 minutes two times a week. I think that we could probably do that in the general education classroom, don't you? We would need to figure out which class it makes the most sense to do this in and then come up with a schedule, but I don't see why we couldn't work on it during class at your desk or in the back of the room for a couple of minutes a week. How do you feel about that, Ms. Davis?

Ms. Davis: That sounds fine to me. What do you think, James?

James: Yeah, that would work, as long as I don't have to miss what the other kids are doing.

Ms. Bonner: I don't think it would work in language arts because of the structure of that classroom, but maybe in math or science. In both of those classes, I believe the teachers begin most class sessions with either an Entrance Slip or Question of the Day that the students have to work on when they first come in to the room. That might be a good time for Mr. Atkins and James to work on his auditory processing and direction words. He wouldn't miss any of the primary instruction, and he would still be able to participate in the opening activity at least three times during the week.

Mr. Atkins: That sounds like a great idea! I'll talk with the teachers in those courses, and we can go from there. What do you think, James?

James: That works for me. Maybe math class would be better because I'm better at math than anything else.

Ms. Davis: I agree.

Mr. Atkins: Okay, so I'll start by talking with your math teacher and then talk to your science teacher if math doesn't work out. Now, let's move on to the next goal. Let's see . . . this one is for your reading fluency. I think this one might be a bit trickier. We wanted to help you improve your reading so that you would enjoy it more and be able to use reading for both information and pleasure.

James: Good luck with that one!

Ms. Lopez: Remember, James, you agreed to help us with this goal.

James: Yeah, I know. But that doesn't mean I'm going to like it.

Mr. Atkins: Okay, on your IEP, we wrote: "When reading leisure material of his choice, written at a sixth-grade reading level, James will read at an average fluency rate of 127 words correct per minute." To work on this goal, we said that we needed to do some reading fluency interventions, having you read more and charting your own progress, as well as doing some flashcard drills and a few other interventions.

               We also decided that we needed to work on this every day. Because we identified leisure reading as the material we would use, I'm not sure we can do that in the general education classroom while there is other instruction going on, but let's walk through a scenario anyway. Okay, so James would be in class, and the teacher would be lecturing or giving directions. When I came in to the class, James and I would go to the back of the room or out in the hall to read and do the various reading interventions. Does that sound right to everyone?

Ms. Davis: What about doing this in language arts. Aren't students reading in there every day?

Ms. Lopez: That's a great question. I know that they do read, but most of the reading is done as homework, and they discuss the reading in class. The teacher also provides advance organizers to the students prior to their reading homework to help them better understand the material, but I don't think they actually spend class time reading. James, does this sound right to you?

James: Yeah, last year that's about what we did, and I've heard that next year it's more of the same, except the books are harder. We have to write stories and research papers, too.

Ms. Lopez: That's what I thought, so I don't think language arts is the place to work on James's reading fluency. Ms. Bonner, do you agree?

Ms. Bonner: From what I understand about that class, I think you both are right.

James: I don't want the other kids to see that I suck at reading.

Mr. Atkins: So, does it make sense that we work on this goal in the resource room, James?

James: I guess so, but I don't want to be in there all day.

Mr. Atkins: Well, you wouldn't, because we agreed that all it would really take is about 10 minutes each day. How about instead of going to homeroom you come to my room for the first 10 minutes, do the reading fluency interventions with me, and then go on to your next class when the bell rings?

James: Just for 10 minutes, right?

Mr. Atkins: That's right. I think that's all that we will need, as long as we do it every day.

James: I'm okay with that.

Mr. Atkins: All right, so now we just have one more goal to talk about, and this one is for reading comprehension. We wrote: "Using a graphic organizer, James will match a minimum of 10 key terms from the content reading material for each unit of instruction with the correct definition in 7 of 10 instances." I think this goal lends itself to being done in the general education classroom because it deals with the content vocabulary that is regularly taught in all of the subjects. Which classes do you feel this is the biggest problem in, James?

James: Well, I'm kinda worried about history next year and science, too. I'm okay with math, but it always sounds like the teachers are talking in a foreign language to me when I'm in history and science classes. I don't have a clue what's going on half the time.

Ms. Davis: Sounds like you could use some help in both classes.

James: Yeah, probably.

Ms. Bonner: It would be fairly easy for the general education teacher to work with Mr. Atkins to identify key words that James would need to know, and teaching some cognitive learning strategies to help James learn the content vocabulary could be done as the instruction is occurring. If we introduced the idea of using graphic organizers to the general education teachers, then they may want to use them for all of their classes, making it a content enhancement. Then, you wouldn't even need it as a modification specific to James, but rather, it would help the teachers and benefit all of their students. I'm sure James isn't the only student confused by the challenging vocabulary.

James: Yeah, everyone's brain is fried in those classes!

Mr. Atkins: So, are we all in agreement that we can work on this goal either in history or science class?

Ms. Davis: It makes sense to me. I don't even think it matters which one, just as long as the teacher is okay with it.

Mr. Atkins: I'll look at a tentative schedule for services and see which one makes the most sense. I could even do 10 minutes a week in each class if you think that would help.

Ms. Davis: It certainly couldn't hurt.

Mr. Atkins: Alright, then. I'll talk to the teachers to figure out how we will make all of this work to best benefit James.

Scenario Reflection

Based on the Challenge Scenario, document and discuss your initial thoughts regarding the following questions:

- In James's scenario, what information did the team use to make their decisions regarding the LRE?

- How did the meeting facilitator, Mr. Atkins, solicit input from all of the team members? Did everyone have an opportunity to participate?

- How was James included in the decision-making aspect of the IEP? Why is it important to include the student in decision-making aspects of the IEP?

- Can you think of a time or an experience when you were embarrassed in front of your peers? What was at the heart of your embarrassment? Why might a student with a disability be embarrassed to receive services in a separate class setting?

- Why do you suppose a law was created and approved to mandate consideration of inclusion in the general education classroom for students with disabilities?

- Why do we sometimes struggle with the notion of inclusion of everyone in the learning community?

IMPLICATIONS FOR INSTRUCTIONAL DECISIONS

With the focus on students with disabilities being involved in the general education curriculum and interacting with and learning alongside peers without disabilities, educators must work collaboratively and creatively to provide the necessary supports and instruction to students with disabilities. The IEP team should begin their conversation by considering a full range of possible supplementary aids and services they could put in place to support the student before considering a more restrictive placement. The LRE for some students may not necessarily mean a physical environment, such as a traditional mortar-and-brick classroom, but rather a virtual environment, such online learning (Sze & Cowden, 2012).

Least Restrictive Environment and the Decision-Making Process

LRE is not an actual place, but a principle that guides the IEP team's decision-making process (Bowe, 2005; Yell et al., 2020). When determining the LRE for a particular student, the IEP team needs to consider the student's personal vision and goals; the student's interests, strengths, and needs; the services and accommodations needed in order for the student to make educational progress; and information about the curriculum and various setting options. Determining the LRE for a student should be the final topic of discussion for an IEP team after they have identified the student's vision, Present Levels of Academic Achievement and Functional Performance, goals (and objectives if needed), evaluation criteria, and needed services. Discussing LRE in light of this information helps the team make the most appropriate decision for and with the student, based on their academic needs.

Each goal should be considered when discussing the LRE for a student, with decisions focused on where each goal might best be addressed. For example, a reading comprehension goal might best be addressed in a history class where students frequently are asked to gain access to various resources and read to discover information. A writing goal might best be addressed in a biology class where students are expected to conduct experiments and write lab reports on a regular basis. A communication goal might best be met in a writing class where students work in small groups to create stories. LRE decisions are not based on the actual course content, per se, but rather on the types of interactions with others and with the content that best lends itself to the student's goals.

The types of educational setting decisions for students with disabilities will vary and should be determined on a case-by-case basis. Two major guideposts of LRE are ensuring that the environment is appropriate and individualized, requiring IEP teams to consider various attributes of the student, curriculum, and learning environments in order to make the most beneficial decisions on behalf of and with the student. Disability labels should not be a factor when making LRE decisions. Considering the vast differences in needs and interests among students with disabilities, there is no single definition of what the LRE would be for any student with any given learning difference.

Students who have mild learning disabilities, such as James, are not the only ones who can be included in a general education classroom. It is the legal and ethical obligation of district staff to consider inclusive settings for all students. Districts must also consider such educational environments for students who have significant issues related to behavior, as well as students with intellectual disabilities.

Stop and Think!

Positive behavior support is a process for understanding and resolving a child's challenging behavior that is based on values and empirical research (Fox & Duda, 2015). This approach has three steps:

1. Bring together a team of concerned, knowledgeable individuals.

2. Conduct a functional behavioral assessment, which should include data collected across a variety of settings and should be focused on determining the function(s) of the student's behavior(s) so that an appropriate intervention plan can be developed. The assessment typically involves observations and the collection of data, such as the frequency of the behavior or ABC (Antecedent-Behavior-Consequence) data. The data should be analyzed to determine what functions the behavior is serving for the student, and the assessment should include recommendations for possible interventions that could help modify the behavior to be more appropriate for school settings.

3. Develop the behavioral intervention plan that includes 1) strategies for modifying the curriculum, environment, activity, or interactions to prevent occurrences of the challenging behavior; 2) procedures to teach a new skill to use in place of the challenging behavior; and 3) strategies to ensure that new skills are learned and acknowledged, and challenging behavior is not maintained.

Behavioral issues are the primary reason students are routinely excluded from the general education environment, demonstrating a prejudice and lack of value for students with issues related to mental health (Howard, 2013). Half of all chronic mental illness begins by age 14, yet only half of these students will receive support. More than 50% of students age 14 and older with a mental health condition who are served by special education leave school—this the highest dropout rate of any disability group (National Alliance on Mental Illness, 2013). When considering ways to support students with behavioral issues in their LRE, it is critical for the IEP team to consider a full range of supplementary aids and services and ensure that the entire school staff are educated on how to implement the supplementary aids and services with fidelity across time and settings.

To support students with behavioral issues, the IEP team must develop a comprehensive positive behavior support plan that provides the student with the structure and reinforcement they need in order to gain access to the curriculum, considering services and strategies to help students with behavioral issues interact with peers in a positive way. By creating structured situations within the general classroom environment in which students can practice their newly developing skills, the team is increasing the likelihood of success with the intervention. If, however, a student is unable to participate in the general education environment at the present time, then the team needs to annually review the interventions and LRE, continually seeking opportunities to increase the student's participation in a less restrictive situation. (For example, as of 2010, the U.S. Department of Education estimated there were more than 10,000 alternative schools in the country.)

Students with developmental delays and/or intellectual disabilities are also often excluded from the general education environment, particularly older students, because of the misperception that the ability gap is too great between the students with disabilities and those without disabilities. Yet, a student does not have to have the ability to master grade-level content in order to be included in the general education environment. The primary consideration of the IEP team must be the ultimate benefit(s) the student will receive by participating in that environment. Even though the curriculum might prove challenging for a student, the benefits might far outweigh the drawbacks. Surrounded by students with age-appropriate expressive language skills, independence, and self-help skills, students with more significant disabilities typically will begin to develop their skills alongside their peers without disabilities, modeling the more sophisticated skills as demonstrated by their peers in a general education classroom (Sugai et al., 2010a). In order to benefit from peer modeling, students with disabilities need to be in proximity to peers, responding and interacting as a member of a classroom community.

Stop and Think!

Consider at least three different scenarios in which a particular academic or behavioral skill would be better taught in a natural environment rather than in a more restricted one. After discussing your scenarios, step back and list the criteria you used to make such determinations.

What is considered the LRE for a student at one point in their educational career may not be that student's LRE at another point in time. All individuals need variations in the time, place, and type of support they receive. For example, when first learning to drive, it is not appropriate for an adult to simply place the individual learning to drive in a car; hand them the keys; say, "Be back in an hour;" and then walk away. New drivers require direct instruction with multiple prompts, various levels of reinforcement, and time to practice before they are able to drive a car solo. Initially, an individual's LRE for driving is likely much more restrictive than it is after the individual has been driving for a while.

This is not to suggest that all skills need to be introduced in a more restrictive setting. For some skills, it may be entirely appropriate to learn the skill in the natural environment, such as in a chemistry lab. For example, imagine a student who struggles to sustain positive peer relationships during school hours. The IEP team members all agree that this student would benefit from regularly scheduled structured social skills training sessions. Although the social skills training could occur in a resource room setting, the training might be more effective if it was conducted in the general education classroom in the form of skits and role plays with other students. It is unlikely that only one student would benefit from the structured instruction for social skills development, so taking time during homeroom once a week to practice role plays could be instructive and engaging for everyone. Not only would the natural environment provide many more role models, but those involved could also help design the lessons and the role plays, promoting higher order thinking skills and fostering leadership in other students as well.

The LRE is the environment most like that of students without disabilities in which the student with a disability can succeed academically and behaviorally, as measured by progress on specific goals in the IEP. When considering the educational benefits of inclusion for a student, the IEP team should ignore the eligibility label that has been placed on a student and instead focus on the individual characteristics of the student and how they learn (Falvey, 1995). The team should also be aware that less restrictive service delivery options, including inclusion in the general education classroom with coteaching, has been shown to contribute to positive outcomes for all students involved (Friend & Bursuck, 2011).

Implementing Self-Checks for the Least Restrictive Environment

Court rulings have resulted in several tests that may be used to check on the appropriateness of a student's LRE. In *Daniel R.R. v. State Board of Education* (1989), two questions were devised to help determine if the LRE requirement has been met: 1) Can an appropriate education in the general education classroom with the use of supplementary aids and services be achieved satisfactorily? and 2) If a student is placed in a more restrictive setting, is the student included to the "maximum extent appropriate"? This second question creates challenges to self-contained school environments such as hospitals, special schools, and programs for adjudicated youth. IEP teams in these settings must periodically reassess the appropriateness of the restrictive setting and weigh the positive and negative outcomes of continued placement in the environment to ensure compliance with IDEA.

In *Sacramento City Unified School District v. Holland* (1994), four additional and perhaps more essential questions were developed for assessing the appropriateness of an LRE decision: 1) What are the educational benefits of inclusive settings versus self-contained settings for this student? 2) What are the nonacademic benefits? 3) What effect will the student with a disability have on the teacher and their peers? and 4) What will the supplementary aids and services cost in order for the student to stay in the inclusive setting?

These questions help teams navigate the balance between the educational and social benefit to all students involved and the fiscal responsibility of the district.

As a result, students with disabilities should receive an appropriate version of the educational and social benefits that students without disabilities routinely receive in school. The next sections provide a more in-depth look at how an IEP team might address these questions.

What are the educational benefits of inclusive settings versus self-contained settings for this student?

It is difficult to determine what a student will or will not gain from any given situation, so the safe assumption is that the student can learn. Consider the example of a third-grade student who was labeled a nonreader but who identified the word "science" from a library catalogue. Consider also the student who had difficulty speaking due to a significant intellectual learning difference but who learned what the term "biodegradable" meant. All a teacher can do is apply evidence-based teaching practices and present the information through the most accessible means possible, provide multiple opportunities to practice, and then problem-solve based on student outcomes. The least dangerous assumption we can make about students with disabilities is that they can learn some aspect of the content, and knowing some aspect of it is better than never having been introduced to it at all. Knowledge should not be kept from certain populations of people, but rather offered willingly to anyone and everyone.

Special consideration in language planning is imperative when considering students with disabilities who are ELLs. An inclusive setting provides the benefit of English role models and opportunities to develop academic language proficiency more than a self-contained setting. The IEP team, however, must take special care in designing IEPs that consider the native language and English proficiency level as well as the necessary supports required in order for the student to benefit from English-only instruction.

What are the nonacademic benefits?

At the core of this question is the team's ability to think beyond restrictive definitions of disability and consider the entire student. Beyond the academic issues the student may have, the team must also consider the implications for social learning if the student were able to regularly interact with same-age peers without disabilities. Not only should the team consider what the student might gain from being in the general education classroom but also what the ramifications might be if the student was not provided this opportunity. Where would the student learn new social skills? Whom would the student be modeling? Is it possible to set up situations and scenarios to support learning social skills in the general education classroom? These questions, along with others, need to be answered as IEP team members contemplate LRE decisions.

Students who spend a majority of time around same-age peers without disabilities develop more age-appropriate social skills and maintain age-appropriate expectations for themselves as contributing members of society. ELLs receiving special education services are not only learning English but also the culture of school and mainstream culture; therefore, it is critical that they also have an opportunity to interact with same-age peers without disabilities. Students with disabilities need to have opportunities to befriend and work with others who do not have disabilities, gaining not only personal development skills but also a strong sense of self from the experience. Katz and Mirenda (2002) found a clear relationship between social interactions with typical peers and the achievement of IEP goals by students with severe disabilities.

What effect will the student with a disability have on the teacher and their peers?   Unfortunately, many IEP teams only address the perceived negative impact a student with a disability might have on a classroom, such as slowing down the pace of the class or repeatedly disturbing or interrupting the class due to either behavioral issues or distractions created by support personnel and services. The IEP team must also consider the broader, positive societal implications for including a student with a disability, however, in order to fully address this question. Would having this student in the class be a potential catalyst for higher order thinking and discussions on social justice and citizenship? What would the students without disabilities gain from this experience? The team should also consider that instructional strategies that are implemented for one or two students may, in fact, benefit other students, as well. For example, providing visual prompts for a student with autism can also benefit other students by allowing them to see the day's outline of events. Our culture is typically uncomfortable with difference. Given limited exposure to difference, this discomfort is perpetuated, with little chance for change, often leading to further isolation and abandonment for the minoritized group (Falvey, 1995; Sapon-Shevin, 2003). In many cases, the positive cultural implications for inclusion are far reaching and worthy of consideration when making LRE decisions. (These implications are discussed more thoroughly at the end of the chapter.)

What will the supplementary aids and services cost in order for the student to stay in the inclusive setting?   This final question is probably what separates the ideology of inclusion from the legal practices of LRE. Congress recognized the financial strain that a district might endure educating a student with a significant disability. Therefore, the decision to include a student in the general education classroom must not put additional undue stress on the district. Quite often, however, the use of consultation services and coteaching to support students with disabilities in the general education classroom is quite fiscally responsible, costing no more or no less than the alternative pull-out services, which can be in and of themselves cost prohibitive. For instance, educating a student with a disability through pull-out services may cost a school district two to four times the average expense of educating a typically developing student in the general education classroom (Hurt, 2012).

THE LEAST RESTRICTIVE ENVIRONMENT CONTINUUM

When making LRE decisions, the IEP team should consider the general education classroom environment and discuss how the student's goals can be met and how services would be provided in that environment. The goal is to keep students with disabilities involved with their typically developing peers as much as possible. When considering students with disabilities who are ELLs, the IEP team needs to be cognizant that addressing language proficiency typically falls under the purview of general education, whereas the disability is typically addressed through special education. Because legislative and litigation mandates require that ELLs not be excluded from participation in school activities, their language needs are addressed in one or more of the following programs:

- Bilingual special education

- Bilingual education

- English as a second language (ESL) instruction

ELLs are typically served in ESL pull-out programs because there is a shortage of bilingual special education and bilingual education teachers. The IEP team needs to be aware that special education teachers do not have the same training or qualifications as ESL and bilingual teachers to address language proficiency. Therefore, coordinated services in the LRE is needed to address the student's disability and language proficiency needs.

　　If a team has determined that the level of support needed is so significant that it would detract from the student's learning or the learning of others in a general education classroom, then more restrictive settings can be considered. Otherwise, the student would receive those services in the general education environment (see Figure 8.1).

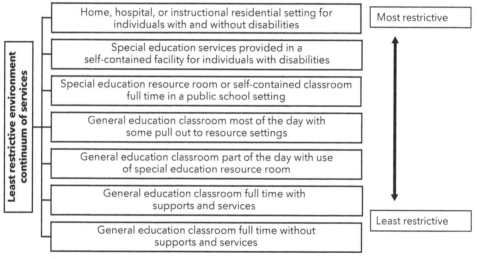

Figure 8.1.　Least restrictive environment continuum of services.

LEAST RESTRICTIVE ENVIRONMENT TECHNOLOGY SUPPORTS

The use of technology is one support that can make a significant difference in the student's independence and ability to participate more fully in the general education curriculum with minimal staffing supports. Technology can be used to support academic areas of deficit, such as an online reader for text above a student's ability level or a graphing calculator and virtual manipulatives for equations above a student's ability level.

　　In addition, teachers can use screencasting technologies—many of which are available for free—to record critical content, learning expectations, vocabulary, examples of solved problems, and more for students to access multiple times throughout their learning day. Although students often have limited face-to-face instructional time with special education teachers, they can increase their learning time exponentially using technology and recorded instruction.

Technologies can also be used as behavioral supports—from online scheduling and calendars that send students reminders of upcoming deadlines and required materials, which are very useful for students with attention-deficit/hyperactivity disorder and/or who struggle with limited working memory, to mindfulness and growth mindset videos and apps that can support calming needs for students with a background of trauma, autism, or acting-out behaviors.

There are a wide array of communication technologies and applications such as Proloquo2go and Speak for Yourself that allow students with autism, apraxia, and other communication disorders to communicate their wants, needs, and thoughts independently or with less adult support. Technologies can also be used for students learning English through translator apps and picture dictionaries.

Some key questions that the IEP team can consider when deciding on the type of assistive technology include the following:

What technology support(s) . . .

- Does the student need in order to acquire or attain needed skills to participate in grade- or age-appropriate learning activities?

- Would allow the student to communicate their thoughts, wants, and needs?

- Would allow the student to search for key vocabulary or find alternate words in their home language?

- Would allow the student to self-calm or request help without disturbing instruction (e.g., sending an e-mail to the school counselor, nurse, or special education teacher)?

- Would read text above ability level or type student thoughts for writing above ability level?

- Would provide recorded instruction to help the student break down or understand a key concept?

INCLUDING A LEAST RESTRICTIVE ENVIRONMENT STATEMENT ON THE IEP

The conversation surrounding LRE should always follow along the continuum in Figure 8.1, beginning with the general education environment and curriculum. If the team does not feel that the services needed for the student to make progress toward their goals can be provided in the general education environment, then alternatives can be discussed. When decisions are made to remove the student with a disability from the general education environment, however, a statement is required to be added to the IEP, describing the extent of that student's exclusion from the general education setting.

The purpose of IDEA was to support an equitable value system for public education. Beginning the LRE conversation in the general education setting, and requiring IEP teams to justify when students will not be included in the general education class, is how inclusive practices are supported through LRE. This process can support change in our beliefs, dispositions, and eventual practices as we demonstrate a philosophy of inclusion versus exclusion in our schools.

INCLUSION VERSUS MAINSTREAMING

Although popular in special education circles, the terms "mainstreaming" and "inclusion" are not found in IDEA. In fact, these terms were coined by educators in an attempt to interpret the law. Although the two terms are often used interchangeably, each represents very different philosophical paradigms, often leading to radically divergent decisions concerning a student's LRE. Knowing the difference between these two terms is tantamount to participation in the LRE decision-making process.

Mainstreaming is the selective placement of students with disabilities in one or more general education class(es). Mainstreaming is an older model that was first implemented when students began to be included in general education classrooms.

Under this philosophical framework, students earn the right to participate in general education classrooms when it is perceived that they need minimal support to engage in instruction in that setting (Rogers, 2006). The courses students are admitted to typically include nonacademic courses, such as lunch, recess, homeroom, study hall, life skill courses (e.g., consumer science, computer basics, word processing, wood shop classes); classes not considered to be core content, such as music, art, and physical education; and courses considered unrelated to the learner's disability, such as social studies and science.

The premise behind these decisions is that the student does not have a disability in these various subjects; therefore, they can participate with minimal support. For example, a student with a learning disability that negatively affects their written language skills does not have a disability in social studies. Therefore, under a mainstreaming philosophy, the IEP team determines the student needs resource room support for language arts but can negotiate the rigors of a social studies classroom. The flaw in this thinking, however, is that written language skills are also needed when learning social studies. Students write reports, complete essay tests, create posters and computerized presentations, and/or take lecture notes in social studies, all requiring a level of competence in writing.

Assuming that a student does not use these skills in courses considered nonacademic devalues the rigor present in these courses. Not only might students be required to write in these courses, but the student's cognitive processing difference that negatively affects their ability to write might also have a negative impact on the student's ability to draw, create multidimensional images, coordinate their body movements, or copy musical notes on a scale.

Unfortunately, this model still occurs for some students with more severe disabilities. The severity of a student's disability plays a role in the decision-making process for LRE when the team is operating under a mainstreaming philosophy. Involvement in a general education class is rarely considered appropriate for students with severe difficulties, unless it is a nonacademic course.

Inclusion refers to a commitment to educate each child in the school and classroom they would otherwise attend if they did not have a disability. Services and supports are brought to the student in the general education classroom, and inclusion requires only that there is an identified benefit for the student to participate in the general education classroom (Rogers, 2006). Instead of focusing on labels, the team examines the goals, objectives (if appropriate), and services and determines the most naturally occurring opportunities during which the goal can be addressed and services provided. If the goal is for the student to initiate an interaction with a peer in an unstructured or informal setting, then the LRE might be during lunch, study hall, or recess. Or perhaps the LRE would be during lab work in biology or in drama class. The team determines which environment is most conducive to instruction in the desired skill and provides supports in that environment. Knowing the potential learning environments is critical when making decisions concerning a student's LRE. This is one of the reasons having general education teachers present at IEP meetings is so essential.

The difference between mainstreaming and inclusion is less about where a student's desk is situated and more about the reasons that underlie the decisions determining the appropriate educational environment for each student. To determine whether or not a teacher, grade-level team, school, or district operate from a mainstreaming or inclusive philosophy, one must eavesdrop on the conversations IEP teams have during the LRE discussion of an IEP meeting. The mathematics teacher who says, "Amy can't be in my class because she is still working on number recognition and number value," is operating from a mainstreaming perspective. Yet, the mathematics teacher who suggests, "Perhaps when I assign algebraic equations for students to compute, Amy could find and circle all of the 3s on the worksheet," is designing instruction based on an inclusive perspective.

Benefits Versus Labels

Decisions involving students in the general education classroom are often based on labels in a mainstreaming philosophy. For example, if a student has a learning disability in written expression, then the IEP team might determine a science class to be an appropriate environment to include the student, disregarding the possibility that students may be asked to write in science. The team is focusing on the specific multifactored evaluation criteria for special education eligibility instead of how the student might benefit from being involved in the general education curriculum and/or classroom environment.

Educators who have an inclusive stance are more compelled to first consider what benefit there might be for the student to be included, whether it be an academic, behavioral, or social benefit. Labels have no place in the discussion, with, instead, the discussion focusing on the student's learning characteristics, strengths, and interests instead of disability label. Although the verbiage of the law falls short of mentioning either mainstreaming or inclusion, it can be inferred that inclusion is at the heart of the LRE mandates, with the focus on bringing services and supports to students with disabilities in the general education classroom whenever possible (Kilanowski-Press et al., 2010). Figure 8.2 provides a checklist of suggestions on how to prepare for the IEP meeting.

Stop and Think!

The No Child Left Behind Act of 2001 (PL 107-110) and Every Student Succeeds Act of 2015 (PL 114-95) require that all school districts maintain the same high standards of academic achievement for all children, including students with limited English proficiency, students with disabilities, those considered to have an economic disadvantage, and students who represent minoritized racial and ethnic groups (Part A, subparagraph [C][v]).

- How might this requirement have an impact on an IEP team's decision concerning a student's LRE?

- Discuss with a colleague how you might approach a situation in which you think that the proposed placement for a student does not adhere to the spirit or letter of the law regarding the LRE. How would you bring this to the attention of the group? What barriers might you face, and what supports might you need in order to move the group forward to help the student?

SUMMARY

This chapter detailed the important role that IEP teams hold in ensuring that students with disabilities are afforded the opportunity to receive their instruction and intervention in the LRE.

Because special education is a service and not a placement, *LRE* refers to the setting in which instruction and intervention will occur in order for a student with a disability to benefit from their education. IDEA 2004 safeguards an inclusive setting by stating that students with disabilities are to be educated with peers without disabilities to the "maximum extent appropriate" (§ 300.114[a]). The IEP team is charged with protecting a student's LRE by explicitly documenting the percentage of time that a student is removed from a general education setting and the rationale as to how the disability affects the student from participating with peers without disabilities in general education settings. Determining instruction and intervention in the LRE is a process and a procedure that requires careful consideration, including the continuum of placements from least to most restrictive and ethical and legal ramifications.

PREPARATION FOR THE IEP MEETING:
LEAST RESTRICTIVE ENVIRONMENT

Prior to the Meeting

☐ Review progress monitoring data to determine if student is making sufficient progress toward meeting IEP goals. Adjust instruction as needed.

☐ Determine if the delivery of instruction alongside peers without disabilities was effective in meeting the annual IEP goal and corresponding short-term objectives. If not, determine what supplementary aids, services, and supports are needed so student is included in the general education environment to the maximum extent appropriate.

☐ For students from culturally and linguistically diverse (CLD) backgrounds, review language proficiency progress monitoring data and opportunities for language development and interaction with peers from similar cultural and language experience.

During the Meeting

☐ Consider and discuss the continuum of services to determine appropriate delivery of services.

☐ Include statement of proposed placement and explanation as to why the placement was proposed.

☐ Include quality English language development into instructional delivery for English language learners.

☐ For students who are CLD, incorporate interactions with peers from similar cultural and language experiences.

☐ Check that classroom materials reflect the culture of the student.

☐ If using an interpreter, be sure to use appropriate interpreter etiquette (see Chapter 2).

After the Meeting

☐ Debrief with all team members, including parents, about the effectiveness of the meeting.

☐ Check with parents on the use of an interpreter and if they understood the meeting and key takeaways.

Figure 8.2. Preparation for the IEP meeting: Least restrictive environment.

THE IEP CHECKLIST: LEAST RESTRICTIVE ENVIRONMENT

The following checklist can be used as an inventory to ensure that the LRE section of the IEP meets IDEA regulations.

Key Area (IEP section): **Least Restrictive Environment (LRE)**	Criteria met	
	Yes	No
L1: A statement is included that students have access to the general curriculum.		
L2: A statement is included that explains and provides the rationale for why a child is not participating in the general education curriculum.		

ACTIVITIES

The activities included in this chapter are intended for the reader to gain a deeper understanding of the content covered. For this chapter, each activity builds on the skills of the previous activity. The activities associated with this chapter include the following:

• Activity 8.1. Least Restrictive Environment Case Study Decision

• Activity 8.2. Identification of a Quality Least Restrictive Environment Section

• Activity 8.3. Culturally Responsive Environment Inventory

Activity 8.1.

Least Restrictive Environment Case Study Decision

Supporting chapter: Chapter 8 (Least Restrictive Environment)

Purpose: The purpose of this activity is to engage the learner in considering the least restrictive environment (LRE).

Directions: After reading the following case study, consider the questions at the end, and discuss your response with a peer.

Alvarro is a fourth-grade student who is a gifted singer but struggles with reading fluency and reading comprehension due to a specific learning disability in reading. During reading instruction, while the other fourth-grade students are studying Greek gods and the mythology surrounding them, Alvarro leaves the general education classroom and goes to the special education resource room to receive intense reading interventions. In the resource setting, Alvarro works on a computer program to review phonemes and morphemes. Then he joins a reading group comprised of other students who have low reading ability, where he takes turns reading aloud and discussing the vocabulary related to the story. Currently, the students are reading a third-grade level book about kids in the future.

Discussion Questions

1. Consider the case of James in the Challenge Scenario in this chapter. How is Alvarro's educational placement different from James's?

_____

_____

_____

_____

_____

2. What was the LRE decision based on in Alvarro's situation?

_____

_____

_____

_____

_____

3. How might Alvarro have been included in the general education classroom and still receive support for improving his reading fluency and comprehension?

_____

_____

_____

_____

_____

Activity 8.2.

Identification of a Quality Least Restrictive Environment Section

Supporting chapter: Chapter 8 (Least Restrictive Environment)

Purpose: The purpose of this activity is to develop the skill of writing statements that reflect the least restrictive environment (LRE).

Directions: Use an IEP to inventory the LRE section and indicate the quality of the information provided. Then, rank the section and provide evidence to support your ranking.

Rubric scale: Use the following scale and circle the number that best ranks the IEP area reviewed in the table that follows.

1 = Standard not met	2 = Standard partially met	3 = Standard met	4 = Standard exceeds
• IEP fails to provide evidence of meeting the IDEA 2004 requirements. • IEP does not address the IDEA 2004 requirements.	• Performance provides evidence of partially meeting IDEA 2004 requirements. • Performance addresses some of the IDEA 2004 requirements.	• Performance provides evidence of meeting most/all of the IDEA 2004 requirements. • Performance addresses most/all of the IDEA 2004 requirements.	• Performance provides evidence of exceeding all IDEA 2004 requirements. • All indicators are addressed in the IEP and go beyond expectations.

Key Area (IEP Section): Least Restrictive Environment	Ranking	Rationale for Ranking
L1: A statement is included that students have **access** to the general curriculum.	1 2 3 4	
L2: A statement is included that explains and provides the rationale for **why a child is not participating** in the general education curriculum.	1 2 3 4	

Rewritten LRE statement:

_____

_____

_____

_____

_____

Activity 8.3.

Culturally Responsive Environment Inventory

Supporting chapter: Chapter 8 (Least Restrictive Environment)

Purpose: This activity affords an opportunity to focus on the least restrictive environment (LRE) that supports students with disabilities who come from culturally and linguistically diverse (CLD) backgrounds.

Directions: There are three parts to this activity. First, identify a student with a disability who comes from a CLD background. Use the following checklist to survey the school and classroom environment, materials, and interactions that the student engages in on a daily basis. Finally, consider any adjustments needed to ensure culturally and linguistically responsive instruction in the LRE.

Criteria	Yes/No	Adjustments to confirm culturally and linguistically responsive instruction in LRE
1. Does the school display items (e.g., bulletin boards, posters, signs) or images that reflect the same culture and home language as the student?		
2. Are school assemblies and other large-group gatherings responsive to the culture and home language of the student?		
3. Are the parents or caregivers of the child involved in school activities?		
4. Does the school provide written communication (e.g., website, policies, newsletters) in the home language of the student?		
5. Does the school and classroom library include books and perspectives that reflect the culture and home language of the student?		
6. Do the environments in which the student participates (i.e., general and special education classrooms) display items (e.g., bulletin boards, posters, signs) that reflect the culture and home language of the student?		
7. Do textbooks and other school materials include images and information that reflect the culture and home language of the student?		
8. Do textbooks and other teaching materials provide a perspective that includes other cultures, including that of the student?		

Criteria	Yes/No	Adjustments to confirm culturally and linguistically responsive instruction in LRE
9. Do the teaching staff and service providers deliver instruction and/or therapy in a culturally and linguistically responsive manner?		
10. Does the student have opportunities to interact with peers without disabilities who come from the same cultural and linguistic background as the student?		
11. For an English language learner, does the student participate in bilingual and/or English as a second language programs?		

Accommodations and Modifications to Meet the Needs of the Learner

Kathleen G. Winterman

After reading this chapter and engaging in activities related to this chapter, you will be able to meet the following outcomes:

- Address the differences between accommodations and modifications.

- Construct meaningful accommodations and modifications to a student's work.

- Discuss meaningful ways to support inclusive education.

Differentiated curriculum is designed to meet the needs of all children; however, this can be confusing when a student has a disability and needs an individualized education. Adaptations to the curriculum are required for some students with disabilities. An **adaptation** is an overarching term that incorporates both accommodations and modifications (Prater, 2018). One component of IEPs that has often been misinterpreted is how decisions related to state and district test accommodations are made and how this applies to the classroom setting. Teachers often hear the word "accommodations," but what does this actually mean? Many people truly do not have a good understanding of the differences between an accommodation and a **modification.** Therefore, these terms are often confused and interchanged, which is a mistake that changes the dynamics of the learning situation. Before beginning the discussion on the accommodation process, it is important to first clarify the differences between accommodations and modifications.

With accommodations, there are no changes to the learning content. An accommodation simply allows a student with disabilities to meet the same standard of learning as their peers but through a different avenue, such as providing an oral response instead of a written response. Other widely used accommodations include providing extended time, allowing preferential seating, providing a copy of the class notes, and so forth. These adaptations allow students to work around their disability.

A modification, however, requires an actual change in the content of what the student is learning and is used when accommodations alone are not sufficient to support the student. An example of this would be a scenario in which a second-grade class is working on beginning multiplication while a child with a disability is still learning addition. In this situation, the curriculum has been modified, meaning the content has been changed to meet the learner's needs. The critical concept behind accommodations and modifications is that children with disabilities receive the supports necessary to be successful in school (Searle & Swartz, 2020).

IDEA'S KEY COMPONENTS

- **Free appropriate public education (FAPE).** Requires that the student be educated in a manner that meets their educational needs by a public educational agency that is free to the family.
  - *Zero Reject.* Mandates that the school cannot deny a child an education due to the severity of their needs.
- **Least restrictive environment (LRE).** The student is educated in a manner that is most like their typical peers.
- **Procedural safeguards** (due process). The family has the right to disagree with the placement, services, and educational plan for their child and can bring the school district to court.
- **Parental participation** (shared decision making). Parents have the right to participate as part of the education team for their child.
- **Nondiscriminatory evaluation.** Requires schools to utilize a team approach in assessing a student in all suspected areas of a disability using measures that are valid, reliable, culturally relevant, and linguistically appropriate.
- **Individualized education program (IEP).** The IEP team assesses current evaluation information and develops a written document designed to meet the unique educational needs of each student with a disability.

CONNECTION TO LEGAL PERSPECTIVE

The supports necessary for students with disabilities to be successful in school often require specially designed instruction that includes accommodations and/or modifications. The Individuals with Disabilities Education Improvement Act (IDEA) of 2004 (PL 108-446) defined *specially designed instruction* as

> (3) . . . adapting, as appropriate to the needs of an eligible child under this part, the content, methodology, or delivery of instruction—
> (i) To address the unique needs of the child that result from the child's disability; and
> (ii) To ensure access of the child to the general curriculum, so that the child can meet the educational standards within the jurisdiction of the public agency that apply to all children. (§ 300.39[b][3])

Therefore, specialized instruction requires adapting curriculum, content, and instructional delivery. Adaptations may come in the form of an accommodation or a modification based on the student's goals and objectives. Examples of adjustments that can be made to a student's learning program include

- *Size:* the number of items the student is expected to learn/complete
- *Time:* the duration of time allotted to the student for learning, task completion, or testing
- *Level of support:* the type of support the student receives (e.g., peer assistance, teacher assistance, group assistance)
- *Input:* the way instruction is delivered to the student
- *Output:* how the student responds to instruction
- *Difficulty:* the degree of difficulty for student work (e.g., skill level, problem type, format)
- *Participation:* the way in which the student is expected to participate (e.g., individual participation, group participation, active listening, physical presence)
- *Alternate goals:* changing the student's goals to meet their abilities (e.g., locating states on a map versus memorizing state capitals)
- *Substitute curriculum:* providing different instruction and materials to meet the student's individual goals

Although the student's academic and functional needs drive the adaptations needed to gain access to the general education curriculum, they do not alter the content standards.

As inclusion of students with disabilities within the general classroom increases, so do the necessary accommodations needed to ensure that these students meet the mandated state content standards, which has resulted in more students participating in high-stakes testing as mandated by the Every Student Succeeds Act (ESSA) of 2015 (114-95), No Child Left Behind (NCLB) Act of 2001, and IDEA. Meeting these individual needs in a manner that enables a student with disabilities to successfully participate in the general education curriculum while still producing viable educational results as demonstrated by high-stakes testing becomes the challenge facing IEP teams. Salend (2008) noted, "Recognizing that many students with disabilities need accommodations in order to participate in high-stakes assessments, IDEA requires that students' individualized education programs (IEPs) delineate testing accommodations for state, district, and teacher-made tests" (p. 14).

Universal design for learning (UDL) is a framework to guide the design of learning environments and instruction that are accessible and challenging for all students (Center for Applied Special Technology [CAST], 2018).

Incorporating the principles of universal design for learning (UDL) into the testing process creates a means for testing materials to meet the needs of a variety of learners (CAST, 2018); yet, these principles must be applied to the student's everyday learning to become an effective means of education. Once the IEP team has determined the student's academic needs, the necessary strategies may be employed throughout the student's day, offering glimpses of success and hope for improved learning for the student. Without fidelity of implementation, teachers, parents, and students are left with the uncertainty of not knowing which strategies are effective and which require revision.

A legal requirement of IDEA is that all students participate in academic assessments to determine their growth and benefit from educational endeavors, which lays the foundation in which students' learning is determined and measured. To understand the legal ramifications of this section of the IEP, it is helpful to know exactly what IDEA states. The verbatim requirement for this component from IDEA (at § 612[a][16]) states that students with disabilities are included in all general, state, and local testing programs.

(A) In general. All children with disabilities are included in all general State and district-wide assessment programs, including assessments described under section 1111 of the Elementary and Secondary Education Act [ESEA] of 1965, with appropriate accommodations and alternate assessments where necessary and as indicated in their respective individualized education programs.

   (i) A statement of any individual appropriate accommodations that are necessary to measure the academic achievement and functional performance of the child on State and district-wide assessments consistent with section 612(a)(16) of the Act; and

(6)

   (ii) If the IEP Team determines that the child must take an alternate assessment instead of a particular regular State or districtwide assessment of student achievement, a statement of why—
     (A) The child cannot participate in the regular assessment; and
     (B) The particular alternate assessment selected is appropriate for the child; and

(7) The projected date for the beginning of the services and modifications described in paragraph (a)(4) of this section, and the anticipated frequency, location, and duration of those services and modifications.

   (x) To support the development and provision of appropriate accommodations for Children with disabilities, or the development and provision of alternate assessments that are valid and reliable for assessing the performance of children with disabilities, in accordance with sections 1111(b) and 6111 of the ESEA. (§ 300.704)

The law clearly states that accommodations for children with disabilities shall be incorporated to provide for valid and reliable assessment of the student's educational performance in accordance with the Elementary and Secondary Education Act of 1965 (PL 89-10). The importance of this mandate cannot be overstated. Its pertinence is so relevant to the child's welfare that the decree is mentioned in numerous locations within the legislation and is restated in NCLB and ESSA as well as the *Endrew F. v. Douglas County School District* case. In the following Challenge Scenario, core issues of equity are discussed and examined through the lens of meeting the needs of every learner.

Challenge Scenario

Mrs. Dugan, a fourth-grade teacher, overhears a few students who are talking outside her classroom door. The students are discussing whether or not it is fair for Jimmy to get extra time to take the math test. If he can have the extra time, then why can't they? As an experienced teacher, she does not approach the students to discuss the issue; instead, she waits for the teachable moment in which the class can have a discussion about meeting the needs of all students. The next day, during the morning class meeting, the teacher begins a discussion about fairness and what that means to different students. Mrs. Dugan tells a story about a mother who had seven children, all of whom had different needs. But because the mother did not want to be unfair to any of her children, all of them had to take tap dancing, all of them had to participate on the swim team, all of them had to use an inhaler for asthma, all of them had to wear glasses, all of them had to watch basketball, and none of them could read nonfiction. By the end of the story, the students were laughing by the absurdity of the story.

It was at this point that Mrs. Dugan truly began the discussion of fairness and meeting the needs of all students or being fair to everyone and not just the majority. As an example, Mrs. Dugan asked her class to think about how a student who broke his arm during a basketball game might need extra help during the school day. These supports and services are provided to meet the learning needs of the students. The same supports are offered if a student has an educational necessity for accommodations based on a documented disability. Mrs. Dugan shared that an example of this could be extended time on a test, but there are many other things that a teacher could do to assist their students. The students began to understand the meaning of fairness—meeting the needs of every student—and appeared to have a sense of relief with the knowledge that their teacher would do the same to meet their educational needs.

ACCOMMODATIONS

Accommodations can be offered to any student and not just students with a 504 plan or an IEP. Accommodations are a means of changing the learning environment and not the content to be learned. For example, a student might be given an untimed test when others must complete the test within a certain time frame, such as a timed addition test in first or second grade. This example would be a means of supporting a student with a processing issue or a writing issue such as dysgraphia. The same adaptation could be made for a student who has an injured arm with no need for a written plan. A different way to accommodate for the same needs could be to offer the student an option of orally responding to the assessment. Specific strategies to determine the best accommodation for the student are listed next.

> ### Stop and Think!
> The kind of open discussion Mrs. Dugan has with students in the Challenge Scenario reveals the students' misconceptions about the socially constructed nature of disability. Its focus on how the nature of the academic task and the skills of the individual intersect to create a need help to demonstrate that the accommodation is not simply one of convenience but of true necessity. Review what fairness meant when you were in school. Do you still agree with your child-like perspective? Why or why not?

Determining Accommodations

When deciding the services needed, the team should be mindful of the federal and state regulations and if the accommodations adhere to these standards. The frequency, location, and duration of services all need to be considered when determining the accommodations. Examples of this might include how often an accommodation will take place and if it is going to be implemented in all classes or only in certain subjects. Discussions of location might include if the student will be provided this accommodation in the general education classroom or within a resource room. In addition, the IEP team must discuss who is implementing the accommodation and how the fidelity of its implementation will be assured and monitored.

Types of Accommodations

Accommodations generally fall into three categories: content, process, and product.

Content   Content accommodations involve what the student will learn. The student has the same academic goal as their peers, but the teacher varies how the content is taught. Variations can include adjusting the assignments by providing a study guide or rubric, changing the levels of support (e.g., offering a word bank), or changing how the student will report the information back to the teacher. For example, if a student with a specific learning disability in the area of dyscalculia has difficulty with mathematics computation, then concrete objects or manipulatives are used as an accommodation when new concepts are introduced.

Process   Process accommodations offer students access to the same academic content but provide the possibility to change how they are exposed to it. Variations can include allowing the student to complete parts of a project with a peer or teacher's support, using the spell check feature on a computer to check their work, or listening to an audiobook to complete a reading assignment (Zascavage & Winterman, 2009). Some of the easiest accommodations to employ are centered on time adjustments, such as allowing multiple breaks, setting a time limit for the amount of work a student needs to complete within the given time, and giving untimed tests. The extensive array of electronic supports available to students should not be ruled out. The IEP team needs to examine the intent of learning activities to determine how to accomplish these learning tasks. By changing the learning process, students are able to demonstrate their knowledge without assessing their disability. For example, if a student is allowed to access an online textbook that reads the book to the student, then the impact of having a specific disability in the area of dyslexia that affects reading is eliminated.

Product   Product accommodations allow teachers to adjust student output. Variations can include reducing the number of problems the student needs to complete or breaking large assignments into smaller subsections for the student, as well as allowing the student to complete sections of an assignment with a partner. Additional product accommodations include allowing a student to complete an assignment or assessment by using speech-to-text software, using a scribe to dictate responses to a problem, or completing written assignments on a computer. For example, a student with a specific learning disability in the area of dysgraphia is provided with a digital recorder as an accommodation to orally dictate responses to written questions.

Special Considerations for Testing Accommodations

The dilemma IEP teams encounter in providing accommodations for a student with a disability is how to assess the student's knowledge of the content without inherently assessing their disability and the affect it has on the student's means of sharing their knowledge. According to Prater (2018), instead of assuming that the student will require testing accommodations, the IEP team must look at the student's strengths and academic needs to determine the provisions required to facilitate the student's testing protocol. To address this challenge, IEP teams must look beyond the testing accommodations to see how these supports bolster the student's instruction on a daily basis (Searle & Swartz, 2020). If these same strategies are not institutionalized as a viable part of the student's educational program, then they will offer little support when testing occurs. Therefore, consistent implementation of accommodations is necessary for the student to benefit from their use during testing situations. The student's educational plan, including academic and testing accommodations, should parallel the educational plan that is in effect on a daily basis. During the IEP meeting, the team determines the necessary accommodations so that accurate measurements of academic achievement and functional performance can be obtained.

MODIFICATIONS

When accommodations are not sufficient, instructional modifications become necessary to adjust the level of difficulty of the learning content. Assignments or tests must be reduced or altered, requiring fewer objectives to be mastered or only parts of an objective. As discussed in Chapter 6, students who require modifications to the curriculum often participate in alternate assessments instead of the traditional state and district testing protocols. The IEP team needs to determine the frequency of the modifications, including which content areas need to be included and the location in which these services should take place. The IEP team must also ask if the student should receive all of their services within the general education classroom or if the least restrictive environment (LRE) is elsewhere (see Chapter 8). The IEP team also needs to establish the duration of the services required to meet the student's learning goals and objectives. These modifications can be reviewed on a predetermined schedule, as decided by the IEP team, and may be short in duration or remain in place for the entire school year.

Alternate Assessments

According to IDEA, some students require such significant curriculum modifications that they are precluded from participating in standardized testing. The number of students eligible to participate in alternate assessment is capped at 1%

of the testing population for both state and local educational agencies. IDEA mandates that

> A student eligible to participate in an alternate assessment based on modified academic achievement standards must be a student with a disability under section 602(3) of the Individuals with Disabilities Education Act (IDEA), and may be in any of the disability categories listed in the IDEA. A student's individualized education program (IEP) team (IEP Team), which includes the student's parent, determines how the student will participate in State and district-wide assessments. If a State chooses to develop modified academic achievement standards, the State must establish clear and appropriate criteria for IEP Teams to apply in determining whether a student should be assessed based on modified academic achievement standards in one or more subjects. These criteria must include, but are not limited to, the following:
>
> 1. There must be objective evidence demonstrating that the student's disability has precluded the student from achieving grade-level proficiency. Such evidence may include the student's performance on State assessments or other assessments that can validly document academic achievement.
>
> 2. The student's progress to date in response to appropriate instruction, including special education and related services designed to address the student's individual needs, is such that, even if significant growth occurs, the IEP Team is reasonably certain that the student will not achieve grade-level proficiency within the year covered by the student's IEP. The IEP Team must use multiple valid measures of the student's progress over time in making this determination.
>
> 3. The student's IEP must include goals that are based on grade-level academic content standards. It is a State's responsibility to establish and monitor implementation of clear and appropriate guidelines for IEP Teams to use when deciding if an alternate assessment based on modified academic achievement standards is appropriate for an individual student. These guidelines should provide parameters and direction to ensure that students are not assessed based on modified academic achievement standards merely because of their disability category or their racial or economic background or the lack of appropriate instruction. (U.S. Department of Education, 2007)

The original goal of alternate assessments was to establish a means of assessing students who have been considered "untestable" in the past. Although the new practices pursue and promise alternatives to tests, labeling a specific practice as an alternative is not a guarantee of meaningful departure from existing practice (Tan, 2013). According to ESSA, all students with disabilities must participate in the annual standardized assessments through the grade level that they are enrolled in or through the Alternate Academic Achievement Standards (AA-AAAS). Those students who participate in general grade-level assessments are to be provided with the appropriate accommodation necessary to ensure that the grade-level measure assess the student's academic achievement. Only those students with the most significant disabilities may participate in AA-AAAS, which ESSA capped at 1% for all students tested. States that may exceed the 1% cap may apply for a waiver for 1 year (U.S. Department of Education, 2016a).

EFFECTIVE INCLUSIVE PRACTICES

Although inclusion may look different in every region, district, school, and classroom, there are certain best practices that effectively support an inclusive classroom that might reduce the need for accommodations or modifications of a student's curriculum. Two of those best practices are briefly presented in this section and include **response to intervention (RTI)** and **UDL**.

Response to Intervention

RTI is a type of multi-tiered systems of support (MTSS). Although it can be used for special education purposes (e.g., determining a specific learning disability), it is designed to provide early intervention and support for all learners. RTI or any MTSS is based on effective teacher instruction using research-validated strategies and curriculum in the general education classroom. The students are monitored on specific skills using frequent curriculum-based assessments. The results of these assessments are then used to guide instruction. RTI is data-driven instruction using a curriculum and instructional methodology that is proven to be effective to increase student learning.

RTI is typically based on a three-tier framework with increasing support or interventions for students who are not making satisfactory academic or behavioral progress. It begins with a universal screening, an assessment in core curriculum or behavioral areas, that identifies students who may need additional support. These students are then progress-monitored based on the specific skills in which they are having difficulties. These students are closely monitored in the areas of need during Tier One instruction. In Tier One, students receive effective instruction in the general education classroom using a research-validated curriculum and methodology. Students are assessed on the curriculum regularly and progress is monitored. Adjustments are made to instruction based on those assessment results to provide additional support to those students who need it. Tier One, and all tiers, also include a fidelity check or an observation of the teacher to ensure that effective instruction is being provided in the way it is designed and validated. It is vitally important that general educators have a depth of knowledge and provide culturally responsive, evidence-based instruction for students who come from culturally and linguistically diverse (CLD) backgrounds. Educators' lack of understanding the instructional needs of students who are CLD often leads to inappropriate referrals and/or ineffective instruction. Furthermore, meeting the needs of students from CLD backgrounds through English as a second language or bilingual education is a general education function (not a special education need); therefore, it is important that Tier One instruction should be provided to all children.

Fidelity of instruction becomes critical for students from culturally and linguistically diverse (CLD) backgrounds to ensure that culturally and linguistically responsive instruction is provided to the student on a consistent basis. This lack of instruction or fidelity in instructional practices often causes academic challenges for the CLD population rather than supporting their learning. It is important that data is gathered to help distinguish between a student's developing English proficiency versus a true underlying disability.

The students whose assessment results indicate a lack of progress in Tier One are moved to Tier Two and provided more intensive interventions targeted to the specific areas of need. This can mean that the student receives any combination of more instruction, smaller group instruction, or different instruction. This more intensive intervention is typically still provided within the general education classroom. Fidelity checks are administered to ensure validity of instruction.

Progress continues to be monitored and instructional decisions are made based on the assessment results. Students who continue to struggle typically either go through a second round of Tier Two instruction or are referred to Tier Three intervention. Tier Three typically includes a referral for special education services. The assessment results from the RTI process can be used to help determine eligibility for special education either independently or in conjunction with standardized, norm-referenced assessments. Schools need to be cautious when determining if lack of progress is a result of a possible underlying disability and not a result of inadequate instruction, poor culturally responsive instruction, and/or a lack of understanding the typical developmental process of acquiring a second language.

RTI has the potential to benefit the school system in many ways. The emphasis on effective instruction and tiers of support allows for appropriate instruction for all learners. Teachers have the opportunity to challenge students at the students' rate of learning. There is shared responsibility between general and special educators and increased accountability for all student learning. RTI allows for earlier intervention when difficulties arise due to the data-driven nature of instruction. RTI has the potential to increase the learning of all students, including those with disabilities, when done effectively and correctly.

Universal Design for Learning

UDL is a way to design instruction in ways that fully engage all learners. UDL is an instructional framework based on the concept that everyone learns differently. UDL offers guidelines to increase students' access to learning through varying means of engagement, representation of their knowledge, and multiple ways to demonstrate that knowledge. The classroom, instructional process, materials, and assessments are designed to facilitate greater learning for all students, including typically developing students, those that have disabilities, and English language learners (ELLs), as well as those who are gifted. ESSA also used UDL as a framework to urge educators to remove barriers in the curriculum for all students (Section 4104). UDL was developed by researchers at CAST as a way to remove barriers to learning and meet the needs of the greatest number of students by allowing them to learn and demonstrate their knowledge through a variety of learning styles or preferences (visual, auditory, kinesthetic, and tactile). Visit the CAST web site for a brief overview of UDL (www.cast.org).

UDL is based on the three main principles of Multiple Means of Representation, Multiple Means of Action and Expression, and Multiple Means of Engagement. Multiple Means of Representation requires that information be presented by the teacher or in a lesson in multiple formats and allows for alternative ways for students to gain access to the information. It incorporates methods of activating background knowledge and providing the required vocabulary and information needed for comprehension before the start of the lesson.

For students with disabilities as well as English language learners, the concept of multiple means of representation supports the importance of comprehensible instruction, which means tapping into a student's background knowledge (i.e., funds of knowledge) and providing supports (e.g., visual and/or audio such as peer readers, audio books, text to speech).

Multiple Means of Action and Expression allows the students to show their knowledge or demonstrate their learning in a variety of ways. These provide students options for the way in which they respond to a question or prompt (e.g., typing, handwriting) and allow options on the method in which an assignment is completed (e.g., essay, project, presentation). Multiple Means of Engagement is designed to better stimulate students' interest and motivation in the learning activity. It increases the relevance and authenticity of an activity (e.g., using money to teach math, culturally responsive pedagogy) and allows for greater peer collaboration and communication.

All students have individual needs, strengths, and interests. The benefit of UDL is that it allows for more flexibility within the curriculum design and teaching process, which then allows students to gain access to the information in ways they learn best. UDL allows students to be challenged and enriched based on individual needs and learning preferences.

Visit the CAST web site for more information on UDL (www.cast.org). View the UDL Guidelines–Educator Worksheet (https://udlguidelines.cast.org/?utm_source=castsite&utm_medium=web&utm_campaign=none&utm_content=footer) and corresponding video for more information on the three main principles of UDL.

SUMMARY

This chapter discussed the accommodation process for students with disabilities. Once the IEP team determines the necessary accommodations and modifications a student requires, these strategies are then put in place. For students to be successful with the classroom and testing settings, IEP teams need to be cognizant of students' strengths and weaknesses and develop a system of services that will meet their learning needs. For some students, this means establishing a series of accommodations to allow that student to participate in the same curricular content as their same-age peers. For other students, modifications or curricular changes need to be determined. These accommodations and/or modifications need to be implemented consistently so that the IEP team can assess their effectiveness. After faithful implementation, the team can evaluate the student's success as well as their own. Students can only achieve within the classroom and testing situation when all members of their IEP team actively participate in the ongoing dialogue to determine how best to meet the students' academic needs. Figure 9.1 provides a checklist of suggestions on how to prepare for the IEP meeting.

PREPARATION FOR THE IEP MEETING:
ACCOMMODATIONS AND MODIFICATIONS

Prior to the Meeting

- [ ] Identify student's current academic strengths and needs.
- [ ] Identify student's home and English proficiency level.
- [ ] Review current IEP goal(s), objectives, and progress monitoring data.
- [ ] Identify areas of strength that can be used to convey student's knowledge.

During the Meeting

- [ ] Discuss whether the student will need accommodations to successfully participate in grade-level curriculum.
- [ ] Identify language supports needed for English language learners so that instruction and classroom materials are comprehensible.
- [ ] Explore what type of accommodation might be needed and when.
- [ ] Determine if curricular modifications will be required (remember this alters the content).
- [ ] Encourage a discussion of how universal design for learning might be used to create lessons to support learning.
- [ ] If using an interpreter, be sure to use appropriate interpreter etiquette (see Chapter 2).

After the Meeting

- [ ] Debrief with all team members, including parents, regarding the effectiveness of the meeting.
- [ ] Review with the student how they did as a self-advocate; discuss ways to improve.
- [ ] Send copies of the meeting documents to all participants.
- [ ] Follow up on any unresolved issues.

Figure 9.1. Preparation for the IEP meeting: Accommodations and modifications.

THE IEP CHECKLIST: ACCOMMODATIONS AND MODIFICATIONS

The following checklist can be used to aid the IEP team in discussing and evaluating the accommodations and modifications within a student's IEP.

Key Area (IEP section): **Accommodations/District Tests**	Criteria met	
	Yes	No
A1: Accommodations match the services delivered in the classroom on a regular basis.		
A2: Accommodations are derived from student needs (Present Levels of Academic Achievement and Functional Performance).		
A3: Accommodations adhere to local and federal guidelines.		

ACTIVITIES

The activities included in this chapter are intended for the reader to gain a deeper understanding of the content covered. For this chapter, each activity builds on the skills of the previous activity. The activities associated with this chapter include the following:

- Activity 9.1. Study Team Exploration

- Activity 9.2. Comparing Quality Accommodations and Universal Design for Learning

- Activity 9.3. Identification of Quality Accommodations and Modifications

- Activity 9.4. Instructional Accommodations for Students From Culturally and Linguistically Diverse Backgrounds With Disabilities

Activity 9.1.
Study Team Exploration

Supporting chapter: Chapter 9 (Accommodations and Modifications to Meet the Needs of the Learner)

Purpose: The purpose of this activity is to help develop the skill and knowledge to identify the accommodations and modifications possibly needed for students with disabilities.

Directions: Consider children with disabilities, and answer the following questions.

1. What accommodations can be made available to all students to access as needed?

_____

_____

_____

2. What accommodations could you make for students with visible disabilities? Visible disabilities are those that can be seen by the casual observer. The accommodations are often more obvious for students with visible disabilities.

_____

_____

_____

3. What accommodations could you make for students with invisible disabilities? Invisible disabilities cannot be easily determined by a casual observer. These disabilities are often not noticed by peers, so the student with the disability is usually more guarded about their need for additional supports.

_____

_____

_____

4. What issues arise when providing accommodations for students with invisible disabilities that do not arise with students with visible disabilities? Why?

_____

_____

_____

5. What relationships may exist between a student's invisible disability and challenging behavior?

_____

_____

_____

Activity 9.2.

Comparing Quality Accommodations and Universal Design for Learning

Supporting chapter: Chapter 9 (Accommodations and Modifications to Meet the Needs of the Learner)

Purpose: The purpose of this activity is to help develop the skill and knowledge to identify the accommodations and modifications possibly needed for students with disabilities.

Directions: Compare quality accommodations with universal design for learning. How do they support the learning of all students?

_____

_____

_____

_____

_____

_____

_____

_____

_____

_____

_____

_____

_____

_____

_____

_____

_____

_____

_____

_____

_____

_____

_____

_____

_____

_____

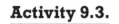

Activity 9.3.

Identification of Quality Accommodations and Modifications

Supporting chapter: Chapter 9 (Accommodations and Modifications to Meet the Needs of the Learner)

Purpose: The purpose of this activity is to develop the skill and knowledge to identify the accommodations and modifications possibly needed for students with a disability and to document these needs in the IEP.

Directions: Use an IEP to inventory the Accommodations and Modifications section and indicate the quality of the information provided. Then, rank the section and provide evidence to support your ranking.

Rubric scale: Use the following scale and circle the number that best ranks the IEP area reviewed in the table that follows.

• 1 = Standard not met • IEP fails to provide evidence of meeting the IDEA 2004 requirements. • IEP does not address the IDEA 2004 requirements.	• 2 = Standard partially met • Performance provides evidence of partially meeting IDEA 2004 requirements. • Performance addresses some of the IDEA 2004 requirements.	• 3 = Standard met • Performance provides evidence of meeting most/all of the IDEA 2004 requirements. • Performance addresses most/all of the IDEA 2004 requirements.	• 4 = Standard exceeds • Performance provides evidence of exceeding all IDEA 2004 requirements. • All indicators are addressed in the IEP and go beyond expectations.

Key Area (IEP Section): Accommodations/District Tests	Ranking	Rationale for Ranking
A1: Accommodations **match** the services delivered in the classroom on a regular basis.	1 2 3 4	
A2: Accommodations are **derived** from student needs (Present Levels of Academic Achievement and Functional Performance).	1 2 3 4	
A3: Accommodations **adhere** to local and federal guidelines.	1 2 3 4	

Rewritten accommodations and modifications statement(s):

_____

_____

_____

_____

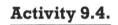

Activity 9.4.

Instructional Accommodations for Students From Culturally and Linguistically Diverse Backgrounds With Disabilities

Supporting chapter: Chapter 9 (Accommodations and Modifications to Meet the Needs of the Learner)

Purpose: The purpose of this activity is to plan instruction that meets the language proficiency needs of a student with a disability who comes from a culturally and linguistically diverse (CLD) background.

Directions: Use the following chart to consider a student with a disability who also comes from a CLD background. List possible linguistic supports and accommodations so that instruction will be comprehensible.

Category of instruction	Linguistic supports	Accommodations
Example: Presentation	**Example:** Modified English (basic vocabulary with less complex grammar structures) Use realia (everyday objects and materials to aid in delivering instruction)	**Example:** Repeat directions, text to speech
Presentation		
Equipment and materials		
Response		
Setting		
Time/scheduling		

Transition Teaming

Meeting Postsecondary Needs

Laura Clarke

After reading this chapter and engaging in activities related to this chapter, you will be able to meet the following outcomes:

• Describe transition requirement for students making the transition from one school program to the next.

• Explain legislation and best practices surrounding transition from age 14 and/ or in Grade 8.

• Identify the continuum of services (least restrictive environment [LRE]) for students at transition age.

When we consider transitions in life, we think about changes from one part of life to another. Transitions for children and students with disabilities can include additional challenges because parents and educators plan the best way to communicate the child's strengths, areas of need, and required supports for the student as they move from one school to another. Transitions in school happen from early childhood (Part C IDEA services) to preschool, from preschool to elementary, elementary to middle (or secondary), and from middle to high school. After completing their primary education, a student makes the transition from high school to their next level of learning, career exploration, or programming. For students with an IEP, it is a recommended practice to begin planning early (several months—or even years—prior to the actual event), which can include having a planning meeting with both sets of educators, letting the child meet teachers and related services providers at the new school, and planning for any needed accommodations, including special equipment and physical changes to a facility. To ensure the best possible outcome for children and students with disabilities, transition works best when thoughtful planning occurs.

IDEA'S KEY COMPONENTS

- **Free appropriate public education (FAPE).** Requires that the student be educated in a manner that meets their educational needs by a public educational agency that is free to the family.
  - *Zero Reject.* Mandates that the school cannot deny a child an education due to the severity of their needs.
- **Least restrictive environment (LRE).** The student is educated in a manner that is most like their typical peers.
- **Procedural safeguards** (due process). The family has the right to disagree with the placement, services, and educational plan for their child and can bring the school district to court.
- **Parental participation** (shared decision making). Parents have the right to participate as part of the education team for their child.
- **Nondiscriminatory evaluation.** Requires schools to utilize a team approach in assessing a student in all suspected areas of a disability using measures that are valid, reliable, culturally relevant, and linguistically appropriate.
- **Individualized education program (IEP).** The IEP team assesses current evaluation information and develops a written document designed to meet the unique educational needs of each student with a disability.

TRANSITION ACCORDING TO THE INDIVIDUALS WITH DISABILITIES EDUCATION ACT

Transition is a crucial planning time to ensure the student's goals and specially designed instruction are uniquely tailored for their specific strengths and needs. Transition planning should be carefully crafted to help the student succeed as they move out of the pre-K–12 learning environment and into the adult world of postsecondary education, work, supported employment, or adult living. Ensuring that a student's transition plan is uniquely tailored to their needs requires educators to engage in a variety of transition-centered conversations and use transition-centered assessments designed to help the student and their family explore postsecondary school options for career and activities of daily living such as finding safe housing, budgeting, connecting with friends; engaging in the political and social systems of their community; and maintaining physical, social, and emotional health.

IDEA requires educators to provide services for students with disabilities in the LRE. LRE must still be considered for transition services and planning, and some of the processes are similar, but the outcomes are different in a postsecondary world. When considering the LRE continuum of services throughout a student's schooling, one looks first at the general education classroom and consider what supports (supplementary aids and services) a student needs to succeed. In the same way during transition planning, the student's support team considers what supports a student needs to succeed in each area of their adult life. The team may consider if the student needs additional instruction or supports for any area (academic skills and functional skills) and develop transition goals around those areas. Transition goals are specific to the student's postsecondary plans. For example, Josh will need to take a bus to his community college each day, so one of his transition goals it to successfully transfer buses to get to the community college. Sara will be moving into an apartment when she graduates and does not know how to do her own laundry, so she has a transition goal for sorting laundry. Max will be attending a community program for adults with disabilities and is using a new communication device to request his favorite snacks, so his transition communication goal focuses on greeting people and making requests. For bilingual students, it is important to consider the language used in specific situations. In the previous example, Sara not only needs a transition goal for sorting laundry, but she also needs a goal that when making requests, such as change for community washing machines, the language of the request will be that of the receiver.

Continuum of services must be viewed in a different way when considering next steps past high school for students with IEPs. At the least restrictive end of services, some students will move from high school to college with minimal accommodations as required by the Americans with Disabilities Act (ADA) of 1990 (PL 101-336). ADA is a civil rights law that prohibits discrimination against people with disabilities in all areas of public life (ADA National Network, 2020). Accommodations on the job can include changing job tasks, providing reserved parking, modifying accessibility of a work area, allowing a flexible work schedule, and providing a product or service to increase ability to complete a job task. ADA supports in a university setting can include supports such as an interpreter or physical supports in the classroom environment.

When considering the LRE continuum for students at transition age, some students choose vocational programs or adult education, and others move directly to work (see Figure 10.1). Many students will be eligible for pre-employment transition services (sometimes referred to as *Pre-ETS*). Pre-ETS provides a comprehensive job exploration curriculum to support students as they consider job or employment opportunities. In addition, many students will utilize vocational rehabilitation (VR) services. VR programs are federally funded agencies that support students as they make the transition from high school to employment and independent living. These adult programs provide support to students as they pursue meaningful employment that aligns with their abilities and interests. To be eligible for services from the VR program, students must "have a physical or mental impairment that constitutes or results in

Figure 10.1. Continuum of placements for postsecondary options. (*Key:* ADA, Americans with Disabilities Act [ADA] of 1990 [PL 101-336].)

a substantial impediment to employment; and requires VR services to prepare for, secure, retain, advance in, or regain employment" (Office of Special Education Programs [OSEP], 2017, p. 12). Students who qualify for VR services may require Pre-ETS services, including counseling in job exploration, work-based experiences, workplace readiness training, self-advocacy, and person-centered planning (OSEP, 2017).

Students with more significant disabilities might move into supported employment or day programs, whereas other adults might require independent living support as part of their transition plans. The IDEA-mandated services specific to adult life provided to students with IEPs from age 16 through graduation are generally termed *transition services.*

According to the Office of Special Education and Rehabilitation Services, "transition services" are an integrated set of activities for students with disabilities that are part of a "results-oriented process" focused on improving academic performance and daily living skills needed for the student to be successful after high school (OSEP, 2017). Each student's transition services, like the rest of the IEP, should be individualized based on the student's strengths, needs, interests, and plans for the future. IEP services should include specially designed instruction as needed. If needed, services should also include required related services. As you read through the chapter, the Challenge Scenarios serve as a guide to help you plan for students with IEPs.

To develop transition services and goals, teams are making data-driven decisions—just as in the rest of the IEP. For this reason, it is critical that the IEP team have rich, meaningful data to help the team make appropriate goals and recommendations for the student's transition plan. Figure 10.2 highlights information that should be included in transition data.

Stop and Think!

If each student with an IEP who is age 16 requires transition services, how do IEP teams meet the student's individual strengths and needs? What do we need to make decisions?

CONNECTION TO LEGAL PERSPECTIVE

IDEA specifically defines *transition* in an IEP to be the time "beginning not later than the first IEP to be in effect when the child is 16 and updated annually thereafter" (20 USC Title 20, Section 1414). Some states require transition services to begin "in the child's eighth grade year or when the child has reached the age fourteen" (704 KAR 3:305). For some students with more significant disabilities, it is best practice to begin planning before age 16. For example, in areas of the country where there are long waiting lists for state Medicaid services, housing, or adult services, it is important to provide families with information to allow them to begin planning early. For students who may need longer than secondary schooling to develop critical communication, social, or behavior skills to enter

Figure 10.2. Transition data. (*Source:* O'Brien and Pearpoint, 1995.) (*Key:* AAC, augmentative and alternative communication.)

competitive employment, IEP teams may need to consider focusing on transition goals in these areas at a younger age. It is okay to begin planning earlier than age 16 for students who have academic or functional skills that will require additional time for development.

Many free transition planning tools are available for IEP teams. The National Technical Assistance Center on Transition (2018) has a free Age-Appropriate Transition Assessment Toolkit 4.0 that includes a list of appropriate assessments for each part of the transition process. LifeCourse Tools are designed to support caregivers and educators as they help plan next steps for students with more significant disabilities (LifeCourse, 2020). LifeCourse's core belief is that "all people have the right to live, love, work, play, and pursue their own aspirations" (p. 3). LifeCourse focuses on high expectations for all students and has several free planning tools that the IEP team and students can use to begin to plan for life after high school.

Required Transition Services IEP Team Members

According to OSEP's (2017) *Transition Guide to Postsecondary Education and Employment for Students and Youth with Disabilities*, the following members are required as part of the IEP transition services team:

- The parents of the child

- At least one general education teacher (if the child is participating in the general education environment)

- At least one special education teacher

- A representative of the public agency (local education agency [LEA]) who is qualified to provide (or supervise the provision of) specially designed instruction and is knowledgeable about the general curriculum and the availability of LEA resources

- An individual who can interpret the instructional implications of evaluation results (which can be one of the previous members)

- An interpreter if English is not the home/primary language for the student and/or family

- At the discretion of the parent or LEA, other individuals with knowledge regarding the child

- Whenever appropriate, the child with a disability

Challenge Scenarios

The following Challenge Scenarios will be used throughout the chapter to better understand transition services required for students with varying disabilities.

Challenge Scenario 1: Marcus

Marcus is a 16-year-old with a specific learning disability in math reasoning. Marcus is able to solve two-step linear equations with a visual model and calculator. He needs significant scaffolding to solve word problems and equations provided in story/real-world scenarios. His strengths lie in following steps in visual models and asking for help when he is not sure of the correct order of operations. Marcus has developed strong self-advocacy skills during middle school and is able to use calculators on his school laptop and his phone to solve problems in class. Marcus shared in his individual learning plan (ILP) that he wants to go to a 4-year university to earn a degree in construction management so he can work at a local construction company.

- *At age 16:* Given a college application, Marcus will complete all sections in a college application in 3 out of 4 opportunities as measured by a teacher-created checklist.

- *At age 17:* Given a monthly budget, Marcus will allocate funds to pay for housing, food, class fees, and social outings with a positive bank balance in 3 out of 4 opportunities as measured by a teacher-created rubric.

Challenge Scenario 2: Elizabeta

Elizabeta is a 17-year-old with an intellectual disability and a diagnosis of Down syndrome. She is bilingual, and Spanish is the language spoken at home. Her social proficiency expressive communication in both languages is considered in the high average range of understandability (meaning most people can understand what she is saying). She would like to work at a local department store shelving clothing and toys. She has a bus schedule app on her phone and is able to ride the local bus system independently to and from her favorite restaurant and store. She can use the next-dollar strategy and her banking app to purchase items at the restaurant and store using a list-making app that she shares with her teacher and mother. Her banking app is set to allow her to purchase items up to $25 without additional permissions from her mother.

- *At age 14:* Given a restaurant menu or store flier, Elizabeta will purchase items within her budget using the next-dollar strategy with 75% accuracy in 3 out of 4 opportunities as measured by a teacher-created checklist.

- *At age 15:* Given a restaurant menu, Elizabeta will choose a lunch that falls within her budget in 3 out of 4 opportunities as measured by a teacher-created checklist.

- *At age 16:* Given a common unknown word or phrase spoken in a store, Elizabeta will use her Spanish-to-English translation app to translate the word or phrase in 3 out of 4 opportunities as measured by a teacher-created checklist.

- *At age 17:* Given a bus schedule and time to be at work or an appointment, Elizabeta will choose the right bus to take with 100% accuracy in 4 out of 4 opportunities as measured by a teacher rubric.

Challenge Scenario 3: Dan

Dan is a 20-year-old with autism and an intellectual disability who also has a diagnosis of epilepsy. He is considered nonverbal and is 5% accurate using a communication app on his tablet. He and his family are looking at adult day programs to provide community experiences and support his continued learning of daily living skills. Dan's teachers and families are modeling communication with his augmentative and alternative communication device, and Dan is at the beginning stages of using a communication app on his iPad to communicate his wants and needs in 5% of given opportunities. Dan also uses some picture symbols to request snacks and his favorite music, and he will travel from one seat to another to get his communication board and ask for snacks or music. His goals are to increase independent communication of his wants and needs (transition and education) and independently prepare meals (activities of daily living).

- *At age 14:* Given a snack or meal, Dan will use a utensil to scoop the food instead of his fingers in 3 out of 4 opportunities as measured by a frequency count.

- *At age 15:* Given a new person who has entered the room (or Dan's line of sight), he will use his communication device to greet the person in 3 out of 4 opportunities as measured by a frequency count (direct measure).

- *At age 16:* Given a desired object (snack item), Dan will use his communication device to request the item with 50% accuracy in 3 out of 4 opportunities as measured by a frequency count (direct measure).

- *At age 17:* Throughout his day, Dan will carry his communication device and place it on a table or surface next to him when he is in the room with 50% accuracy in 3 out of 5 days as measured by a checklist (direct measure)

TRANSITION-RELATED COMPONENTS OF THE IEP

The following are required components for a student's IEP from the time they are 16:

- Measurable postsecondary goals related to transition, education, employment, and (when appropriate) independent living skills

- Transition services needed to assist the student to reach those goals (including courses of study)

- A statement that the student has been informed of their rights that will transfer when they reach the age of majority (age 18 in most states). This statement must be in place beginning no later than 1 year before they reach the age of majority under their state's law (20 U.S.C 1414[d][1][A][i][VIII]; 34 C.F.R. §§ 300.320[b]; and 34 C.F.R. § 300.3210[b]).

Let's take a look at each of these elements in detail.

Developing Measurable Postsecondary Goals

It is crucial that the IEP team begin with a firm foundation when they think about writing postsecondary goals: accurate and complete assessment data that is stated in the student's Present Levels of Academic Achievement and Functional Performance (PLAAFP) within their IEP. Collect a variety of transition data across a period of time to ensure the IEP team has enough data to make decisions. Planning for the rest of a student's life takes students and parents some time to process and gather information, so giving them time to review any assessment tools and have conversations will be important. For example, if a student is considering going to a 4-year college, then the family might need to investigate which schools are appropriate, funding for education, accommodations for the student's academic work, and more. For a student who will be attending a supported day program, the family might need to investigate all the potential providers in their area, review funding sources, and meet with state Medicare office staff.

Given the intricate and multilayered considerations for planning a successful transition to adult life, it is crucial that teachers give plenty of time in advance of the IEP meeting for families to review and complete needed assessments. Some families will need support completing these assessments, and the assessments should be provided in the family's home language. Some examples of assessments that an IEP team might consider in the transition process might include

- Student and parent/guardian surveys

- Person-centered planning tools

- ILP
- College and career readiness such as Trajectory for Planning and Trajectory for Exploring (LifeCourse, 2020)
- Employability skills assessment results

After this data is collected and analyzed, the IEP team often drafts a transition statement of the student's overall plan for life in the first years after high school for the PLAAFP. An example of a PLAAFP transition statement is: "After high school, (insert student name)'s goal is to (insert either employment focus or education/ training needed) to be able to become (list ideal job here)." A few sample transition statements include

- *Marcus:* After high school, Marcus' goal is to attend a 4-year university to earn a degree in construction management so he can work at a local construction company.
- *Elizabeta:* After high school, Elizabeta's goal is to obtain on-the-job training to work at Kohl's stocking the children's department.
- *Dan:* After high school, Dan's goal is to participate in the adult services program at Redwood, a local service agency for adults with disabilities.

Using the BEST (behavior, evaluation, specific, timely) strategy when writing a measurable postsecondary goal provides both compliant and measurable goals. According to IDEA, transition planning begins at 16; however, it is best practice to begin transition planning earlier for students with more significant disabilities. Following are examples of transition goals for a series of the scenarios using the BEST strategy.

- **B**ehavior: Describe the intended behavior using concrete, sensory-specific language that can be seen or heard.
- **E**valuation: Indicate the assessment measure and specify the key quantifiable performance (i.e., criteria) indicator that will determine if the desired behavior was met.
- **S**pecific: Use precise language that describes the condition for when the student will demonstrate the desired behavior.
- **T**imely: State the time line or date.

Additional Considerations   Keep in mind that for employment, the transition team should focus on the specific job the student wants to do. The focus for the education/training area is on the specific training or education a student needs to help them obtain the specific job they want. When considering employment opportunities, there is an extensive continuum of services, including community-based work experience, internship, mentorship, apprenticeship, paid employment, and career pathways (OSEP, 2017).

Extensive career exploration is needed for students to know enough about available job options. This can include in-person or virtual visits to different jobs, career fairs, and other opportunities to see different types of work opportunities in action.

Transition Services

When considering appropriate transition services, it is crucial for the IEP team to consider all areas of life needed for a student to be safe and successful. They must also consider if any public agencies are available to support the student in the acquisition of these skills. For example, the Office of Vocational Rehabilitation can support students in the development of work-appropriate skills. For areas where a student needs support and no outside agency is available, the special education teacher and IEP team need to work together to develop appropriate instruction to help the student gain needed skills. Consider Figure 10.3 and check the areas in which transition services might be needed for a student. It is important for the IEP team to consider both academic and functional (life) skills to support the student's successful life after high school.

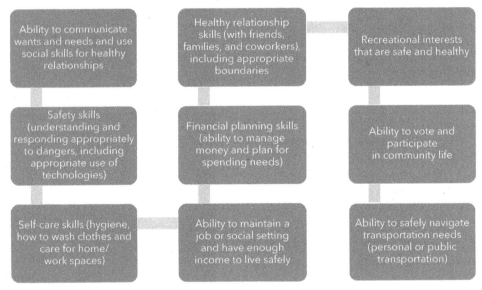

Figure 10.3. Postsecondary areas of life to consider in IEP transition plans.

USING A FRAMEWORK FOR PLANNING

Helping students develop self-advocacy skills is a key component of transition planning. Students need to be able to advocate for themselves at home, work, and in the community to be successful, and that advocacy needs to focus on using their strengths and supporting any skill deficits with appropriate accommodations. For example, if a student is reading below grade level, then requesting to use an online reader can be a great way to advocate for their needs. This section focuses on helping students develop key self-advocacy skills through the IEP team process, including involving the student's family and appropriate community services.

Stop and Think!

Max and his IEP team used the tool in Figure 10.3 and responded to the matrix with the following responses.

Max is proficient at these skills:

- Ability to communicate wants and needs, social skills for healthy relationships

- Safety skills (understanding and responding appropriately to dangers, including appropriate use of technologies)

- Self-care skills (hygiene, how to wash clothes, cares for home/workspaces)

- Healthy relationship skills (with friends, families, and coworkers, including appropriate boundaries)

- Recreational interests that are safe and healthy

- Ability to vote and participate in community life

- Ability to safely navigate transportation needs (personal or public transportation)

Max will need support in the following areas:

- Ability to maintain a job or social setting and have enough income to live safely

- Financial planning skills (ability to manage money and plan for spending needs)

- Max needs support in financial planning, balancing a checkbook, and creating a budget

How do educators and service providers work with each student and their family to ensure that goals are aligned with the student's life plans?

Starting Strong With Student Self-Advocacy

Throughout a student's school journey with special education services, it is best practice to teach self-advocacy skills to empower students to have a voice in their own academic and functional strengths and needs. The first step for teachers when teaching self-advocacy skills is to assess a student's current strengths and needs in identifying their plans for the future, including completing interest inventories and interviewing the student and family. It can also include specific career and life skills inventories to clearly identify student strengths and needs. Language proficiency and strengths should be assessed for students who are bilingual or English language learners. An assistive technology assessment is likely needed for students who use a communication system or who have not adopted a communication system. Technologies for accommodations should also be assessed to discover the least intrusive and most accessible ways for a student to increase their independence in speaking, listening, communicating in writing, managing finances, and managing their social, emotional, and behavioral needs.

Once a clear understanding and baseline data regarding a student's strengths and needs has been established, the team can work with the student to identify areas where the student can begin to advocate for themself. Self-advocacy can include teaching students to

- Plan the agenda for their IEP meeting

- Present their own progress monitoring data

- Share the direction for their IEP transition goals

Reframing the IEP Team

As you consider the IEP team composition during transition planning, it is important to also consider additional team members who might be able to support the student in their transition, education, employment, or activities of daily living needs. For example, would it be beneficial to invite VR specialists to the table at an earlier age for students who might be pursuing several areas of interest? Would it be good to have a community parks and recreation person be part of a meeting for a student who wants to participate in adult sports leagues? For students who might need activities of daily living support, could the IEP team invite local agencies who provide these services to discuss best practices in making the transition to adult services?

It is crucial for the IEP team to have all needed data to be able to discuss the student's current areas of strength and make plans for their areas of need. Take another look at Figure 10.3 to review each area in which a student might need support. As you review each area of possible need, it is important to consider who within the school district team or the community may be able to assist in teaching needed skills. As the team considers a student's area(s) of need, it is crucial to keep parent and student input a priority in the conversation. It is also best practice to begin the planning with parent and student input and engage them throughout the planning process to ensure their questions, comments, and concerns are addressed, which can be done by developing a checklist like the one in Table 10.1.

Engaging Family and Community Supports

The *Endrew F. v. Douglas County School District* (2017) ruling made clear the vital importance of engaging family in the development of a student's IEP. As data is being collected for IEP meetings for transition-age students, it is crucial for teachers to engage family in the conversation. Parents can offer vital insights into a student's future support network and areas of need. Considering the areas in Figure 10.3, parents can include key insights into a student's ability to communicate their wants and needs, organize their time, make plans with family and friends, advocate for their future, and navigate key life decisions (Feldman et al., 2018). In addition, family can share how much familial support is available over the long term. This allows the IEP team time to work with the family in providing supports for any areas of need in which the family might not have the time, resources, or knowledge to support the student. Parent involvement is a critical principle of IDEA; however, the appearance of involvement for families who are culturally and linguistically diverse (CLD) is often different from the expectations of the transition team. This difference should not be interpreted as a lack of interest, but rather as a difference in the family's understanding of the ways they might be involved. In addition, the goals for students after graduation may also be different for families who are CLD from that of the transition team. For example, transition teams often focus on student's independence, whereas families who are CLD might focus on interdependence. Therefore, the transition team must be mindful of these differences and seek the valuable input from families who are CLD in a manner that is culturally responsive, accepting of differences, and respectful of the of the families' goals.

There are many possibilities for an IEP team to consider when looking at community support (Feldman et al., 2018). The IEP team should be composed of members who can contribute to making data-driven decisions in helping the student successfully transition from IDEA-mandated services and secondary programming to successful adult endeavors (OSEP, 2017). Remember to follow state and district guidelines for inviting members to attend an IEP meeting.

Table 10.1. Family involvement checklist

Time line	Questions to ask family and student	Where to document
A few weeks prior to the IEP meeting (contact by phone, text, or e-mail, based on family comfort and your district contact policies) *Note:* It is important to communicate in the home language of the student and family. If not already known, discuss with family their views on fluency/comfort of home language for communication.	What plans do you have for (student's) future? What type of (schooling/job/ community setting) are you considering for (student)? What types of activities does (student) plan to do when they are not at work (recreation activities)? What language is (student) most comfortable/fluent to communicate with others? (Make plans for an interpreter if needed.)	On an IEP planning form or district-required documentation form for family contact
During IEP meeting	Plan an agenda in which you ask for the family's input at the beginning of the meeting, as you discuss goals, and as you discuss services.	IEP conference summary notes
After the IEP meeting	Document progress toward IEP goals following IEP time line.	IEP progress notes

Addressing Key Transition Needs

It is important for IEP team members to think through each potential area of transition services to consider what specific areas a student might need to be successful in their postsecondary life. Beginning at age 16, it is a federal requirement under IDEA to address transition needs and services for students who qualify for special education services. These transition services should focus on skills and strategies needed for the student to be successful once they leave school-based services. The three main areas for transition services are training or education, employment, and, when appropriate, independent living skills (OSEP, 2017). Areas to consider in transition planning include the following:

- Postsecondary education

- Vocational education

- Employment (independent)

- Employment (supported)

- Independent living skills

- Adult community programming

As part of a student's transition planning process, it is important to teach self-advocacy skills for receiving ADA accommodations in future educational and/or work situations. The student's daily living skills are also critical. The team must ask if the student can

- Gain access to and manage housing

- Communicate wants or needs in the home language and/or English

- If a communication device or system is used, use the communication system to communicate wants, needs, and express thoughts

- Manage a personal budget

- Maintain safe relationships

- Advocate for their wants and needs (self-advocacy)

- Navigate transportation needs (independent driving, public transportation, or supported public transportation)

- Engage in safe leisure activities

- Participate safely in community life

- Access and utilize technology to support independence (Test et al., 2014)

One additional transition need that should be addressed is a student's right to make education decisions when reaching the legal age of majority in that state. Once a student reaches their state's age of majority (age 18 in many states), they have rights to all of their educational records and to make decisions regarding their education. For students who have significant intellectual disabilities, students and their families follow the state's requirements for determining competence, often through a legal guardianship process.

SUMMARY

This chapter walked through the key aspects to consider when planning the transition section of the IEP for students age 16 and older. As students enter the transition period of their special education programming, IEP teams begin to transition from a school-focused lens to helping the student develop key life skills to be successful in their life after high school. Student strengths and needs must be considered through conversation with the student and their family, and transition-focused assessments need to focus on the student's future plans. Data needs to be collected and analyzed and must include the multifaceted possibilities of work, leisure, and home life and provide the foundation for age-appropriate transition IEP goals and specially designed instruction that will support the student in their next steps. Foremost in this process must be a culturally respectful, student-centered planning process that emphasizes a focus on building on the student's strengths and providing instruction and support for areas of need specific to employment, education, transition to adult life, and activities of daily living. The resources in Figure 10.4 provide supports to IEP teams as they construct transition IEPs, and the checklist in Figure 10.5 may be used to prepare for the transition IEP meeting.

THE IEP CHECKLIST: TRANSITIONS

The following checklist can be used as an inventory to ensure the IEP contains the required components for students who are age 16 or older.

Key Area (IEP section): **Transitions Beginning at Age 16, Coordinated Activities That Meet These Criterias**	Criteria met	
	Yes	No
T1: Statement of quality-of-life goals: The statement is results-oriented; focused on improving academic and functional achievement; facilitates movement from school to postschool activities, including postsecondary education, vocational education, integrated employment (supported employment), continuing and adult education, adult services, independent living, or community participation.		
T2: Vision: The vision is based on the child's needs, taking into account the child's strengths, preferences, and interests.		
T3: Resources and interagency collaboration: The individualized education program (IEP) includes a description of the course of study needed to reach stated goals, including instruction, related services, community experiences, development of employment and other postschool adult living objectives, and, when appropriate, acquisition of daily living skills and vocational evaluation.		
T4: Stakeholders: Parents of a child making the transition from Part C services (early childhood) to Part B services (school-age) can request an invitation to the initial IEP meeting be sent to representatives of the Part C system to assist with a smooth transition of services.		

1. Americans with Disabilities National Network provides guidance on legal requirements and supports available to adults with disabilities in the workplace and access to community resources.

2. *IDEA 2004 Secondary Transition Questions and Answers Resource* (Office of Special Education and Rehabilitative Services, 2011) provides clarification on IDEA specific to students at transition age.

3. National Clearinghouse of Rehabilitation Training Materials (funded by the Rehabilitation Services Administration [RSA]) has training materials specific to supporting rehabilitation needs of students who have vision, hearing, or mobility differences.

4. National Deaf Center on Postsecondary Outcomes (funded by the Office of Special Education Programs [OSEP]) has resources to support students who experience deafness or hearing loss in their postsecondary plans for work or further schooling.

5. National Technical Assistance Center on Transition (funded by OSEP and RSA) has research- and evidence-based practices specific to increasing outcomes for students with disabilities who are transition age.

6. *Transition Guide to Postsecondary Education and Employment for Students and Youth with Disabilities* (OSEP, 2017) includes guidance for students, families, and educators in planning the transition to postsecondary learning and employment.

7. *Transition of Students with Disabilities to Postsecondary Education: A Guide for High School Educators* (U.S. Department of Education's Office for Civil Rights, 2011) includes supports for high school teachers, counselors, and families in planning for transition to adult life, including the role of vocational rehabilitation in the transition process.

Figure 10.4. Transition resources.

ACTIVITIES

The activities included in this chapter are intended for the reader to gain a deeper understanding of the content covered. For this chapter, each activity builds on the skills of the previous activity. The activities associated with this chapter include the following:

- Activity 10.1. Transition Supports Identification

- Activity 10.2. Person-Centered Planning

- Activity 10.3. Stakeholders Planning

- Activity 10.4. Identification of a Quality Transition Plan

PREPARATION FOR THE IEP MEETING:
TRANSITION

Prior to the Meeting

☐ Communicate student transition plans and goals with families or caregivers.

☐ Review transition assessment data (Examples: daily living, career interest, college and/or career readiness, employment skills, communication and/or augmentative and alternative communication, gross and/or fine motor skills, mobility and/or movement, technology).

☐ If transition assessment has not occurred, then ensure that transition assessment occurs.

☐ Identify student's strengths and funds of knowledge.

☐ Ascertain the student's home language and/or English language proficiency level.

☐ Determine if student qualifies for pre-employment transition services and/or vocational rehabilitation services.

☐ Plan an agenda for the meeting and share with all participants.

During the Meeting

☐ Be mindful of the student's and family's postsecondary goals.

☐ Review transition assessment data.

☐ Consider language proficiency and the student's funds of knowledge as strengths while constructing IEP goal.

☐ Update or develop postsecondary goals related to transition skills (e.g., communication, safety, self-care, healthy relationships, financial planning, voting, transportation, self-advocacy, education, employment, independent living skills). Use BEST (behavior, evaluation, specific, timely) to check that goal(s) are meaningful and compliant.

☐ Identify transition services that will assist the student to reach goals.

☐ Include a statement of transfer of rights at least 1 year prior to student meeting age of majority.

☐ If using an interpreter, be sure to use appropriate interpreter etiquette (see Chapter 2).

After the Meeting

☐ Prepare progress monitoring to reflect IEP goal.

☐ Debrief with all team members, including parents, about the effectiveness of the meeting.

☐ Check with parents on the use of an interpreter and if they understood the meeting and key takeaways.

Figure 10.5. Preparation for the IEP meeting: Transition.

Activity 10.1.

Transition Supports Identification

Supporting chapter: Chapter 10 (Transition Teaming: Meeting Postsecondary Needs)

Purpose: The purpose of this activity is to practice identifying transition supports.

Directions: Given the key transition areas discussed in this chapter, identify the transition area to support the students in the scenarios provided in the chapter.

Challenge Scenario 1: Marcus

Marcus is a 16-year-old with a specific learning disability in math reasoning. Marcus shared in his individual learning plan that he wants to go to a 4-year university to earn a degree in construction management so he can work at a local construction company. Marcus is heading to a university and planning to work at a local construction company.

    Areas of Support (choose all that apply):

- Postsecondary education

- Vocational education

- Employment (independent)

- Employment (supported)

- Independent living skills

- Adult community programming

Challenge Scenario 2: Elizabeta

Elizabeta is a 17-year-old with an intellectual disability and a diagnosis of Down syndrome. She is bilingual, and Spanish is the language spoken at home. Her social proficiency expressive communication in both languages is considered in the high average range of understandability (meaning most people can understand what she is saying). She would like to work at a local department store shelving clothing and toys. She has a bus schedule app on her phone and is able to ride the local bus system independently to and from her favorite restaurant and store. She is able to use the next-dollar strategy and her banking app to purchase items at the restaurant and store using a list-making app that she shares with her teacher and mother. Her banking app is set to allow her to purchase items up to $25 without additional permissions from her mother.

    Elizabeta is planning to work at a local department store and ride the bus system to work.

    Areas of Support (choose all that apply):

- Postsecondary education

- Vocational education

- Employment (independent)

- Employment (supported)

- Independent living skills

- Adult community programming

Challenge Scenario 3: Dan

Dan is a 20-year-old with autism and an intellectual disability who also has a diagnosis of epilepsy. He is considered nonverbal and is 5% accurate using a communication app on his tablet. He and his family are looking at adult day programs to provide community experiences and support his activities of daily living skills. His goals are to increase independent communication of his wants and needs (transition and education) and help him independently prepare meals (activities of daily living). Dan is planning to attend an adult day program and live at home with his family.

Areas of Support (choose all that apply):

- Postsecondary education
- Vocational education
- Employment (independent)
- Employment (supported)
- Independent living skills
- Adult community programming

Tips for Identifying Effective Transition Services

Tip 1: Consider whether the transition service(s) are coordinated and focused on improving the student's academic and functional achievement to support the student's postschool activities:

- Postsecondary or vocational employment
- Integrated or supported employment
- Continuing adult education or adult services
- Independent living
- Community participation

Tip 2: Assess if the transition service(s) are based on the child's individual needs, taking into account their strengths, preferences, interests, and needs including

- Instruction
- Related services
- Community experiences
- Development of employment and postsecondary goals
- Acquisition of daily living skills and functional vocational evaluation

Tip 3: Determine whether the transition service(s) are recommended practice for transition. Does the IEP meeting conversation include

- Parent input on student plans and progress
- Student input on their postschool plans
- A discussion and a note on the IEP that the student and family have been informed that student rights will transfer when they reach the age of majority in their state

Tip 4: Remember that all transition IEPs should include

- Present levels, including student-specific data of strengths and needs specific to transition
- Considerations of special factors, which may include student-specific data and needs in relation to communication, behavior, English language proficiency, and vision and/or hearing differences
- Goals that include transition needs based on student's transition plans

- Specially designed instruction created to support student transition needs (with a focus on increased independence for student)

- Special education and related services to meet transition plans

- Accommodations or modifications to support student transition plans

Tip 5: At the final IEP meeting before a student ages out of IDEA-related services, provide the student with a Summary of Performance (a summary of academic and functional performance to support postschool goals and education). The summary should be provided either when the student graduates with a regular diploma or when the student ages out of IDEA-related services.

Activity 10.2.

Person-Centered Planning

Supporting chapter: Chapter 10 (Transition Teaming: Meeting Postsecondary Needs)

Purpose: The purpose of this activity is to develop the skills and knowledge to collaborate in transition planning.

Directions: Use the following Person-Centered Planning Chart to observe a transition planning meeting and document your observations of the stages observed.

Stages	Student responsibilities	Team responsibilities	Observation documentation
Planning the meeting	Shares strengths	Student, along with parent(s) and facilitator, identifies the agenda, location, and participants.	
Meeting			
1. Dream	Shares their big dream (e.g., becoming a race car driver)	Facilitator and team brainstorm the vision for the future. All ideas are considered viable choices.	
2. Now	Shares what is happening in their life currently, including the positive as well as challenging situations	The team supports the student in being authentic with what is really happening (e.g., if the student is unable to read, then that is a reality).	
3. Enroll	Identifies supportive people in their life who can help them achieve goals	The team helps the student identify key individuals in their life.	
4. Building strength	Determines what types of activities would support them in achieving their goals Building strength might mean the student needs to build academic skills such as reading or math in order to accomplish the dream	The team shares additional activities that build capacity for the student to be successful in reaching the dream.	
5. First steps	Shares their first activities to achieve goals	The team supports the process and suggests activities that align with the first steps.	

Stages	Student responsibilities	Team responsibilities	Observation documentation
6. Charting actions	Identifies actions that help them move closer to the goal at periodic points of time	The team helps the student become specific about their goals, identifying dates, people, and places that will be involved in each of the actions.	
7. One-year goal	Student determines a goal to be achieved within 1 year and updates the team at the 1-year anniversary about the progress they have made toward achieving their goal	Team members celebrate the realization of the goal.	

Activity 10.3.

Stakeholders Planning

Supporting chapter: Chapter 10 (Transition Teaming: Meeting Postsecondary Needs)

Purpose: The purpose of this activity is to develop the skills and knowledge needed to identify the roles and responsibilities of stakeholders.

Directions: Use the following Stakeholders Chart to observe a transition planning meeting and identify the roles and responsibilities of each stakeholder involved in the transition plan.

Stakeholders/person who addresses these needs	Roles and responsibilities
Employment (could include current or future employer)	
Disability services coordinator	
Medical professional/person to speak to medical needs	
Transportation professional/person to speak to future transportation plans	
Vocational rehabilitation professional/job training coach	
Special education teacher	
General education teacher(s)	
Paraprofessional	

Other members may include friend(s), community member(s) (e.g., person representing a spiritual, volunteer, hobby, or recreational interest), or legal representation.

Other: _____	
Other: _____	
Other: _____	

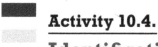
Activity 10.4.

Identification of a Quality Transition Plan

Supporting chapter: Chapter 10 (Transition Teaming: Meeting Postsecondary Needs)

Purpose: The purpose of this activity is to develop the skills and knowledge to identify the key elements of transition plans.

Directions: Use an IEP and inventory the Transition Plan section to determine if it meets IDEA requirements.

Rubric scale: Use the following scale and circle the number that best ranks the IEP area reviewed in the table that follows.

• 1 = Standard not met • IEP fails to provide evidence of meeting the IDEA 2004 requirements. • IEP does not address the IDEA 2004 requirements.	• 2 = Standard partially met • Performance provides evidence of partially meeting IDEA 2004 requirements. • Performance addresses some of the IDEA 2004 requirements.	• 3 = Standard met • Performance provides evidence of meeting most/all of the IDEA 2004 requirements. • Performance addresses most/all of the IDEA 2004 requirements.	• 4 = Standard exceeds • Performance provides evidence of exceeding all IDEA 2004 requirements. • All indicators are addressed in the IEP and go beyond expectations.
Key Area (IEP Section) **Transitions Beginning at Age 16, Coordinated Activities That Meet These Criteria**	**Ranking**	**Rationale for Ranking**	
T1: Statement of quality-of-life goals: The statement is results oriented; focused on improving academic and functional achievement; and facilitates movement from school to postschool activities, including postsecondary education, vocational education, integrated employment (supported employment), continuing and adult education, adult services, independent living, or community participation.	1 2 3 4		
T2: Vision: The vision is based on the child's needs, taking into account the child's strengths, preferences, and interests.	1 2 3 4		
T3: Resources and interagency collaboration: The IEP includes a description of the course of study needed to reach stated goals, including instruction, related services, community experiences, development of employment and other postschool adult living objectives, and, when appropriate, acquisition of daily living skills and vocational evaluation.	1 2 3 4		

Key Area (IEP Section) **Transitions Beginning at Age 16, Coordinated Activities That Meet These Criteria**	Ranking	Rationale for Ranking
T4: Stakeholders: Parents of a child making the transition from Part C services (early childhood) to Part B services (school age) can request an invitation to the initial IEP meeting be sent to representatives of the Part C system to assist with a smooth transition of services.	1 2 3 4	

Rewritten statement of transition:

_____

_____

_____

_____

_____

_____

_____

_____

Designing Behavioral Intervention Plans

Kathryn Doyle and Stephen Kroeger

After reading this chapter and engaging in activities related to this chapter, you will be able to meet the following outcomes:

- Explain the importance of using positive intervention when designing IEPs to help a student learn acceptable behaviors.

- Defend how positive behavior interventions and supports (PBIS) provide a framework that addresses disruptive behavior and improves student outcomes.

- Compose a goal that focuses on an alternative behavior for a student who exhibits challenging behaviors.

The teaching profession has made dramatic strides in what we know about how to support students to be successful academically, socially, and emotionally. This chapter is positioned to guide school teams in an overview of the current state of the field and serve as a practical guide into the two widely used tools that help us understand student behavior and what to do when student behaviors become a concern. It is important to keep in mind that change is never mono-directional; sometimes educators, community members, and parents have to examine our behaviors and how we design our learning and home environments to determine how we contribute to unproductive student behaviors.

CONNECTION TO THE LEGAL PERSPECTIVE

The Individuals with Disabilities Education Improvement Act (IDEA) of 2004 (PL 108-446) is a law that ensures a free appropriate public education (FAPE) to eligible children with disabilities. IDEA requires that for students with disabilities who exhibit challenging behavior, schools must consider the use of positive interventions to help students learn acceptable alternative behaviors if the behavior is a manifestation of their disability. IDEA advocates a proactive response to student behavior and requires the IEP team to assess the needs for behavioral

> ## IDEA'S KEY COMPONENTS
>
> - **Free appropriate public education (FAPE).** Requires that the student be educated in a manner that meets their educational needs by a public educational agency that is free to the family.
>   - *Zero Reject.* Mandates that the school cannot deny a child an education due to the severity of their needs.
> - **Least restrictive environment (LRE).** The student is educated in a manner that is most like their typical peers.
> - **Procedural safeguards** (due process). The family has the right to disagree with the placement, services, and educational plan for their child and can bring the school district to court.
> - **Parental participation** (shared decision making). Parents have the right to participate as part of the education team for their child.
> - **Nondiscriminatory evaluation.** Requires schools to utilize a team approach in assessing a student in all suspected areas of a disability using measures that are valid, reliable, culturally relevant, and linguistically appropriate.
> - **Individualized education program (IEP).** The IEP team assesses current evaluation information and develops a written document designed to meet the unique educational needs of each student with a disability.

support. A functional behavioral assessment (FBA) and a behavioral intervention plan (BIP) are the two tools available to IEP teams according to IDEA. These tools are defined and explained, as well as their connection to the IEP, in this chapter.

THE NEED FOR EQUITABLE PRACTICES

It was pointed out in a *Dear Colleague Letter* (U.S. Department of Education, 2015) that during the 2013–2014 school year, 10% of all students ages 3–21 with disabilities were removed for disciplinary reasons for 10 school days or less. Alarmingly, students of color with disabilities faced disproportionately higher rates of removal. The letter also stated that 19% of Black students with disabilities ages 3–21 were removed for disciplinary reasons 10 school days or less within a single school year (U.S. Department of Education, 2014). This means that Black children with disabilities were removed at almost twice the rate of their peers. Receiving a school suspension leads to a host of negative outcomes, including lower academic performance, interrupted school attendance, lower self-esteem, and decreased graduation levels. In addition, school suspensions significantly increase the odds of imprisonment during young adulthood (Hemez et al., 2020). Implications of these policies are that Black students with disabilities are far more likely to end up in correctional facilities than their White counterparts. It is imperative to emphasize the need for culturally responsive behavioral support and system change. Therefore, we urge you as a reader to be prepared to study not only the behavior of concern in a school, a group, or an individual, but also be prepared to examine the learning environment and teacher beliefs and attitudes. Behavior change in others always includes behavior change in teachers, leadership, and staff.

CULTURALLY RESPONSIVE PBIS

Positive behavior interventions and supports (PBIS) is a framework supported by research focused on improving student behavioral outcomes. The PBIS framework focuses on proactively teaching students safe and positive behaviors. PBIS includes the student's team, in collaboration with administrators and behavior specialists, working to provide the training, policy support, and organizational support needed for successful student behavioral outcomes. PBIS is constructed as a three-tiered support framework that is a data-driven, problem-solving framework to improve outcomes for all students. It is important to note that the three tiers of support refer to levels of support students receive, not to students themselves. Consistent with person-first language protocols, students receive Tier 2 supports, they are not Tier 2 students (Horner et al., 2017).

Tier 1 refers to universal prevention and is foundational for behavior and academics. Schools provide these universal supports to all students. Quality Tier 1 programming gives most students what they need to be successful and prevent future problems. The approach in Tier 2 is a targeted prevention that focuses on improving specific skill deficits. Groups of students with similar targeted needs will typically receive this level of intervention, which provides increased opportunities for practice and feedback while keeping the intervention maximally efficient. Tier 2 supports help students develop the skills they need to benefit from Tier 1 interventions at the school. Tier 3 supports are the most intensive that the school offers and require individualized interventions and student plans that include goals related to academics and behavioral support. See Figure 11.1 for a visual representation of universal prevention and supports.

Cultural responsiveness is a defining feature of PBIS (Center on Positive Behavioral Interventions & Supports, 2015). Leverson et al. (2019) provided a PBIS

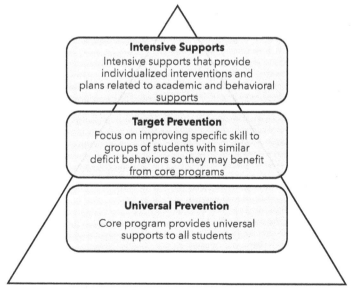

Figure 11.1. Universal prevention and supports.

cultural responsiveness field guide, which emphasized that effective school environments help the vast majority of students to be successful; however, for students who are not from the dominant culture, the school environment can expose them to unintentional slights, which devalue their backgrounds and diminish school connectedness. Given this reality, it is imperative that school staff engage students through validation and affirmation of their identity, which includes their cultures and individual learning histories. Failing to take this kind of action risks disengaging underrepresented racial minorities from the school through unintentional slights and actions.

Positive Behavior Interventions and Supports Web Resources

- Center on Positive Behavioral Interventions & Supports (https://www.pbis.org)
- What Is PBIS? (https://www.understood.org/en/learning-thinking -differences/treatments-approaches/educational-strategies/pbis-how -schools-support-positive-behavior)
- PBIS World (https://www.pbisworld.com)
- U.S. Department of Education School Climate and Discipline (https:// www2.ed.gov/policy/gen/guid/school-discipline/index.html)
- IDEAs That Work (http://ccrs.osepideasthatwork.org/about-us)

Cultural responsiveness consists of five components (see Table 11.1): identity, voice, supportive environment, situational appropriateness, and data for equity (Leverson et al., 2019). Leverson and colleagues specified that behavior is learned and context specific. They also noted that shared beliefs and behaviors serve purposes that may be difficult to understand by those who

---

How to Create a Culturally Responsive Classroom

1. Discover your students' assets
   - What are your student's strengths, interests, funds of knowledge, culture, cultural values, and language?
2. Construct a supportive classroom environment
   - Grow authentic, caring relationships
   - Design a welcoming classroom
3. Analyze the curriculum
   - Look for ways to increase relevance
   - Look for ways to increase and support rigor
4. Maintain your own learning
   - Investigate resources to deepen your own understanding (Breiseth et al., 2020)

are outside of that culture or context. Furthermore, cultural responsiveness requires that educators hold high expectations for all students, use students' cultures and experiences to enhance their learning, and provide all students with access to effective instruction and adequate resources for learning (Klingner et al., 2005).

Table 11.1. Cultural responsiveness as defined by positive behavior interventions and supports (PBIS)

Element	Description
Identity	Each of our identities is complex. We draw on who we are from our race, ethnicity, abilities, gender identity, language, marital status, religion, socioeconomic context, and geographic location. Together they provide a sense of self and history, and they influence how we interact in society. Not only do practitioners need to explore their own multifaceted identities but they also need to develop a thick understanding of the other person. Seeing a student for 45 or 50 minutes a day can lend itself to a thin description of who we are to each other. No one set of experiences are universal.
Voice	*Intellectual mattering* (Schwartz, 2019) is a term that denotes that your and my presence and participation helps shape what happens in the environment. Walker (2020) explained this as a dynamic mutuality in which we share an interest in others as whole people, that we are willing to be influenced by the other. In the context of cultural responsiveness, voice suggests that teachers and administrators look for opportunities to hear from those who have been historically underrepresented.
Supportive environment	*Supportive environment* refers to the expectation that the community must develop fluency and expertise rather than a system in which infractions are delivered. Staff in a supportive environment hold each other accountable, and all members of the learning community feel valued. Students will see themselves in the classroom because diversity is welcome.
Situational appropriateness	*Situational appropriateness* is defined in the *PBIS Cultural Responsiveness Field Guide* (Leverson et al., 2016) as the ability to determine what types of behavior will ensure positive outcomes in a given setting and demonstrate those skills with fluency. We also know that situations and contexts change, so behavior in one environment might be perceived as acceptable, but the perception or expectations for behavior changes in another setting. This is referred to as *code switching*, and individuals must learn how, when, and why behavioral expectations change depending on the context.
Data for equity	*Data for equity* refers to a two-fold aspect of data—student outcomes and fidelity of implementation of evidence-based practices. Implementation of an evidence-based practice is directly in the sphere of influence of teachers and leaders. Rather than relying on statements that rely on overgeneralizations, such as comments that begin with "those kids . . .," we turn to data to disaggregate and examine it in meaningful ways. For example, the *PBIS Cultural Responsiveness Field Guide* (Leverson et al., 2016) highlighted the Wisconsin Risk Ratio calculator, which was designed to compare an identified group's risk with that of the dominant enrollment group.

Technical and Adaptive Change

Cultural responsiveness in the context of PBIS suggests that those committed to implementing change in their learning environment should be sensitive to the kind of changes that are needed. There are two types of change to consider within the PBIS framework—technical and adaptive changes. Heifetz et al. (2009) noted that technical change involves learning and implementing new strategies or tools to use with students. Technical change tends to be easier to make, at least on the surface, but it may have a diminished effect if it is not accompanied by adaptive changes.

An FBA is a process for identifying unexpected behaviors as well as interventions that will support a student trying to improve or eliminate a behavior. An FBA can be seen as an example of a technical change. A staff member can learn to collect data and formulate a hypothesis about a student's specific behavior, but if the evaluator's underlying biases have not also been examined, then the results of such an assessment may give rise to a faulty or misguided approach to what is needed to support the student. How we interpret data is influenced by our beliefs and preconceived notions of a given situation.

Adaptive change, however, represents changes in values, beliefs, roles, relationships, and approaches to work. For example, implementing effective culturally responsive practices might begin with staff members exploring their personal journey in understanding how their own culture shapes their beliefs about instruction and student interactions. This kind of exploration often leads to changes in the way staff manage the dynamics of difference or diverse cultures and norms in the classroom and/or school (Rose et al., 2020). Adaptive change requires authentic engagement from everyone involved in the learning environment.

Educators can take actions to begin the technical and adaptive work of creating a culturally responsive PBIS system. Leverson and colleagues (2019) recommended that teachers and leaders begin this process by increasing identity awareness, which involves enacting strategies to learn about and affirm the cultures and experiences of families, students, and communities. Examining lesson plans together is one way a group of teachers and administrators might increase their identity awareness. Nandakumas and colleagues (2021) discussed how a lesson plan embodies many of the beliefs of the planners. In their exchange about increasing opportunities to respond in the classroom, they closely examined how teachers can plot a change in their practice by writing a script that clearly documents learning intentions and specific evidence-based practices designed to be culturally responsive. Organizational studies have demonstrated that the cultures within organizations cannot be adequately understood if the sole focus is on an individual's discrete acts and cognitive or moral qualities (Blackler & McDonald, 2000). The implications are that we need to simultaneously address technical and adaptive changes that a person-centered educational system aspires to implement.

FUNCTIONAL BEHAVIORAL ASSESSMENT

Many students who have behavioral needs will be successful at school with evidence-based Tier 1 and Tier 2 supports. A good benchmark for evaluating your school's behavioral supports is to determine if about 95% of the students are successful with Tier 1 and Tier 2 supports. Around 5% of students will need the most intensive supports the school offers; these students may also benefit from an FBA. School teams should be proactive when assessing the function of behavior for a student. Teams that wait until the student is in crisis are often left with fewer options if the behavior escalates to dangerous levels.

An FBA is a research-based approach to helping school staff understand why students engage in different behaviors across all settings and how these behaviors are regularly reinforced in the settings in which they occur. FBAs are mandated by IDEA as a component of PBIS. An FBA helps determine the function of the targeted challenging behaviors across school settings so interventions can be executed effectively in a behavioral support plan. The learning principle behind an FBA is that all behavior exhibited by a student serves a purpose to either 1) give the individual access to something desirable (positive reinforcement) or 2) allow them to escape or avoid something unpleasant (negative reinforcement). A student may be disruptive in class because they have learned that the teacher will quickly put them on a classroom technology device to limit the disruption (i.e., positive reinforcement of undesired behavior). Conversely, a student may find an academic assignment challenging and will give the teacher the middle finger, which they know will result in them being sent out of the classroom (i.e., negative reinforcement of undesirable behavior). Many escape/avoidance behaviors can be reduced or eliminated by addressing academic needs. The CEEDAR Center has created an excellent resource that provides possible intervention strategies for escape or avoidance behaviors: https://ceedar.education.ufl.edu/wp-content /uploads/2014/09/Handout-16-Function-Based-Intervention-Strategies.pdf

An FBA can be requested within the evaluation process for the student or by a member of the school team (family included) if the student's behavior is becoming more of a concern and the student is not responding to Tier 1/Tier 2 interventions. It is important to note that parental/guardian consent must be obtained to move forward with the FBA. The FBA process should be individualized based on the student's areas of strength, needs, and behavior.

Once the team has agreed that the student would benefit from an FBA and consent is obtained, the behavior of concern must be operationally defined. This means it is described in a clear, observable, and measurable way. Clear definitions allow the team to collect more reliable data. The team will want to avoid subjective or vague terms such as *mad, defiant, bad attitude, lazy, loses control,* and *apathetic.* A good rule of thumb is that the definition should pass the "stranger test," meaning that any school professional could pick up the team's definition and understand the behavior of concern and collect data on it.

Stop and Think!

Mr. Robbins, a sixth-grade English language arts teacher, has Daniel in class. Mr. Robbins proudly announces at staff meetings that he does not believe in positive behavior interventions and supports (PBIS) and he does not understand rewarding kids to do what is right. The rest of Mr. Robbin's core teams implements PBIS with high fidelity. Mr. Robbins has the most office referrals in the school. Daniel has started exhibiting some challenging behaviors in Mr. Robbins' classroom, but nowhere else. Mr. Robbins comes to you as the special education teacher (also known as the *intervention specialist*) and demands that you write "one of those behavior plan things that will get him out of my classroom."

• How would you address Mr. Robbins' request within a PBIS framework?

What happens if the student has multiple behaviors of concern? It is up to the team to prioritize which behaviors should be addressed. Behaviors that should be prioritized are those that occur at a high intensity or frequency or that are dangerous to the student or others. One should also look for keystone behaviors. Questions that are helpful to ask include 1) How often does the behavior occur? 2) Does the behavior interfere with learning? 3) Does the behavior present a danger to others? and 4) If one behavior is addressed first, will it lead to better outcomes with the other behaviors of concern?

After the team has focused on and operationally defined the behavior of concern, they will collect data. Data can be collected via direct and indirect methods. Indirect methods include interviews, checklists, questionnaires, and record reviews. Interviews, checklists, and questionnaires should be shared with key stakeholders such as parents, general education teachers, paraprofessionals, and the student, if possible. The records-review process can give insight to past school successes and areas of need. Indirect measures should always be used in conjunction with direct observation measures. Research has shown that indirect measures can often be highly subjective or inaccurate.

Recoding antecedent, behavior, and consequence data (ABC method) is the most common way to collect direct observation data. There are narrative recording and checklist formats available. The ABC method allows the observer to record what happened right before the behavior occurred (the antecedent), as well as what happens right after the behavior occurred (the consequence). The team can then analyze this data to look for patterns in the student's behavior. Are there events that trigger the behavior? Are there consistencies in how the team responds to the challenging behavior? The team can then develop a hypothesis about the function, or purpose, of the student's behavior. Other data that should be collected to assist with progress monitoring includes frequency (how many times it occurs); rate (how often a behavior occurs in a specified time period); duration (how long the behavior lasts); latency (how long it takes a student to start something); and momentary time sampling (if the behavior occurs or does not occur in an interval). These data collection tools provide the team with the data needed to identify patterns and contexts that make the behavior more or less likely to occur in the future.

Examples of Data Sheets

Initial steps in an FBA are designed to pinpoint the behavior of concern and settings in which the behavior occurs. This behavior will be considered important and meaningful for the individual and others involved. Once this behavior focus has been achieved, staff collects data about various aspects of the behavior, such as what was occurring just before the behavior took place, a description of the behavior, and an accounting of all the consequences of the behavior. These data can point to events and occurrences in the setting that almost always benefit from examination. Sometimes staff will note that a behavior will occur when new academic content is presented or when a student is asked to work independently after recently learning a new skill. At the consequence end of the behavioral pathway, staff may notice that the behavior of concern is consistently reinforced in some way, either positively or negatively. An ABC chart (see Figure 11.2) is a form designed to capture this behavioral pathway. Other data collection tools that teachers and staff will find helpful include check-off data (see Figure 11.3), frequency data (see Figure 11.4), duration data (see Figure 11.5), and interval data (see Figure 11.6).

FBA forms will vary from state to state and district to district; however, they will often contain the same or similar information:

- What triggers the behavior

- Setting events, or where the behavior is likely to occur

- How often or how long the behavior occurs

- Where the behavior is least likely to occur

- Person(s) with whom the behavior is most/least likely to occur

- The adult response to the behavior

- The outcomes or consequences of the behavior

- A hypothesis on the function of behavior

- Other relevant information

In the end, the team will have established a behavioral pathway. A behavioral pathway is a portrait of the many aspects of a given behavior such as the triggering events, both within and outside of the context; a clear and measurable description of the behavior; the consequences of the behavior; and the team's hypothesis of how the behavior functions for the individual. Once this pathway has been described, the team is ready to develop ways to support the student and make related changes in the learning environment. This often requires professional development for everyone involved with the individual.

Date/Time	Setting/Staff	Antecedent (what happened before the behavior)	Behavior (clear, observable definition of the behavior)	Consequence (what happened after the behavior)
Comments:				
Comments:				

Figure 11.2.   Blank ABC data chart.

Behavioral Intervention Plan

Once an FBA has been completed by the team, which often includes staff, teachers, a case manager, and family members, they are ready to develop a BIP. The FBA will have clearly identified a working hypothesis of how the behavior is functioning for the individual. The FBA will also explain how various settings and events play a part in the behavior's function for the individual. Having this information in hand, the team is prepared to develop a BIP whose aim is to support the student's behavior change and guide educational professionals as they work to make shifts in the learning context.

A BIP is created by the team to help reduce the prevalence of challenging behaviors and teach the student socially acceptable alternative replacement behaviors. The goal for these replacement behaviors is for the new behavior to serve the same function as the challenging behaviors. This approach supports the development of a different behavioral pathway that supports academic success. Replacement behaviors should be observable, measurable, and teachable. Instead of throwing books on the floor, a replacement behavior may include requesting a break, raising a hand, or using a speech-generating device. The research and evidence-based interventions chosen should correlate with the student's function of behavior. Figure 11.7 provides many resources to support you in this process. The BIP should clearly articulate antecedent strategies, behavior teaching strategies, and reinforcement strategies.

Date/Time	Antecedent (what happened before the behavior)	Behavior (clear, observable definition of the behavior)	Consequence (what happened after the behavior)	Hypothesized Function
	• Work demand placed • Attention restricted • Item/activity restricted • Transition • Other _____	• Work refusal • Left desk • Cursing • Hitting peer • Hitting staff • Elopement • Kicking • Other _____	• Redirected • Prompted • Ignored • Removed item • Other ____	• Attention • Tangible • Escape • Sensory
	• Work demand placed • Attention restricted • Item/activity restricted • Transition • Other _____	• Work refusal • Left desk • Cursing • Hitting peer • Hitting staff • Elopement • Kicking • Other _____	• Redirected • Prompted • Ignored • Removed item • Other ____	• Attention • Tangible • Escape • Sensory

Figure 11.3. Check-off data sheet.

BIP requirements will vary from state to state and district to district but will generally contain the same information: 1) a strength-based profile, 2) the behavior of concern and baseline data gathered from the FBA, 3) interventions that will be put in place by the school team, 4) what data will be collected, 5) who will implement the interventions and collect the data, 6) when progress monitoring data will be shared with the team, and 7) a clear and measurable goal statement. This goal statement should support the behavior IEP goal for the student.

The IEP team determines if the school discipline policies need to be amended for a student and whether consequences need to be different from those written into school discipline policy. The team should always be using data to determine if the consequences chosen are changing the student behavior.

Time Lines

IDEA does not address a specific time line for an FBA and BIP to be completed and written. It is generally addressed in individual state rules. State rules vary from 30 to 90 days to start the process once an FBA has been requested. As a general best practice, FBAs and BIPs should be reviewed annually with progress monitoring occurring as it is stated in the IEP.

Student:				
Target behavior:				
Date	Start time	End time	Tally of occurrences	Total

Figure 11.4. Frequency data.

Stop and Think!

Refer to a behavioral intervention plan, whether it is one you have written yourself or that was prepared by a colleague or a mentor teacher.

Consider following the checklist in order to complete a brief analysis of the plan.

1. Focus and function

   • Challenging behavior is defined or described in specific language that anyone can recognize when it is occurring.

   • There are summaries of at least three sources of data on the challenging behavior. Data collection may include ABC observations, event recording, records review, and personal interviews. If not, information that is still needed has been prioritized and assigned to team members to obtain immediately.

   • Based on the data, a hypothesis is written to state the conclusions and the function or purpose of the challenging behavior.

2. Instructional and preventive

   • Specific antecedent procedures that change aspects of the environment to prevent behaviors from occurring are described in full.

   • Changes made in the current curricular design, process, and/or delivery are specifically described. These changes are intended to create a better match between the present skills of the individual and the demands of the setting.

(continued)

Stop and Think! *(continued)*

- Crisis management procedures, if needed, are explicitly listed, including which adult will carry out each phase of the plan.

3. Positive and equivalent

  - At least one replacement or alternative behavior is listed (i.e., a social skill or behavior that is useful to the student and is functionally equivalent). The new behavior must render the challenging behavior ineffective and/or inefficient.

  - A teaching plan, including instructions on how to teach the replacement behavior, and any other social skills lessons are written out.

  - There is a clear description of positive reinforcement procedures designed to increase the desired behavior. A reinforcement schedule and a follow-up review date to check the progress of the desired behavior is also included in this part of the support plan.

4. Long term and comprehensive

  - The plan considers goals and outcomes over the span of years verses short-term behavioral outcomes.

  - The support plan provides the individual with opportunities to demonstrate generosity, responsibility, and mastery in interactions and work with adults and peers in school, the workplace, and the community.

  - An ongoing data collection process is described and includes time lines for collecting and reviewing data to check for improvement. The support plan is adjusted in conjunction with these findings.

Answer the following questions:

- What are the strengths of the document?

- Are revisions needed to improve the document? (Kroeger & Phillips, 2007)

WRITING QUALITY BEHAVIORAL IEP GOALS

The behavioral goals addressed in the IEP should correspond directly with the student's FBA and BIP. It often makes the most sense to have the behavioral goal written directly from the BIP goal statement. The IEP goal should target an observable replacement behavior that is amenable to change and will contribute to the student's academic success (see Figure 11.8). It is important to note that the goal should focus on student behavior, not educator behavior, even though the professional development of the members of the team are frequently involved to support the changes needed in the learning environment. According to Marx and Miller (2020), quality behavioral IEP goals include the following components: 1) time frame, 2) assessment condition, 3) target behavior, 4) supports needed, 5) level of proficiency/criteria, and 6) measurement (see Table 11.2). IEPs should always comply with district regulations first.

An annual IEP goal should target the student using the replacement skill 90%–100% of the time. That being said, the goal should be realistic. If peers are unable to perform the goal at 100% accuracy, then it is unfair to expect that from the target student. Benchmarks, however, can be set at a lower threshold. The decision on how to write the benchmarks should come from the student's baseline data. If the student has a very low repertoire of replacement and coping behaviors in baseline, then it is unreasonable to expect the student to start using them 100% of the time without intensive intervention. Interventions should be scaffolded to build success for the student across the IEP year.

Student:			
Target behavior:			
Date	Start time	End time	Total time

Figure 11.5. Duration data.

BEHAVIORAL PROGRESS MONITORING

It is important to collect behavioral data in an ongoing, systematic, and frequent manner which allows the team to make data-based decisions about what behavioral supports are needed. As a team, the following questions should be addressed:

- How often will data be collected?
- In what contexts will the data be collected?
- Who will collect the data?
- Where will the data be entered to allow the team to analyze it?

The school team should choose assessment measures based on the BIP and IEP behavioral goals. It is key that the school team maintain fidelity to the interventions written in the BIP. If the interventions are used inconsistently, or for too short of a period of time, then the data collected will be meaningless and not lead to behavior change for the student.

Direct Systematic Observation

In direct systematic observation data collection, the school staff watches a person or environment and systematically records the replacement and/or targeted behavior. Behavior is measured in terms of the following: rate, frequency, duration, latency, and intensity. This allows the data collected to be closely aligned with targeted behavioral goals. Another advantage is that many resources exist that provide data collection sheets and training for school staff (see Figure 11.9).

Student:		
Target behavior		
Interval time:		
Interval number	Behavior occurrence	Comparison peer
	Y N	Y N
	Y N	Y N
	Y N	Y N
	Y N	Y N
	Y N	Y N
Percentage of intervals with behavior: number of intervals with behavior divided by the total number of intervals data was collected x 100		

Figure 11.6. Interval data sheet.

Monitoring Student Progress for Behavioral Interventions (DBI Professional
    Learning Series Module 3): https://intensiveintervention.org/resource
    /monitoring-student-progress-behavioral-interventions-dbi-training
    -series-module-3

Defining, Measuring and Monitoring Behaviors (Behavior Support for
    Intensive Intervention: Module 6): https://intensiveintervention.org
    /defining-measuring-and-monitoring-behaviors-behavior-course

Data-Based Decision Making (Intensive Intervention in Behavior: Module 7):
    https://intensiveintervention.org/behavior-data-based-decision-making
    -behavior-course

Marx, T. A., & Miller, F. G. (2020). *Strategies for setting data-driven behavioral
    individualized education program goals.* U.S. Department of Education,
    Office of Special Education Programs, National Center on Intensive
    Intervention.

Functional Behavioral Assessment: Identifying the Reasons for Problem
    Behavior and Developing a Behavior Plan: https://iris.peabody
    .vanderbilt.edu/module/fba

Addressing Disruptive and Noncompliant Behaviors (Part 2): Behavioral
    Interventions: https://iris.peabody.vanderbilt.edu/module/bi2

Classroom Behavior Management (Part 2, Elementary): Developing a
    Behavior Management Plan: https://iris.peabody.vanderbilt.edu
    /module/beh2/#content

Figure 11.7. Resources to support developing quality functional behavioral assessments (FBAs) and behavioral intervention plans (BIPs).

Direct Behavior Rating

Although systematic direct observation is considered the gold star of data collection, a school may not always have the resources to maintain this level of data collection. Another option is direct behavior rating (DBR), which is an evaluative rating that focuses on a range of target behaviors while also targeting more general outcomes. DBR should be defensible, flexible, repeatable, and efficient (Christ et al., 2009). The rating is completed by school staff such as teachers, paraprofessionals, and therapists. Schools will often refer to this tool as a daily behavior report card or a points sheet. The advantage of this approach is that it does not require constant recording or attention on the teacher's end. The team can choose to monitor the student's behavior at an interval that reflects the needs of the student (e.g., every hour, twice a day, at the end of the day).

An example DBR would be that a student checks in with a teacher midmorning, at lunch, and at the end of the day to fill out their behavior sheet. The target behavior the student is working on is raising their hand instead of blurting out. The teacher awards the student points based on the criteria agreed on, such as raising their hand in class. The student will have a goal number they are working

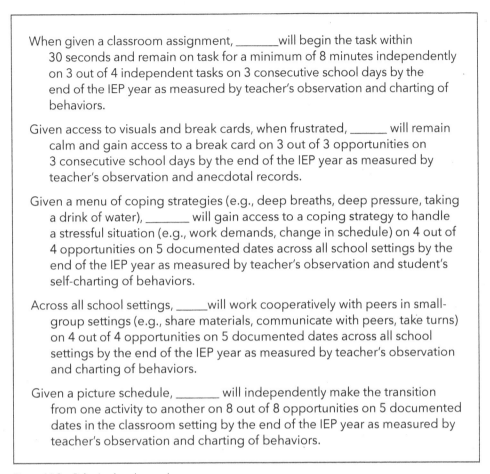

When given a classroom assignment, _____will begin the task within 30 seconds and remain on task for a minimum of 8 minutes independently on 3 out of 4 independent tasks on 3 consecutive school days by the end of the IEP year as measured by teacher's observation and charting of behaviors.

Given access to visuals and break cards, when frustrated, _____ will remain calm and gain access to a break card on 3 out of 3 opportunities on 3 consecutive school days by the end of the IEP year as measured by teacher's observation and anecdotal records.

Given a menu of coping strategies (e.g., deep breaths, deep pressure, taking a drink of water), _____ will gain access to a coping strategy to handle a stressful situation (e.g., work demands, change in schedule) on 4 out of 4 opportunities on 5 documented dates across all school settings by the end of the IEP year as measured by teacher's observation and student's self-charting of behaviors.

Across all school settings, _____will work cooperatively with peers in small-group settings (e.g., share materials, communicate with peers, take turns) on 4 out of 4 opportunities on 5 documented dates across all school settings by the end of the IEP year as measured by teacher's observation and charting of behaviors.

Given a picture schedule, _____ will independently make the transition from one activity to another on 8 out of 8 opportunities on 5 documented dates in the classroom setting by the end of the IEP year as measured by teacher's observation and charting of behaviors.

Figure 11.8. Behavioral goal examples.

toward to earn a reinforcing activity or item at the end of the day or week. The teacher will keep the points as a form of data to progress monitor the student's goal. An added benefit of this procedure is that the student is supported in their efforts at self-evaluation and goal setting.

Although data collection for the IEP should focus on an observable replacement behavior (e.g., asking for a break, raising hand, asking for help), it is appropriate to simultaneously collect data on the student's behavior of concern (e.g., hitting, blurting out, cursing) in order to monitor if a change in programming is needed.

Representing the Data Visually

By visually representing data, school teams can describe student progress in a way that helps to illuminate the written goals. Data can be represented visually in graphs, charts, or checklists. Visual data will allow the school team to determine if the student is making progress toward the goal and responding to the intervention. Visual data is frequently prepared by an intervention specialist for various users. The teacher and classroom staff use it to track processes, students use it to support self-regulation and self-evaluation skills, and a team will use it to assess present processes and make plans for future supports. An IEP team can use these data to report present levels of functional performance.

Table 11.2. Guide for constructing behavioral goals

Components	Definition	Example
B = Behavior	Replacement behavior is stated in observable and measurable terms. Behavior is selected based on the student's most recent functional behavioral assessment that is objective and can be observed.	Student will gain access to a break card to request a break from instruction. Student will increase their use of hand raising. Student will ask for help.
E = Evaluation	Assessment measures and criteria for evaluating the goal are included. • Frequency counts • Duration measures • Latency measures • Intensity measures • Direct behavior ratings What criteria needs to be met to indicate mastery?	Using 20-minute momentary time sampling observation Measured by weekly frequency reporting from direct observations From 45% to 90% accuracy on 9 out of 10 opportunities
S = Specific	Provides precise information: who, what, when, and where What prompts or supports are needed? Where is this happening? What is the setting?	Given a visual schedule . . . Independently . . . When given a verbal reminder . . . In the general education classroom . . . During recess . . . During small-group reading instruction . . .
T = Timely	Date by which the desired behavior will be achieved When mastery will be met?	By May 2023 . . . At the end of the first academic quarter . . .

Challenge Scenario

Mr. Thomas is a new intervention specialist at Regis Elementary School. He is excited for his new position and has a strong background in working with students with behavioral needs. At his old school, he was primarily in charge of supporting the FBA and BIP process. He always made sure his IEP goals corresponded directly with the goals on the BIP. The school psychologist is primarily in charge of supporting the FBA and BIP at Regis Elementary. As Mr. Thomas reads through one of his new student's, LeeAnn, FBA and BIP, he notes that it is well written and the interventions in the BIP are tailored to the function of the behavior. When he gets to LeeAnn's IEP, however, he sees there are no behavioral goals that are connected to the BIP. He is happy he is meeting with LeeAnn's intervention specialist (the special

IRIS Behavior Modules (11 modules total)

https://iris.peabody.vanderbilt.edu/resources/iris-resource-locator

Evidence-Based Practices (Part 3): Evaluating Learner Outcomes and Fidelity

https://iris.peabody.vanderbilt.edu/module/ebp_03/#content

Intervention Central: Direct Behavior Ratings

https://www.interventioncentral.org/direct-behavior-ratings

Direct Behavior Rating Overview

https://intensiveintervention.org/resource/direct-behavior-rating-overview

Behavior Strategies to Support Intensifying Intervention

https://intensiveintervention.org/intervention-resources/behavior-strategies
-support-intensifying-interventions

Briesch, A. M., Riley-Tillman, T. C., & Chafouleas, S. M. (2016). *Direct behavior rating: Linking assessment, communication, and intervention*. Guilford Press.

Figure 11.9. Direct observation resources.

education teacher) from last year, Mr. Frankel, to discuss the transition. The conversation that ensued follows:

Mr. Thomas: Hi, Mr. Frankel. Thanks for taking the time to meet with me today. I am excited to get started with the students. It looks like a good group.

Mr. Frankel: Yeah, we're glad you're here. You are really going to have your hands full with one of them. That LeeAnn, she really gave me a run for my money last year.

Mr. Thomas: I'm glad you brought her up. I was reading through her documents, and I had some questions for you. I noticed she had a really great FBA and BIP, but she didn't have a goal related to that on her IEP.

Mr. Frankel: Well, I'm pretty old school. I don't really think there is a way to measure any of that kind of stuff.

Mr. Thomas: Yeah, measuring behavior can be tricky. I have some ideas I can share with you if you are interested.

Mr. Frankel: Sure. The school psychologist wrote out a BIP. I tried it for a week and clearly it wasn't working, so I used some of my own methods. It's easier to just put her in time-out in the hallway when she starts acting out. Then we can keep teaching. Sometimes she would start cursing the minute she walked in the door. I put her right back in the hallway, and she was happy as a clam.

Mr. Thomas: Thanks for your time, Mr. Frankel. I have some ideas for LeeAnn. I look forward to working with her this year.

Mr. Frankel: Good luck.

Scenario Reflection

Based on the challenge scenario, document and discuss your initial thoughts regarding the following questions:

- Is it a red flag that no behavioral goals are on the IEP? Why or why not?

- How would you respond to Mr. Frankel's comment, "Well, I'm pretty old school. I don't really think there is a way to measure any of that kind of stuff"? What are the methods to measure data?

- Mr. Frankel said he attempted the BIP for a week. What is the issue with this? If the BIP was difficult to implement, what should he have done?

- Did Mr. Frankel's own methods likely consider the function of behavior?

SUMMARY

This chapter focused on best practices and resources to support students with behavioral needs within the IEP process. Teams trying to interpret challenging behaviors in the school setting can be demanding because the interpretation of the behavior requires an examination of a range of factors, including the specific behavior of the individual, the settings the behavior occurs in, and the antecedents and reinforcing consequences that sustain the behavior. Using the framework of PBIS with a culturally responsive lens establishes the climate and builds the skills that all school teams need to successfully support students who have behavioral needs. The legally required use of the FBA and a BIP will guide the team in developing meaningful IEP goals and implementing effective supports for students with challenging behavior. Teams who efficaciously support students with behavioral needs rely on data and research-based interventions to change behavior and support school staff in the change process. Incorporating a PBIS framework, sound FBAs, quality BIPs, professionally written IEP goals, and an effective progress monitoring system will allow students with behavioral needs to flourish and grow as contributing members of the school community and at the community at large. The list in Figure 11.10 can be used in preparation for the IEP meeting.

PREPARATION FOR THE IEP MEETING:
BEHAVIORAL INTERVENTIONS

Prior to the Meeting

☐ Identify student's strengths and list triggers to the student's behavior.

☐ Determine setting(s) where behavior is most/least likely to occur.

☐ Determine frequency of the behavior and with whom it is most/least likely to occur.

☐ Discuss the outcomes or consequence of the behavior.

☐ Identify whether you need to add anyone to the team.

During the Meeting

☐ Create an atmosphere of open communication.

☐ Encourage members to use jargon-free language so all can understand.

☐ Monitor the involvement of each member and their emotional level.

☐ Develop goals and objectives to address the behavioral needs of the student.

☐ Check to see if members agree with the present levels, goals, objectives, and the least restrictive environment.

☐ If using an interpreter, be sure to use appropriate interpreter etiquette (see Chapter 2).

After the Meeting

☐ Debrief with all team members, including parents, regarding the effectiveness of the meeting.

☐ Review with the student how they did as a self-advocate; discuss ways to improve.

☐ Send copies of the meeting documents to all participants.

☐ Follow up on any unresolved issues.

Figure 11.10. Preparation for the IEP meeting: Behavioral interventions.

THE IEP CHECKLIST: BEHAVIORAL GOALS

The following checklist can be used as an inventory to ensure the IEP contains the required components for behavioral goals.

Key Area (IEP section): **Behavioral Goals**	Criteria met	
	Yes	No
BG1: The goal includes a functionally relevant replacement behavior that is observable.		
BG2: The goal includes an assessment measure and criteria for evaluating the goal.		
BG3: The goal includes specific context and condition when the desired behavior is to occur.		
BG4: The goal includes the time line or date when the goal will be mastered.		

ACTIVITIES

The activities included in this chapter are intended for the reader to gain a deeper understanding of the content covered. The activities associated with this chapter include the following:

- Activity 11.1. Adaptive Behavior Practice
- Activity 11.2. ABC Data Collection
- Activity 11.3. Behavioral Intervention Plan Review

Activity 11.1.
Adaptive Behavior Practice

Supporting chapter: Chapter 11 (Designing Behavioral Intervention Plans)

Purpose: The purpose of this activity is to help develop the skill and knowledge to identify adaptive elements in order for a strategy to be effective.

Directions: Read the Jack Pritchard scenario by Heifetz and Laurie (1997). Then, answer the following question.

Heifetz and Laurie (1997, p. 124) presented the following scenario to their readers.

> To stay alive, Jack Pritchard had to change his life. Triple bypass surgery and medication could help, the heart surgeon told him, but no technical fix could release Pritchard from his own responsibility for changing the habits of a lifetime. He had to stop smoking, improve his diet, get some exercise, and take time to relax, remembering to breathe more deeply each day. Pritchard's doctor could provide sustaining technical expertise and take supportive action, but only Pritchard could adapt his ingrained habits to improve his long-term health. The doctor faced the leadership task of mobilizing the patient to make critical behavioral changes; Jack Pritchard faced the adaptive work of figuring out which specific changes to make and how to incorporate them into his daily life.

Adaptive work is required when our deeply held beliefs are challenged, when the values that made us successful become less relevant, and when legitimate yet competing perspectives emerge. It is easy to confuse technical change with adaptive change. Real change efforts must be adopted by everyone involved, and such changes require skills such as collaborating, listening, and responding.

Question: Think about a behavioral challenge that you and your colleagues face. Instead of thinking of strategies to address the challenge, what adaptive elements must be addressed for a given strategy to work effectively?

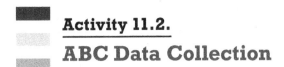

Activity 11.2.
ABC Data Collection

Supporting chapter: Chapter 11 (Designing Behavioral Intervention Plans)

Purpose: To gain experience conducting an ABC analysis and documenting observed behavior

Directions: Observe a child who displays disruptive behavior. You may need to ask a teacher and/or a parent for permission to observe the child's behavior. Use the data collection forms provided in this chapter (Figures 11.2, 11.3, 11.4, 11.5, and 11.6) to record the observation. Finally, analyze the observation by answering the following questions.

- How many instances of the disruptive behavior did you observe?

- What happened prior (antecedent) to the disruptive behavior observed?

- What happened after (consequence) the disruptive behavior ceased?

- What is the function of the observed behavior? (This is a hypothesis regarding your observation.)

- What relevant replacement behavior could be considered?

- Write a replacement behavior IEP goal using the BEST (behavior, evaluation, specific, timely) strategy (see Table 11.2).

Activity 11.3.

Behavioral Intervention Plan Review

Supporting chapter: Chapter 11 (Designing Behavioral Intervention Plans)

Purpose: The purpose of this activity is to gain experience on how the district in your home state provides intensive support for individuals who displays problematic school behavior.

Directions: Obtain a copy of a behavioral intervention plan used in your district. You may need to ask a special education teacher and/or parent for permission to review. Next, review the plan, identify issues, and answer the following questions.

- Was a strength-based profile provided? Summarize the information provided.

- Was there a clear statement of the behavior of concern with baseline data gathered from the functional behavioral assessment? State the behavior of concern and summarize the baseline data provided.

- What intervention will the school team provide?

- What data will the school team collect to ensure that the intervention is working?

- Who will implement the intervention and collect the data?

- When will the progress monitoring data be shared with the IEP team?

- Is the goal clear and measurable? Did it include the BEST (behavior, evaluation, specific, timely) strategy? Why or why not?

12

Supporting Students With Disabilities in Private and Parochial Schools

Kathleen G. Winterman and Rosemary Rotuno-Johnson

After reading this chapter and engaging in activities related to this chapter, you will be able to meet the following outcomes:

- Define services that are provided to students with disabilities at private and parochial schools.

- Explain Child Find, free appropriate public education (FAPE), and qualifying for services at private and parochial schools.

- Discuss the differences between IEPs and individualized service plans (ISPs).

Having parents as active participants in their child's education is a critical component of schooling within the United States. As discussed in Chapter 3, parental participation is not only recommended but also required in every aspect of schooling in the United States. The ultimate parent choice is where to send their child to school. This chapter's intent is to provide parents, teachers, and related services personnel with the information necessary to make an informed decision regarding the placement of a child with a disability in private or parochial schools. In addition, the services available for students with disabilities attending nonpublic schools is discussed as well as the differences between an IEP and an ISP.

CONNECTION TO LEGAL PESPECTIVE

As discussed throughout the book, the Individuals with Disabilities Education Improvement Act (IDEA) of 2004 (PL 108-446) is a federal law that requires each state to ensure that FAPE is available to all eligible children with disabilities residing in that state. The information in this chapter explains the provisions related to, and benefits available to, children with disabilities who are enrolled by their parents in private schools, including religious schools, when the provision of FAPE is not at issue. In IDEA, these children are often referred to as parentally placed private school children with disabilities, and the benefits available to them differ from the benefits for children with disabilities in public schools. IDEA is designed to improve educational results for all children with disabilities. Therefore, it provides benefits and services to children with disabilities in public schools and requires school districts to make services and benefits available to children with disabilities enrolled by their parents in nonpublic (private) schools. The law includes language requiring state education agencies (SEAs) and local education agencies (LEAs) to ensure the equitable participation of parentally placed children with disabilities in programs assisted by or carried out under the equitable participation requirements that apply to them (U.S. Department of Education, 2011).

> Equitable Participation: The 2004 Amendments to IDEA expand upon the 1997 reauthorization and include new requirements to ensure that LEAs provide parentally placed private school children with disabilities an opportunity for equitable participation in programs assisted or carried out under IDEA, the foundation of which is the consultation process. The major provisions regarding children with disabilities enrolled by their parents in private, including religious, elementary, and secondary schools are located in the statute at section 612(a)(10)(A) and in the regulations at 34 CFR §§300.130-300.144 and are listed in the sections below.
>   They concern:

- Agency responsibility for conducting child find activities and determining equitable services (34 CFR §§300.131–300.132);
- Consultation requirements (34 CFR §300.134);
- Written affirmation of timely and meaningful consultation (34 CFR §300.135);
- Child find activities (34 CFR §300.131);
- Data collection requirements (34 CFR §300.132[c]);
- Determination and provision of equitable services (34 CFR §§300.137-300.138);
- Services plans for children with disabilities receiving equitable services (34 CFR §§300.132[b], 300.137[c] and 300.138[b]);
- Permission for delivery of services at the private schools by LEAs, to the extent consistent with law (34 CFR §300.139[a]);
- Determination of the proportionate share of federal IDEA funds to be spent on equitable services (34 CFR §300.133);
- Non-availability of an individual entitlement of parentally placed private school students to special education and related services (34 CFR §300.137[a]); and
- Complaint procedures for private school officials regarding consultation (34 CFR §300.136) (U.S. Department of Education, 2011).

Parents of a child with a disability who wish to send their children to a religious-based or nonpublic school have a decision to make: Send their child to a public school where they will receive needed services or send their child to the nonpublic school where they may receive some, but often not all, needed services. IDEA does not provide protections for students educated in nonpublic schools; therefore, most nonpublic schools do not follow the FAPE regulations.

Stop and Think!

Free appropriate public education (FAPE) refers to specially designed educational services provided at the public's expense to meet a student's educational needs as stated in their IEP. These services are provided without charge to the parent (U.S. Department of Education, 2010).

- How will children at private schools be affected if their parents sign off on their right to FAPE by attending a private school?

IDEA'S KEY COMPONENTS

- **Free appropriate public education (FAPE).** Requires that the student be educated in a manner that meets their educational needs by a public educational agency that is free to the family.
  - *Zero Reject.* Mandates that the school cannot deny a child an education due to the severity of their needs.
- **Least restrictive environment (LRE).** The student is educated in a manner that is most like their typical peers.
- **Procedural safeguards** (due process). The family has the right to disagree with the placement, services, and educational plan for their child and can bring the school district to court.
- **Parental participation** (shared decision making). Parents have the right to participate as part of the education team for their child.
- **Nondiscriminatory evaluation.** Requires schools to utilize a team approach in assessing a student in all suspected areas of a disability using measures that are valid, reliable, culturally relevant, and linguistically appropriate.
- **Individualized education program (IEP).** The IEP team assesses current evaluation information and develops a written document designed to meet the unique educational needs of each student with a disability.

Although there are some services made available to students with disabilities through the LEA, the quantity of services is limited and may vary based on state and district. IDEA requires that public schools utilize a portion of their federal special education funding to provide services to students enrolled in private schools within their school district boundaries (Samuels, 2017). In 2016, approximately 2% of the school-age population with disabilities (85,000) were parentally enrolled in private schools (Samuels, 2017).

A Difficult Decision

Each family's situation is different, as are their values, goals, and aspirations for their child; the extent of the child's disability adds to this complexity. A common scenario follows. Attending the private school is a family tradition, and children are expected to follow in the footsteps of their relatives. The pressure can be palpable; homes are decorated with spirit wear from a beloved alma mater, and the child has accompanied parents to sporting competitions from an early age as a demonstration of the family's intent to carry on the tradition. The child often goes on to attend the elementary and secondary school of the parents' choice, and the family legacy endures. However, when a child has a physical, emotional, or learning difference that requires specialized instruction, the parents may need to decide if the private school is the best educational choice. Another common scenario involves the siblings of the child with a disability attending the nonpublic school, but the child with the disability attends a public school because the nonpublic school has limited special education services. The resulting different academic calendars, sports teams, school expectations, and school communities can fracture a family's time and energies. One final scenario is the family who wishes to send their child to a faith-based school to catechize the child into their faith tradition. When a child with a disability is unable to attend the religious school, the parents' religious wishes may go unfulfilled. Nonpublic schools are not bound by the requirements of IDEA and often do not have the needed special education services for the child with a disability.

PRIVATE SCHOOL PLACEMENT

Parents have the right to educate their children in the school(s) of their choice. Yet, additional safety measures are enacted to protect a child with a disability. When children with disabilities are placed in private schools, the level of support and responsibilities the LEA must offer changes based on how the child was placed in the private school (Clark, 2021). According to the National Center for Learning Disabilities (2020), there are three categories of placements: 1) students parentally placed in private schools prior to being found eligible for special services under IDEA; 2) students placed in private schools after being found eligible to receive services under IDEA; and 3) students with disabilities placed in private schools by the public school district or a public agency. Depending on who and how the student is placed in the private setting may determine who is responsible for paying for the student's tuition.

Child Find

A key responsibility of the local education agency (LEA) is to conduct **Child Find** and ensure the provision of equitable services are available to all children. The most recent provisions require the LEA with jurisdiction over the district in which the private school is located to be the responsible agency for implementing IDEA requirements for parentally placed children with disabilities. The term *Child Find* includes a mandate in which each state is obligated to locate, identify, evaluate, and spend a proportionate share of IDEA funds for equitable services for children with disabilities enrolled by their parents in private schools—including religious, elementary, and secondary schools—located in that district (34 CFR §300.131).

Children who are educated in private schools who are struggling academically and who are deemed to need an evaluation to determine if the child has a disability represent the first group of students parentally placed in private schools. The LEA is responsible to complete the evaluation within a prescribed time line as mandated by IDEA. The LEA must receive parental consent and complete the assessments within 30 days of receiving the consent. In addition, a meeting must be held within 45 days of receiving parental consent to review the assessment data. Parents are responsible for transporting their child to the public school for testing if requested by the public school. Once the child is found eligible for services, the public school should write an IEP within 30 days of the Evaluation Team Report meeting if the child is found eligible for services, which should include the services recommended to meet the child's unique needs. These services can be provided at the public school, or the parent may request the private school develop an ISP to offer some services. Again, parents are highly encouraged to examine the services provided by their state because services are not mandated from public schools for private school students. This is an act of good faith but is not required.

Students who enter the private school with an existing IEP do so with the parents' knowledge that they have waived their IDEA rights to a FAPE for their child. The services the student needs can be received by the parents transporting the child to the public school, or the parents and the private school team can develop an ISP and offer the services according to their resources given team and parental agreement.

Finally, some students are unilaterally placed in private settings (34 CFR §300.145-147). In this case, the public school or other public agency has placed the student in a private school setting to receive their specialized education services because it has been determined that the child's needs cannot be met in the public setting. The LEA is responsible for the financial obligation incurred by this need and placement. Rarely does the LEA agree to such a placement without extensive discussions and often legal battles, but with that stated, this may be what is necessary to meet the unique needs of the child.

Special Education Vouchers

Some states have offered families educational vouchers for children who have varying disabilities as a means of financial support. The amount of the voucher can differ based on the severity of the child's disability. According to Farrell and Marx (2018), as of 2017–2018 school year, 15 states have some type of voucher program, 13 of which are specifically for students with disabilities. The states that provide public funding for nonpublic school students identified with a disability include Arkansas, Florida, Georgia, Indiana, Louisiana, Maryland, Mississippi, North Carolina, Ohio, Oklahoma, Utah, and Wisconsin. Students who are parentally placed in nonpublic schools are not guaranteed the provisions that are included in FAPE. For this reason, the Council for Exceptional Children (CEC), objects to the usage of special education vouchers. CEC's mission is to protect the rights of children with disabilities. Public schools are mandated to provide services, whereas private schools are not, and parents often do not realize the services their child could be entitled to if they were to remain in the public schools (Apling et al., 2003). For this reason, CEC takes a strong stance against the use of special education vouchers for students to attend private schools.

Service Plans

LEAs are required to expend the proportionate share of federal IDEA funds to provide special education and related services to eligible parentally placed children with disabilities. This includes direct services to children. Services may be provided directly by the LEA or by a contract with a third-party vendor, such as a therapist from an agency. Each parentally placed private school child with a disability who has been designated to receive special education and/or related services must have an ISP. The ISP describes the specific special education and/or related services that the LEA will provide to the child. The LEA must ensure that a representative of the private school attends each meeting to develop the ISP. If the private school representative cannot attend, then the LEA must use other methods to ensure participation, including individual or conference telephone calls. This will help ensure communication about the child's needs among key stakeholders. An ISP should reflect only the services the LEA will provide to a parentally placed private school child with a disability who is designated to receive services. It must meet the applicable IEP content requirements to the extent appropriate. The service plan also must, to the extent appropriate, be developed, reviewed, and revised consistent with the requirements related to the IEP team, parent participation, and when IEPs must be in effect, as specified in the Part B regulations.

ISP VERSUS IEP

Following are some crucial differences between an ISP and an IEP:

- The equitable services may be fewer than those received at a public school because limited money flows through the LEA

- No assurance of FAPE

- The services may need to be provided at a public school setting as determined by the LEA in collaboration with the ISP team

- Parents have due process procedural rights only for Child Find (evaluation and reevaluation) but not for any other aspect of the IEP process (Morin, 2020)

To summarize, families always have the right to choose where they will send their child to attend school, but the difference in the services offered might vary dramatically for a student with disabilities. The actual difference between the two is that a student in a public school with an IEP receives all the needed services, including specially designed instruction, whereas the services provided to the student with an ISP at a private school are limited by the amount of money that flows through the LEA to their private school. Parents have the option to keep their child in public school, or they may feel it is best to send their child to private school. Services at private schools may mirror that of a public school or may require parents to pay for the service, such as speech-language therapy. Some schools may charge parents based on the services the child requires. Table 12.1 shows some of the differences between an IEP and an ISP. It is critical that parents are aware of the important questions they must ask regarding the needs of their child. Most identified disabilities have advocacy groups for parents to seek support and guidance.

SUMMARY

Knowledge regarding the legal differences entitled to a child with disabilities in a nonpublic versus a public school is required for all private school parents, special educators, related services providers, and administrators. Perhaps more important, parents of students with disabilities who are contemplating the best educational choice need to know that there are differences in the type and quantity of services their child will receive in the public versus the nonpublic school. Until there is a change in the federal laws and/or the practices of nonpublic schools so that all children with disabilities are protected, it is incumbent on those interested in both private schooling and students with disabilities to advocate for a more robust educational system that meets the needs of all children. The list in Figure 12.1 can be used to prepare for the IEP meeting.

Table 12.1. Individualized service plan (ISP) verses individualized education program (IEP)

Service	ISP	IEP
Measurable annual goals	√	√
Specially designed services	√	√
State- and districtwide testing	√	√
Exemptions	√	√
Meeting participants	√	√
Signatures	√	√
Future planning		√
Extended school year		√
Postsecondary transition		√
Nonacademic and extra-curricular		√
Transportation		√
General factors		√
Least restrictive environment		√
Profile		√

THE IEP CHECKLIST: PRIVATE AND PAROCHIAL SCHOOLS

The following checklist can be used by private and parochial schools as an inventory to ensure that students with disabilities are receiving services that best support their academic, behavioral, and social-emotional needs.

Conversations about best practices regarding the child's needs.	Discussion needed	
	Yes	No
Service Needed		
Measurable Annual Goals		
Specially Designed Services		
Statewide and Districtwide Testing		
Exemptions		
Future Planning		
Extended School Year		
Postsecondary Transition		
Nonacademic and Extra Curricular		
Transportation		
General Factors		
Least Restrictive Environment		

PREPARATION FOR THE IEP/ISP MEETING:
PRIVATE SCHOOLING

Prior to the Meeting

☐ Identify student's strengths and needs (i.e., funds of knowledge).

☐ Identify the possible supports that might be available at the private school.

☐ Determine participants from the private and public school.

☐ Secure interpreter, if needed, and meet with interpreter to review focus of meeting.

During the Meeting

☐ Share the prerequisite skills or behaviors that are required to meet the ISP goal.

☐ Determine the prerequisite skills or behaviors that the learner has mastered.

☐ Construct short-term objectives that address the prerequisite skill(s) that the learner has not mastered.

☐ Consider language proficiency and the student's funds of knowledge as strengths while constructing the objective.

☐ Use BEST (behavior, evaluation, specific, timely) to check to make sure that the objectives are meaningful and compliant.

☐ If using an interpreter, be sure to use appropriate interpreter etiquette (see Chapter 2).

After the Meeting

☐ Prepare the progress monitoring plan to be shared with the team.

☐ Determine the type and frequency of communication regarding the student's progress.

☐ Debrief with all team members, including parents, regarding the effectiveness of the meeting.

☐ Share all documents with the local public school to ensure funding of academic supports.

Figure 12.1. Preparation for the IEP/ISP meeting: Private schooling.

ACTIVITIES

The activities included in this chapter are intended for the reader to gain a deeper understanding of the content covered. The activities associated with this chapter include the following:

- Activity 12.1. Supporting Chapter, Private, and Parochial Schools and IDEA
- Activity 12.2. ISP and IEP Comparison

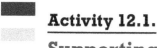

Supporting Chapter, Private, and Parochial Schools and IDEA

(page 1 of 1)

Supporting chapter: Chapter 12 (Supporting Students With Disabilities in Private and Parochial Schools)

Purpose: The purpose of this activity is for the reader to apply their knowledge of the differences between the services provided to students with disabilities in private and public schools.

Directions: Interview three parents of children who attend a private or parochial school who have a disability and ask them about their understanding of IDEA. Do they know the difference between an ISP and an IEP? What is their understanding of free appropriate public education and least restrictive environment?

The IEP Checklist: Your Guide to Creating Meaningful and Compliant IEPs, Second Edition, by Clarissa E. Rosas and
Kathleen G. Winterman. Copyright © 2023 by Paul H. Brookes Publishing Co., Inc. All rights reserved.

258

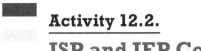

Activity 12.2.

ISP and IEP Comparison

Supporting chapter: Chapter 12 (Supporting Students With Disabilities in Private and Parochial Schools)

Purpose: The purpose of this activity is for the reader to apply their knowledge of the differences between the services provided to students with disabilities in private and public schools.

Directions: Contact a local private school and request an ISP for a student with a learning disability. Please be sure to ask them to redact any identifying information. Then, request an IEP from your local public school, again asking that all private information is removed. Finally, review the documents and brainstorm three ways that the ISP differs from the IEP and the changes you would make if possible.

References

Adger, C. T., Snow, C. E., & Christian, D. (2018). *What teachers need to know about language* (2nd ed.). Multilingual Matters.

American Association on Intellectual and Developmental Disabilities. (2018). *Self-determination: Position statement of AAIDD and The ARC.* https://www.aaidd.org/news-policy/policy/position-statements/self-determination

American Speech-Language-Hearing Association. (2019). *Final report: Ad hoc committee on language proficiency.* https://www.asha.org/siteassets/reports/ahc-language-proficiency.pdf

Americans with Disabilities Act (ADA) of 1990, PL 101-336, 42 U.S.C. §§ 12101 *et seq.*

Americans with Disabilities National Network. (2020). *What are a public or private college-university's responsibilities to students with disabilities?* https://adata.org/faq/what-are-public-or-private-college-universitys-responsibilities-students-disabilities

Anderson, L. W., & Krathwohl, D. R. (2001). *A taxonomy for learning, teaching and assessing: A revision of Bloom's taxonomy of educational objectives: Complete edition.* Longman.

Apling, R. N., Jones, N. L., & Smole, D. P. (2003). Individuals with Disabilities Education Act (IDEA): Possible Voucher Issues: RL31489. *Congressional Research Service: Report, 1.*

Baca, L. M., & Cervantes, H. T. (2004). *The bilingual special education interface* (4th ed.). Pearson Prentice Hall.

Beringer, M. L. (1976). *Ber-Sil Spanish Test* (Rev. ed.). The Ber-Sil Company.

Biegun, D., Peterson, Y., McNaught, J., & Sutterfield, C. (2020). Including student voice in IEP meetings through use of assistive technology. *TEACHING Exceptional Children, 52*(5), 348–350. https://doi.org/10.1177/0040059920920148

Blackler, F., & McDonald, S. (2000). Power, mastery and organizational learning. *Journal of Management Studies, 37,* 833–852.

Blackwell, W. H., & Robinson, J. M. (2017). School choice vouchers and special education in Indiana Catholic diocesan schools. *Journal of Catholic Education, 21*(1), 170–191. http://dx.doi.org/10.15365/joce.2101082017

Bloom, B., Englehart, M., Furst, E., Hill, W., & Krathwohl, D. (1956). *Taxonomy of educational objectives: The classification of educational goals. Handbook I: Cognitive domain.* Longmans and Green.

Board of Education of the Hendrick Hudson Central School District v. Amy Rowley, 458 U.S. 176,102 (1982).

Boehm, A. E. (2001). *Boehm Test of Basic Concepts* (3rd ed.). Pearson.

Bowe, F. (2005). *Making inclusion work.* Pearson.

Breiseth, L., Garcia, S., Butler, S. (2020). *Culturally responsive teaching: What you need to know.* https://www.understood.org/en/school-learning/for-educators/universal-design-for-learning/what-is-culturally-responsive-teaching

Briesch, A. M., Riley-Tillman, T. C., & Chafouleas, S. M. (2016). *Direct behavior rating: Linking assessment, communication, and intervention.* Guilford Press.

Burlington School Committee v. Massachusetts Department of Education, 471 U.S. 359 (1985).

Burstein, N., Sears, S., Wilcoxen, A., Cabello, B., & Spagna, M. (2004). Moving toward inclusive practices. *Remedial and Special Education, 25*, 104–116.

Cavendish, W., Connor, D. J., & Rediker, E. (2017). Engaging students and parents in transition-focused individualized education programs. *Intervention in School and Clinic, 52*(4), 228–235. https://doi.org/10.1177/1053451216659469

Center for Applied Technology. (2018). *The UDL guidelines.* http://udlguidelines.cast.org

Center on Positive Behavioral Interventions & Supports. (2015). *PBIS implementation blueprint.* University of Oregon. https://www.pbis.org/resource/pbis-implementation-blueprint

Chafouleas, S. M., Riley-Tillman, R. W., Christ, T. J., & Sugai, G. (2009). *DBR standard form.* University of Connecticut School of Education. https://dbr.education.uconn.edu

Chappuis, S., Chappuis, J., & Stiggins, R. (2009). The quest for quality: Quality tests and a balanced system are the keys to sound assessment. *Educational Leadership, 67*(3), 14–19.

Childre, A., & Chambers, C. R. (2005). Family perceptions of student centered planning and IEP meetings. *Education and Training in Developmental Disabilities, 40*(3), 217–233.

Christ, T. J., Riley-Tillman, T. C., & Chafouleas, S. M. (2009). Foundation for the development and use of Direct Behavior Rating (DBR) to assess and evaluate student behavior. *Assessment for Effective Intervention, 34*(4), 201–213.

Christle, C. A., & Yell, M. L. (2010). Individualized education programs: Legal requirements and research findings. *Exceptionality, 18*(3), 109–123.

Clark, D. R. (2013). *Bloom's taxonomy of learning domains.*

Clark, S. G. (2000). The IEP process as a tool for collaboration. *TEACHING Exceptional Children, 33*(22), 56–66.

Clarke, L. S., Columbia Embury, D., Jones, R., & Yssel, N. (2014). A teacher's guide to support students with disabilities during crises. *TEACHING Exceptional Children, 46*(6), 169–178.

Collier, C. (2011). *Seven steps to separating difference from disability.* Corwin Press.

Collier, C. (2016). *Classroom Language Interaction Checklist.* Cross Cultural Developmental Education Services.

Comprehensive, Integrated Three-Tiered Model of Intervention. (n.d.). *Professional learning.* https://www.ci3t.org/pl

Compton, D. L., Fuchs, D., Fuchs, L. S., Bouton, B., Gilbert, J. K., Barquero, L. A., & Crouch, R. C. (2010). Selecting at-risk first-grade readers for early intervention: Eliminating false positives and exploring the promise of a two-stage gated screening process. *Journal of Educational Psychology, 102*, 327–341.

Council for Exceptional Children. (2011). *CEC's position on school vouchers.* https://eric.ed.gov/?id=ED400634

Council for Exceptional Children. (2013). *Supporting paraeducators series for teachers and administrators.* http://www.cec.sped.org

Cramer, E. D., Pellegrini-Lafont, C., & Gonzalez, L. (2014, Summer). Towards culturally responsive and integrated instruction for all learners: The integrated learning model. *Interdisciplinary Journal of Teaching and Learning, (4)2*, 110–124.

Cummins, J. (1980). The cross-lingual dimensions of language proficiency: Implications for bilingual education and the optimal age issue. *TESOL Quarterly, 14*(2), 175–187.

Cummins, J. (1981). The role of primary language development in promoting educational success for language minority students. In California State Department of Education (Ed.), *Schooling and language minority students: A theoretical framework* (pp. 3–49). California State Department of Education.

Cummins, J. (1994). The acquisition of English as a second language. In K. Spangenberg-Urbschat & R. Pritchard (Ed.), *Reading instruction for ESL students* (pp. 36–64). International Reading Association.

Cummins, J. (2000). *Language, power and pedagogy: Bilingual children in the crossfire.* Multilingual Matters.

Cunningham, T. H., & Graham, C. R. (2000). Increasing native English vocabulary recognition through Spanish immersion: Cognate transfer from foreign to first language. *Journal of Educational Psychology, 92*, 37–49.

Curriculum Associates. *Brigance Assessment of Basic Skills-Revised, Spanish Edition.* Author.

Daggett, L. M. (2014). "Minor adjustments" and other not-so-minor obligations: Section 504, Private religious K–12 schools, and students with disabilities. *University of Louisville Law Review, 52*, 301–330.

Daniel R.R. v. State Board of Education, 874 F. 2d at 1048 (1989).

Darrow, A. A. (2016). The Every Student Succeeds Act (ESSA): What it means for students with disabilities and music educators. *General Music Today, 30*(1), 41–44. https://doi.org /10.1177/1048371316658327

Davis, M. T., & Cummings, I. K. (2019). Planning and implementing student-led IEPs for students with EBD. *Behavior and Beyond, 28*(2), 90–98. https://doi.org/10.1177/1074295619850569

DeAvila, E. A., & Duncan, S. E. (1991). *Language Assessment Scales—Oral.* DRC. http://www .datarecognitioncorp.com

Demont, E. (2001). Contribution of early 2nd-language learning to the development of linguistic awareness and learning to read. International *Journal of Psychology, 36*, 274–285.

DeMonte, T. M. (2010). Finding the least restrictive environment for preschoolers under the IDEA: An analysis and proposed framework. *Washington Law Review, 85*(157), 157–191.

Diana v. California State Board of Education, No. C-70, RFT, (N. D. Cal. 1970).

Dunn, L. M., Padilla, E. R., Lugo, D. E., & Dunn, L. M. (1986). *Test de vocabulario en imagenes Peabody.* Pearson.

Education for All Handicapped Children Act of 1975, PL 94-142, 20 U.S.C. §§ 1400 *et seq.*

Education of the Handicapped Act Amendments of 1986, PL 99-457, 20 U.S.C. §§ 1400 *et seq.*

Elementary and Secondary Education Act of 1965, PL 89-10, 20 U.S.C. §§ 241 *et seq.*

Emily Thomas, Plaintiff-appellee, Cross-appellant, v. Cincinnati Board of Education, Defendant-appellant, Cross-appellee, 918 F.2d 618 (6th Cir. 1990).

Endrew F. v. Douglas County School District RE–1, 137 S.Ct 988, 580 U.S. (2017). https:// supreme.justia.com/cases/federal/us/580/15-827

Every Student Succeeds Act of 2015, PL 114-95, 20 U.S.C. §§ 1001 *et seq.*

Farrell, I., & Marx, C. (2018). The fallacy of choice: The destructive effect of school vouchers on children with disabilities. *American University Law Review, 67*(6), 1797–1910.

Feldman, E. F., Feldman, M. F., & Fialka, J. (2018). Inclusion includes belonging: How to create and sustain a circle of support. https://unh.app.box.com/s/5mt26mxvciv1n1nq4a5m7t rkrqj1hp1x

Fish, W. W. (2008). The IEP meeting: Perceptions of parents of students who receive special education services. *Preventing School Failure, 53*(1), 8–14.

Florence County School Dist. Four v. Carter, 510 U.S. 7 (1993).

Fox, L., & Duda, M. (2012). *Positive behavior support.* http://www.challengingbehavior.org

Fox, L., & Duda, M. (2015). *Complete guide to positive behavior support: Young children.* Technical Assistance Center on Social Emotional Intervention for Young Children. https://www .researchgate.net/publication/299461771_Complete_Guide_to_Positive_Behavior_Support -Young_Children

Friend, M. (2011). *Special education: Contemporary perspectives for school professionals* (3rd ed.). Allyn & Bacon.

Friend, M., & Bursuck, W. D. (2011). *Including students with special needs: A practical guide for classroom teachers.* Pearson.

Fuchs, D., Fuchs, L., & Compton, D. (2012). Smart RTI: A next-generation approach to multi-level prevention. *Exceptional Children, 78*(3), 263–279.

Fuchs, L., & Vaughn, S. (2012). Responsiveness-to-intervention a decade later. *Journal of Learning Disabilities, 45*(3), 195–203.

Gartin, B. C., & Murdick, N. L. (2005). IDEA 2004: The IEP. *Remedial and Special Education, 26*(6), 327–331.

Greer v. Rome City School District, 967 F. 2d. at 470 (1992).

Grossman, E. G. (2020). Taking control of your child's IEP experience. *Exceptional Parent, 50*(1), 43–46.

Harr-Robins, J., Song, M., Hurlburt, S., Pruce, C., Danielson, L., Garet, M., & Taylor, J. (2012). *The inclusion of students with disabilities in school accountability systems: Interim report.* American Institutes for Research. http://ies.ed.gov/ncee/pubs/20124056/pdf /20124056.pdf

Heifetz, R. A., Grashow, A., & Linksy, M. (2009). *The practice of adaptive leadership: Tools and tactics for changing your organization and the world.* Harvard Business Press.

Heifetz, R. A., & Laurie, D. L. (1997). The work of leadership. *Harvard Business Review, 75*, 124–134.

Hemez, P., Brent, J. J., & Mowen, T. J. (2020). Exploring the school-to-prison pipeline: How school suspensions influence incarceration during young adulthood. *Youth Violence and Juvenile Justice, 18*(3), 235–255. https://doi.org/10.1177/1541204019880945

Hensel, W. (2015). The limits of federal disability law: State educational voucher programs. *Journal of Law and Education, 44,* 199–229.

Herbert, C. H. (1986). *Basic Inventory of Natural Languages.* CHECpoint Systems Inc.

Honig v. Doe, Supreme Court of the United States, 484 U.S. 305 (1988).

Horner, R. H., Sugai, G., & Fixsen, D. L. (2017). Implementing effective educational practices at scales of social importance. *Clinical Child and Family Psychology Review, 20*(1), 25–35.

Howard, V. F. (2013). *Very young children with special needs: A foundation for educators, families, and service providers.* Pearson.

Hurt, J. M. (2012). *A comparison of inclusion and pullout programs on student achievement for students with disabilities.* http://dc.etsu.edu/etd/1487

Individuals with Disabilities Education Act Amendments (IDEA) of 1997, PL 105-17, 20 U.S.C. §§ 1400 *et seq.*

Individuals with Disabilities Education Act (IDEA) of 1990, PL 101-476, 20 U.S.C. §§ 1400 *et seq.*

Individuals with Disabilities Education Improvement Act (IDEA) of 2004, PL 108-446, 20 U.S.C. §§ 1400 *et seq.*

Irving Independent School District v. Amber Tatro, 468 U.S. 883 (1984).

Janney, R., & Snell, M. E. (2013). *Teachers' guides to inclusive practices: Modifying schoolwork* (3rd ed.). Paul H. Brookes Publishing Co.

Karger, J., & Hitchcock, C. (2004). *Access to the general curriculum for students with disabilities: A brief legal interpretation.* http://aim.cast.org/learn/historyarchive/backgroundpapers /brief_legal_interpretation

Katz, J., & Mirenda, P. (2002). Including students with developmental disabilities in general education classrooms: Educational benefits. *International Journal of Special Education, 17*(2), 14–25.

Kentucky Department of Education. (2019). *Individualized education program.* https://education .ky.gov/specialed/excep/forms/Pages/IEP-Guidance-and-Documents.aspx

Kilanowski-Press, L., Foote, C. J., & Rinaldo, V. J. (2010). Inclusion classrooms and teachers: A survey of current practices. *International Journal of Special Education, 25*(3), 43–56.

Klingner, J. K., Artiles, A. J., Kozleski, E., Harry, B., Zion, S., Tate, W., Zamora Durán, G., & Riley, D. (2005). Addressing the disproportionate representation of culturally and linguistically diverse students in special education through culturally responsive educational systems. *Education Policy Analysis Archives, 13*(38), 1–40.

Korte, G. (2015). The Every Student Succeeds Act vs. No Child Left Behind: What's changed? *USA Today.* https://www.usatoday.com/story/news/politics/2015/12/10/every -student-succeeds-act-vs-no-child-left-behind-whats-changed/77088780/

K. R. v. Anderson Community School Corporation, 81 F. 3d 673 (7th Cr. 1996), granted and vacated, 117 S. Ct. (1997).

Kroeger, S. D., & Phillips, L. J. (2007). Positive behavior support assessment guide: Creating student-centered behavior plans. *Assessment for Effective Intervention, 32*(2), 100–112.

Kurth, J. A., Love, H., & Pirtle, J. (2020). Parent perspectives of their involvement in IEP development for children with Autism. *Focus on Autism and Other Developmental Disabilities, 35*(1), 36–46. https://doi.org/10.1177/1088357619842858

Lachman v. Illinois State Board of Education, 852 F. 2d at 297 (1988).

Larry P. v. Riles, Civil Action No. C-70-37 (N.D. Cal. 1971)

Lee-Tarver, A. (2006). Are individualized education plans a good thing? A survey of teachers' perceptions of the utility of IEPs in regular education. *Journal of Instructional Psychology, 33*(4), 263–272.

Leverson, M., Smith, K., McIntosh, K., Rose, J., & Pinkelman, S. (2019). *PBIS cultural responsiveness field guide: Resources for trainers and coaches.* Office of Special Education Programs Technical Assistance Center on Positive Behavioral Interventions and Supports.

LifeCourse. (2020). *What can charting the LifeCourse do for you?* https://www.lifecoursetools.com

Lo, L., & Xu, Y. (2019). *Family, school, and community partnerships for families of individuals with disabilities.* Springer.

Lynch, E. W., & Hanson, M. J. (2011). *Developing cross-cultural competence: A guide for working with children and their families* (4th ed.). Paul H. Brookes Publishing Co.

Mager, R. (1962). *Preparing instructional objectives.* Fearon Publishers.

Mager, R. (1975). *Preparing instructional objectives* (2nd ed.). Lake Publishing.

Martin, J. E., Van Dycke, J. L., Christensen, W. R., Greene, B. A., Gardner, J. E., & Lovett, D. L. (2006). Increasing student participation in IEP meetings: Establishing the self-directed IEP as an evidenced-based practice. *Exceptional Children, 72*(3), 299–316.

Martin, N. (2017). *10 conflict-busters for IEP meetings.* https://blog.brookespublishing.com /10-conflict-busters-for-iep-meetings

Marx, T. A., & Miller, F. G. (2020). *Strategies for setting data-driven behavioral individualized education program goals.* U.S. Department of Education, Office of Special Education Programs, National Center on Intensive Intervention.

Mason, C. Y., McGahee-Kovac, M., & Johnson, L. (2004). How to help students lead their IEP meetings. *TEACHING Exceptional Children, 36*(3), 18–24.

McCabe, K. M., Ruppar, A., Kurth, J. A., McQueston, J. A., Johnston, R., & Toews, S. G. (2020). Cracks in the continuum: A critical analysis of least restrictive environment for students with significant support needs. *Teachers College Record, 122*(5), 1–10.

McLeskey, J., Landers, E., Williamson, P., & Hoppey, D. (2010). *Are we moving toward educating students with disabilities in less restrictive settings?* http://education.ufl.edu/disability-policy -practice/files/2012/05/McLeskey-et-al-JSED-LRE-8.pdf

Mills v. Board of Education of the District of Columbia, 348 F. Supp. 866 (D. D.C. 1972).

Morin, A. (2020). *The difference between IEPs and service plans.* https://www.understood.org/en /school-learning/special-services/special-education-basics/the-difference-between-ieps -and-service-plans?_ul=1*1nupx5f*domain_userid*YW1wLVhMcC13MURIZklDMmZ2R zZvNjhmZnc

Mueller, T. G. (2017). Promoting collaborative partnerships with families. In J. M. Kauffman & D. P. Hallahan (Eds.), *Handbook of special education* (2nd ed.; pp. 773–792). Routledge.

Mueller, T. G., & Buckley, P. C. (2014). The odd man out: How fathers navigate the special education system. *Remedial and Special Education, 35*(1), 40–49. https://www.academia.edu/26632469 /The_Odd_Man_Out_How_Fathers_Navigate_the_Special_Education_System

Myers, A., & Eisenman, L. (2005). Student-led IEPs: Taking the first step. *TEACHING Exceptional Children, 37*(4), 52–58.

Nandakumas, V., McCree, N., & Green, A. L. (2021). Evidence-based and culturally sustaining practices for diverse students with emotional and behavioral disorders. *Intervention in School and Clinic.* https://doi.org/10.1177/10534512211051073

National Alliance on Mental Illness. (2013). *Mental illness: Facts and numbers.* https://namieasysite .com/wp-content/uploads/sites/2/2013/05/mentalillness_factsheet.pdf

National Center for Education Statistics. (2019). *Status and trends in the education of racial and ethnic groups.* https://nces.ed.gov

National Center for Learning Disabilities. (2017). *Understanding learning and attention issues.* https://www.ncld.org

National Center for Learning Disabilities. (2020, October 19). *Significant disproportionality in special education.* https://www.ncld.org/sigdispro

National Center on Educational Outcomes. (2013). *Alternate assessments for students with disabilities.* https://nceo.info/Assessments/aa-aas#:~:text=Alternate%20assessments%20are%20 assessments%20based,general%20assessments%20even%20with%20accommodations

National Center on Intensive Intervention. *Progress monitoring tools chart.* https://intensive intervention.org/resource/academic-progress-monitoring-tools-chart

National Center on Universal Design for Learning. (2013). *About universal design for learning.* http://www.udlcenter.org/aboutudl/whatisudl

National Child Traumatic Stress Network. (2012). *The 12 core concepts of understanding traumatic stress responses in children and families: Core curriculum on childhood trauma.* UCLA-Duke University National Center for Child Traumatic Stress.

National Defense Education Act of 1958, PL 85-864, 72 Stat. 1580, 20 U.S.C. §§ 401-589 *et seq.*

National Technical Assistance Center on Transition. (2018). *Transition planning.* https:// transitionta.org/topics/secondary-education/transition-planning/

No Child Left Behind Act of 2001, PL 107-110, 115 Stat. 1425, 20 U.S.C. §§ 6301 *et seq.*

Oberti v. Board of Education of the Borough of Clementon School District, 995 F 2d. 1204 (3d Cir. 1993).

O'Brien, J., & Pearpoint, J. (1995). *Person centered planning with MAPS and PATH. A workbook for facilitators.* Inclusion Press.

Office of Special Education Programs. (2017). *Transition guide to postsecondary education and employment for students and youth with disabilities.* https://www2.ed.gov/about/offices/list /osers/transition/products/postsecondary-transition-guide-may-2017.pdf

Ohio Department of Education. (2017). *A guide to parents' rights in special education: Special education procedures and safeguards notice.* Office for Exceptional Children.

Osborne, A. G. (2022, February 24). *Cedar Rapids Community School District v. Garret F. Encyclopedia Britannica.* https://www.britannica.com/topic/Cedar-Rapids-Community-School -District-v-Garret-F

Palley, E. (2006). Challenges of rights-based law: Implementing the least restrictive environment mandate. *Journal of Disability Policy Studies, 16,* 229–235.

Pennsylvania Association for Retarded Children (PARC) v. Commonwealth of Pennsylvania, 334 F. Supp. 1247 (E.D. PA 1971).

Pinderhughes, H., Davis, R., & Williams, M. (2015). *Adverse community experiences and resilience: A framework for addressing and preventing community trauma.* Prevention Institute.

Prater, M. A. (2018). *Teaching students with high-incidence disabilities: Strategies for diverse classrooms.* Sage Publications.

Pugach, M., Blanton, L., & Correa, V. (2011). A historical perspective on the role of collaboration in teacher education reform: Making good on the promise of teaching all students. *Teacher Education and Special Education, 34*(3), 183–200. https://doi:10.1177/0888406411406141

Rehabilitation Act of 1973, PL 93-112, 29 U.S.C. §§ 701 *et seq.*

Reusch v. Fountain, 21 Individuals with Disabilities Education Law Report 1107 (D. Md. 1994).

Reyes, J. (2017). RtI: Response to intervention or rushing to identify? In T. Torres & C. Barber (Eds.), *Case studies in special education* (pp. 153–171). Thomas.

Robertson, K., & Ford, K. (n.d.). Language acquisition: An overview. https://www.colorin colorado.org/article/language-acquisition-overview#h-stages-of-language-acquisition

Rogers, J. O. Y. (Ed.). (2006). *Revisiting the inclusion revolution: A decade of changes.* Center for Evaluation Development and Research Phi Delta Kap.

Roncker v. Walter, 700 F. 2d 1058 (6th Cir. 1983).

Rosas, C. E., & Winterman, K. (2012, Winter). The use of a rubric as a tool to guide pre-service teachers in the development of IEPs. *Journal of the American Academy of Special Education Professionals,* 136–147. https://doi-org.concordia.idm.oclc.org/https://files.eric.ed.gov /fulltext/EJ1135727.pdf

Rose, J., Leverson, M., & Smith, K. (2020, April). *Embedding culturally responsive practices in Tier I.* Center on PBIS, University of Oregon.

Roseberry-McKibbin, C. (2007). *Language disorders in children.* Pearson Education.

Rotter, K. (2014). *IEP use by general and special education teachers. Sage Open, 4*(2), 1–8. https:// doi:101177/2158244014530410

Sacramento City School District v. Rachel H., 14 F. 3d 1398 (9th Cir. 1994).

Sacramento City Unified School District v. Holland, 14 F 3d. at 1398 (1994).

Salend, S. (2008). Determining appropriate testing accommodations. *TEACHING Exceptional Children, 40*(4), 14–22.

Samuels, C. A. (2012). Special education look to the IEPs to Common Core. *Education Week, 30*(15), 8–9.

Samuels, C. (2017). *What states have special education vouchers, and how are they working?* http:// blogs.edweek.org/edweek/speced/2017/03/what_states_have_special_education_vouchers.html

San Jose Unified School District. (2019). *Student Oral Language Observation Matrix (SOLOM).* https://outreach.ou.edu/educational-services/education/edutas/comp-center-landing-page /knowledgebases/english-language-learners/ell-admin-teachers/4-2-4-gather-academic -data-ell-and-former-ell-students/student-oral-language-observation-matrix-solom/

Sapon-Shevin, M. (2003). Inclusion: A matter of social justice. *Educational Leadership, 61*(2), 25–28.

Schwartz, H. L. (2019). *Connected teaching: Relationships, power, and mattering in higher education*. Stylus Publishing.

Schwebel, M. (1979). Review of mind in society: The development of higher psychological processes [Review of the book Mind in society: The development of higher psychological processes, by L. S. Vygotsky, M. Cole, Ed., V. John-Steiner, Ed., S. Scribner, Ed., & E. Souberman, Ed., 1978]. *American Journal of Orthopsychiatry, 49*, 530–536.

Searle, M., & Swartz, M. (2020). Solving academic and behavioral problems: A strengths-based guide for teachers and teams. Association for Supervision and Curriculum Development.

Shealey, M. W., McHatton, P. A., & Wilson, V. (2011). Moving beyond disproportionality: The role of culturally responsive teaching in special education. *Teaching Education, 22*(4), 377–396.

Short, D. J., & Echevarria, J. (2016). *Developing academic language with the SIOP model*. Pearson.

Singleton, G. E., & Linton, C. (2015). *Courageous conversation about race: A field guide for achieving equity in schools*. Corwin Press.

Smith, T. E. C. (2005). IDEA 2004: Another round in the reauthorization process. *Remedial and Special Education, 26*(6), 314–319.

Snyder, T. D., & Dillow, S. A. (2012). *Digest of education statistics 2011* (NCES 2012-001). Institute of Education Sciences, National Center for Education Statistics, U.S. Department of Education.

Stiggins, R. J. (Ed.). (2011). *Classroom assessment for student learning: Doing it right-using it well*. Pearson Education.

Sugai, G., Horner, R. H., Algozzine, R., Barrett, S., Lewis, T., Anderson, C., & Simonsen, B. (2010). *School-wide positive behavior support: Implementers' blueprint and self-assessment*. University of Oregon.

Sugai, G., Horner, R. H., Fixsen, D., & Blase, K. (2010). Developing systems-level capacity for RTI implementation: Current efforts and future directions. In T. A. Glover & S. Vaughn (Eds.), *The promise of response to intervention: Evaluating current science and practice* (pp. 286–309). Guildford Press.

Sze, S., & Cowden, O. P. (2012). Using asynchronous online instruction to maximize learning. *Academy of Information and Management Sciences, 16*(1), 43–47.

Tan, K. (2013). Variation in teachers' conceptions of alternative assessment in Singapore primary schools. *Educational Research Policy and Practice, 12*(1), 21–41.

Technology-Related Assistance for Individuals with Disabilities Act of 1988, PL 100-407, 29 U.S.C. §§ 2201 *et seq.*

Test, D. W., Smith, L. E., & Carter, E. W. (2014). Equipping youth with autism spectrum disorders for adulthood: Promoting rigor, relevance, and relationships. *Remedial and Special Education, 35*(2), 80–90.

Timothy W. v. Rochester School District, 875 F. 2d 954 (1st Cir. 1989).

Toronto, A. S. (1973). *Screening Test of Spanish Grammar*. Northwestern University Press.

Tucker, V., & Schwartz, I. (2013). Parents' perspectives of collaboration with school professionals: Barriers and facilitators to successful partnerships in planning for students with ASD. *School Mental Health: A Multidisciplinary Research and Practice Journal, 5*(1), 3–14. https://doi.org/10.1007/s12310-012-9102-0

U.S. Census Bureau. (2017). *New detailed statistics on race, Hispanic origin, ancestry and tribal groups*. https://www.census.gov/newsroom/press-releases/2017/acs-selected-population-tables-aian.html

U.S. Department of Education. (2006, August 14). *Federal Register: Part II: Department of Education: Assistance to states for the education of children with disabilities and preschool grants for children with disabilities: Final rule*. http://idea.ed.gov/download/finalregulations.pdf

U.S. Department of Education. (2007, May 20). *Final regulations on modified academic achievement standards*. http://www2.ed.gov/policy/speced/guid/modachieve-summary.html

U.S. Department of Education. (2010). *Questions and answers on individualized education programs (IEPs), evaluations, and reevaluations*. https://sites.ed.gov/idea/files/policy_speced_guid_idea_iep-qa-2010.pdf

U.S. Department of Education. (2014). *IDEA Part B discipline collection.*

U.S. Department of Education. (2016a, December 8). *Title I: Improving the academic achievement of the disadvantaged: Academic assessments.* https://www.govinfo.gov/content/pkg/FR-2016-12-08/pdf/2016-29128.pdf

U.S. Department of Education. (2016b). *Tools and resources for providing ELs with a language assistance program.* https://ncela.ed.gov/files/english_learner_toolkit/2-OELA_2017_language_assist_508C.pdf

U.S. Department of Education. (2019). *Projections of Education Statistics to 2027* (Forty-sixth Edition). https://nces.ed.gov/pubs2019/2019001.pdf

U.S. Department of Education, Office of Innovation and Improvement, Office of Non-Public Education. (2011). *The Individuals with Disabilities Education Act: Provisions related to children with disabilities enrolled by their parents in private schools.* https://www2.ed.gov/admins/lead/speced/privateschools/report_pg2.html

U.S. Department of Education, Office of Special Education and Rehabilitative Services. (2015). *Dear colleague letter.* https://sites.ed.gov/idea/idea-files/osep-dear-colleague-letter-on-free-and-appropriate-public-education-fape/

Vygotsky, L. S. (1962). *Thought and language.* The MIT Press.

Vygotsky, L. S. (1978). *Mind in society: The development of higher psychological processes.* Harvard University Press.

Vygotsky, L. S. (1986). *Thought and language* (2nd ed.). The MIT Press.

Walker, M. (2020). *When getting along is not enough: Reconstructing race in our lives and relationships.* Teachers College Press.

Waterstone, J. (2017). Endrew F. symbolism v. reality. *Journal of Law and Education, 46*(4), 527–538.

Wilkinson, L. M. (2010, February 9). Council of Parent Advocates and Attorneys (COPAA) Conference in St. Louis March 11–14. *St. Louis Examiner (MO).*

Williams, E. R. (2007). Unnecessary and unjustified: African-American parental perceptions of special education. *Educational Forum, 71*(3), 250–261. http://dx.doi.org/10.1080/00131720709335009

Winterman, K. G., & Rosas, C. (2016). Re-examining progress monitoring: Are we reporting what we think we are? *Ohio Journal of Teacher Education, 30*(1), 13–34.

Wisconsin Center for Education Research at University of Wisconsin, Madison. (n.d.). *WIDA Screener.* https://wida.wisc.edu/assess/screener

Woodcock, R. W., Alvarado, C. G., Ruef, M., & Schrank, F. A. (2017). *Woodcock-Muñoz Language Survey* (3rd ed.). Riverside.

Wright P., & Wright, P. (2011). *From emotions to advocacy.* Harbor House Law Press.

Yell, M. L., & Bateman, D. (2020). Defining educational benefit. *TEACHING Exceptional Children, 52*(5), 283–290.

Yell, M. L., & Drasgow, E. (2010). The continuing influence of the law in special education: Introduction to the special issue. *Exceptionality, 18*(3), 107–108. http://doi.org/10.1080/09362835.2010.491739

Yell, M. L., Katsiyannis, A., Ennis, R. P., Loinski, M., & Bateman, D. (2020). Making legally sound placement decisions. *TEACHING Exceptional Children, 52*(6), 291–303.

Yell, M. L., Shriner, J. G., & Katsiyannis, A. (2006). Individuals with Disabilities Education Improvement Act of 2004 and IDEA regulations of 2006: Implications for educators, administrators, and teacher trainers. *Focus on Exceptional Children, 39*(1), 2–24.

Yell, M. L., & Stecker, P. M. (2003). Developing legally correct and educationally meaningful IEPs using curriculum-based measurement. *Assessment for Effective Intervention, 28*(34), 73–88.

Zascavage, V., & Winterman, K. G. (2009). Assistive technology and universal design for learning: What does the middle school educator need to know? *Middle School Journal, 4*(4), 46–52.

Zirkel, P. A. (2020). An updated primer of special education law. *TEACHING Exceptional Children, 52*(4), 261–265. https://doi.org/10.1177/0040059919878671

Zelman v. Simmons-Harris, 536 U.S. 639, 662 (2002).

Zobrest v. Catalina Foothills School District, 509 U.S. 1 (1993).

Glossary

accommodation   Refers to an adaptation that allows a student with disabilities to meet the same standard of learning as their peers but through a different avenue.

ADA   *see* Americans with Disabilities Act.

adaptation   Term used to refer to accommodation and modifications.

Americans with Disabilities Act (ADA)   A law that prohibits discrimination on the basis of disability.

basic interpersonal communication skills (BICS)   Refers to basic language proficiency necessary for social-communication or interactions.

CALP   *See* cognitive academic language proficiency.

CBM   *See* curriculum-based assessment/measurement.

checklists   Refers to a list of certain skills or criteria, which educators and students may use to gauge their development or progress.

Child Find   Legal requirement under IDEA that requires states and local agencies to identify children with disabilities who may be entitled to special education services.

CLD   *See* culturally and linguistically diverse.

cognitive academic language proficiency (CALP)   Refers to advanced language proficiency necessary for academic achievement.

culturally and linguistically diverse (CLD)   Individuals who differ ethnically and linguistically from mainstream culture.

curriculum-based assessment/measurement (CBM)   Repeated measures from the student's curriculum to assess student achievement.

English language learners (ELLs)   Individuals who come from non–English-speaking homes who are in the process of learning English as a second language.

Every Student Succeeds Act (ESSA) of 2015 (PL 114-95)   The Every Student Succeeds Act passed by President Obama in December 2015 continued the reauthorization of the Elementary and Secondary Education Act of 1965 (PL 89-10) but furthered the initiatives of the No Child Left Behind Act of 2001 (PL 107-110). ESSA includes provisions that will help ensure success for students and schools.

extended written response   This type of assessment requires a student to produce evidence of learning by constructing a written response to a question or task. An extended written response is at least several sentences in length.

externalizing behaviors   An individual who exhibits outward physical aggression. Terms such as *conduct problems* and *antisocial* are often used to describe these overt behaviors.

free appropriate public education (FAPE)   FAPE is the acronym used to refer to free appropriate public education, which is guaranteed in Individuals with Disabilities Education Act (IDEA) of 1990 (PL 101-476) and Section 504 of the Rehabilitation Act of 1973 (PL 93-112).

functional performance   Skills that can be applied to a variety of settings, including nonacademic environments.

high-context culture   Refers to those individuals whose communication is implicit and relies on nonverbal communication and relationships.

IEP   *See* individualized education program.

inclusion   Refers to serving the needs of all learners within a classroom setting, including students with disabilities and students who come from culturally and/or linguistically diverse backgrounds.

individualized education program (IEP)   Legal document developed by a team of district personnel, including a child's parent or guardian, that outlines the individualized education, including special education services, to address the needs of a child who has been identified as having a disability.

internalizing behaviors   Behaviors that are described as hidden. Terms such as *quiet, withdrawn, anxious,* and *depressed* are often used to describe these covert behaviors.

least restrictive environment (LRE)   LRE is the acronym referred to in many documents and requires students who receive special education services to be educated alongside peers without disabilities in the general education environment as much as possible.

low-context culture   Refers to those individuals whose communication is direct and relies on explicit verbal skills.

LRE   *See* least restrictive environment.

modification   Refers to an actual change in the content of what the student is learning and is used when accommodations alone are not sufficient to support the student.

No Child Left Behind (NCLB) Act of 2001 (PL 107-110)   In 2001, President Bush reenacted the Elementary and Secondary Education Act of 1965 (PL 89-10). This law is based on four pillars—stronger accountability for results, more freedom for states and communities, proven education methods, and more choices for parents.

PALS   *See* peer-assisted learning strategies.

PBIS   *See* positive behavior interventions and supports.

peer-assisted learning strategies (PALS)   A structured peer tutoring program in which students work together on reading and mathematics.

people-first language   Used to communicate appropriately and respectfully with and about an individual with a disability. People-first language emphasizes the person first, not the disability.

performance assessment   Requires a student to produce evidence of learning by either creating or developing a product or performance. This type of assessment generally requires students to demonstrate something that meets specific criteria.

personal communication assessment   Requires a student to produce evidence of learning by speaking or writing.

PLAAFP   *See* Present Levels of Academic Achievement and Functional Performance.

positive behavior interventions and supports (PBIS)   A framework supported by research and focused on improving student outcomes.

Present Levels of Academic Achievement and Functional Performance (PLAAFP)   The first part of the IEP that discusses the child's current skills and abilities.

procedural due process   Ensures that children with disabilities will receive a proper hearing, notification, and impartiality regarding their eligibility for special needs education.

selected response assessments   Requires a student to produce evidence of learning by selecting a correct response from a select number of choices. Selected response assessments include multiple choice, true/false, and matching questions.

short-cycle assessments   Frequent or daily formative assessments specific to an instructional goal.

substantive due process   Involves acts that deny or inhibit a person's life, liberty, and property rights.

Appendix

The IEP Checklist

The IEP Checklist

	Discussion needed	
Special Instructional Factors	Yes	No
Does the child have behavior that impedes their learning or the learning of others?		
Does the child have limited English proficiency?		
Is the child blind or visually impaired?		
Does the child have communication needs (required for individuals who are deaf or hearing impaired)?		
Does the child need assistive technology devices and/or services?		
Does the child require specially designed physical education?		
Will the child participate in statewide testing?		

Key Area (IEP section): **Student's Present Levels of Academic Achievement and Functional Performance**	Criteria met	
	Yes	No
P1: Present levels are prioritized based on student's needs.		
P2: A statement is included that explains the effect of a student's disability on their educational performance and involvement and progress in the general education curriculum.		
P3: A statement is included that clearly indicates the student's actual performance in academic and functional areas (e.g., behavioral, communication).		
P4: A statement is included that describes the student's strengths and needs (Present Levels of Academic Achievement and Functional Performance).		
P5: Sufficient details are provided on the student's level of functioning to develop goals.		

Key Area (IEP section): **Goal(s)**	Criteria met	
	Yes	No
G1: Goals are listed in the order that reflects the priority of the student's needs in the Present Levels of Academic Achievement and Functional Performance (PLAAFP) section.		
G2: Measurable annual goals are included in academic and/or functional areas.		
G3: Goals are written using specific, observable, and measurable terms.		
G4: Goals describe skills that can realistically be achieved within 1 year.		
G5: Goals are clearly connected to the statement(s) in the PLAAFP section of the student's IEP.		
G6: All goals reflect the criteria listed here.		

Key Area (IEP section): **Short-Term Objectives and Benchmarks**	Criteria met	
	Yes	No
O1: Objectives/benchmarks are listed in the order that reflects the priority of the student's needs in the Present Levels of Academic Achievement and Functional Performance (PLAAFP) section.		
O2: At least two objectives are written for each goal.		
O3: Each objective includes a condition and measurable behavior.		
O4: Specific criteria that match the skills being measured are written for each objective.		
O5: Objectives are clearly connected to the student's PLAAFP and address the student's abilities and needs.		

Key Area (IEP section): **Measuring and Reporting Progress**	Criteria met	
	Yes	No
M1: A statement is included that describes how a student's progress toward meeting their annual goals will be measured. (Select all measures identified below.)		
☐ Curriculum-based assessment ☐ Portfolios		
☐ Observations ☐ Rubric		
☐ Anecdotal records ☐ Checklists		
☐ Running records ☐ Inventories		
☐ Short-cycle assessments ☐ Work samples		
☐ Performance assessments ☐ Other		
M2: A statement is included describing when and how periodic reports will be provided to the student's parents. (Select all measures identified below.)		
How: *When:*		
☐ Written report ☐ Each time report cards are issued		
☐ Journal ☐ Reported every ___ weeks		
☐ E-mail ☐ Other:		
☐ Phone calls		
☐ Other:		
M3: A statement is included that informs the reader that the reports are issued as frequently as students in general education receive their report cards.		

Key Area (IEP section): **Least Restrictive Environment (LRE)**	Criteria met	
	Yes	No
L1: A statement is included that students have access to the general curriculum.		
L2: A statement is included that explains and provides the rationale for why a child is not participating in the general education curriculum.		

Key Area (IEP section): **Accommodations/District Tests**	Criteria met	
	Yes	No
A1: Accommodations match the services delivered in the classroom on a regular basis.		
A2: Accommodations are derived from student needs (Present Levels of Academic Achievement and Functional Performance).		
A3: Accommodations adhere to local and federal guidelines.		

Key Area (IEP section): **Transitions Beginning at Age 16, Coordinated Activities That Meet These Criterias**	Criteria met	
	Yes	No
T1: Statement of quality-of-life goals: The statement is results-oriented; focused on improving academic and functional achievement; facilitates movement from school to postschool activities, including postsecondary education, vocational education, integrated employment (supported employment), continuing and adult education, adult services, independent living, or community participation.		
T2: Vision: The vision is based on the child's needs, taking into account the child's strengths, preferences, and interests.		
T3: Resources and interagency collaboration: The individualized education program (IEP) includes a description of the course of study needed to reach stated goals, including instruction, related services, community experiences, development of employment and other postschool adult living objectives, and, when appropriate, acquisition of daily living skills and vocational evaluation.		
T4: Stakeholders: Parents of a child making the transition from Part C services (early childhood) to Part B services (school-age) can request an invitation to the initial IEP meeting be sent to representatives of the Part C system to assist with a smooth transition of services.		

Key Area (IEP section): **Behavioral Goals**	Criteria met	
	Yes	No
BG1: The goal includes a functionally relevant replacement behavior that is observable.		
BG2: The goal includes an assessment measure and criteria for evaluating the goal.		
BG3: The goal includes specific context and condition when the desired behavior is to occur.		
BG4: The goal includes the time line or date when the goal will be mastered.		

IEP Checklist:

PRIVATE AND PAROCHIAL SCHOOLS

The following checklist can be used by private and parochial schools as an inventory to ensure that students with disabilities are receiving services that best support their academic, behavioral, and social-emotional needs.

Conversations about best practices regarding the child's needs.	Discussion needed	
	Yes	No
Service Needed		
Measurable Annual Goals		
Specially Designed Services		
Statewide and Districtwide Testing		
Exemptions		
Future Planning		
Extended School Year		
Postsecondary Transition		
Nonacademic and Extra Curricular		
Transportation		
General Factors		
Least Restrictive Environment		

Index

Page numbers followed by *f* and *t* indicate figures and tables, respectively.